THE WAR OF THE AUSTI

MODERN WARS IN PERSPECTIVE

General Editors: *H.M. Scott and B.W. Collins*

ALREADY PUBLISHED

Mexico and the Spanish Conquest
Ross Hassig

The Wars of French Decolonization
Anthony Clayton

The Spanish-American War: Conflict in the Caribbean and the
Pacific 1895–1902
Joseph Smith

The War of the Austrian Succession, 1740–1748
M.S. Anderson

THE WAR OF THE AUSTRIAN SUCCESSION, 1740–1748

M. S. ANDERSON

LONGMAN
London and New York

Longman Group Limited,
Longman House, Burnt Mill,
Harlow, Essex CM20 2JE, England
and Associated Companies throughout the world.

*Published in the United States of America
by Longman Publishing, New York*

© Longman Group Limited 1995

First published 1995

ISBN 0 582 05951 8 CSD
ISBN 0 582 05950 X PPR

British Library Cataloguing-in-Publication Data

A catalogue record for this book is
available from the British Library

Library of Congress Cataloging-in-Publication Data

Anderson, M.S. (Matthew Smith)
The War of the Austrian Succession, 1740–1748 / M.S. Anderson.
p. cm – (Modern wars in perspective)
Includes bibliographical references and index.
ISBN 0–582–05951–8 (CSD). – ISBN 0–582–05950–X (PPR)
1. Austrian Succession, War of, 1740–1748. I. Title. II. Series.
D292.A32 1995   94–15591
940.2'532–dc20   CIP

Set by 7 in 10/12 Sabon
Produced by Longman Singapore Publishers (Pte) Ltd.
Printed in Singapore

CONTENTS

LIST OF MAPS

ACKNOWLEDGEMENTS

This book, which covers relatively briefly a large and complex subject and is intended in the main for students, is the product of reading and teaching which has extended over many years, sometimes intermittently, and to which many friends have contributed, sometimes unconsciously. I should like, however, to pay tribute to the memory of my former teachers, David Horn and Richard Pares, who did most of all to awaken my interest in history in general and that of the eighteenth century in particular, and also record my debt to the editor of this series, Hamish Scott, to whose perceptive and illuminating comments I owe much. As always, I am also deeply indebted to the British Library, the British Library of Political and Economic Science and the London Library. Without their bountiful resources and helpful staffs my task would have been much more difficult.

ABBREVIATIONS

Arneth, *Geschichte*	A. von Arneth, *Geschichte Maria Theresias* (10 vols, Vienna, 1863–79)
Barbier, *Chronique*	*Chronique de la Régence et du Règne de Louis XV (1718–1763), ou Journal de Barbier* (4 vols, Paris, 1885)
Baudi di Vesme, *La Pace*	C. Baudi di Vesme, *La Pace di Aquisgrana (1748)* (Turin, 1969)
Baudrillart, *Philippe V*	A. Baudrillart, *Philippe V et la Cour de France* (5 vols, Paris, 1890–1902)
Berney, *Friedrich*	A. Berney, *Friedrich der Grosse: Entwicklungsgeschichte eines Staatsmannes* (Tübingen, 1934)
Butler, *Choiseul*	R. Butler, *Choiseul*, i, *Father and Son, 1719–1754* (Oxford, 1980)
Carutti, *Storia*	D. Carutti, *Storia della Diplomazia della Corte di Savoia* (4 vols, Turin, 1875–80)
Guglia, *Maria Theresia*	E. Guglia, *Maria Theresia: Ihre Leben und ihre Regierung* (2 vols, Munich–Berlin, 1917)
Lodge, *Studies*	Sir R. Lodge, *Studies in Eighteenth-Century Diplomacy, 1740–8* (London, 1930)
Mediger, *Moskaus Weg*	W. Mediger, *Moskaus weg nach Europa: Der Aufstieg Russlands zum europäischen Machtstaat im Zeitalter Friedrichs des Grossen* (Braunschweig, 1952)

Pares, *War and Trade*	R. Pares, *War and Trade in the West Indies, 1739–1763* (Oxford, 1936)
Pol. Corr.	*Politische Correspondenz Friedrichs des Grossen*, ed. J. G. Droysen *et al.* (46 vols, Berlin, 1879–1939)
Richmond, *The Navy*	Sir H. W. Richmond, *The Navy in the War of 1739–48* (3 vols, Cambridge, 1920)
Sautai, *Préliminaires*	M. Sautai, *Les Préliminaires de la Guerre de la Succession d'Autriche* (Paris, 1907)
Sautai, *Débuts*	M. Sautai, *Les Débuts de la Guerre de la Succession d'Autriche* (one vol. only published; Paris, 1909)
Wilkinson, *Defence*	S. Wilkinson, *The Defence of Piedmont, 1742–8: A Prelude to the Study of Napoleon* (Oxford, 1927)

INTRODUCTION

The war of the Austrian Succession is not an easy subject for the historian. Its difficulty lies in its lack of unity of theme, in the fact that it does not centre around any one clearly defined and predominant issue. It has, therefore, no single narrative spine around which secondary aspects of the story can be grouped. It was a series of struggles, interrelated indeed but sometimes quite loosely so, the product of widely differing ambitions cherished by different rulers and governments. These interreacted in complex and changing ways which are not always easy to make intelligible to the reader. The fact that many of the states involved – Bavaria, Saxony, Sardinia-Piedmont, the Dutch Republic, even to some extent Prussia – were of relatively secondary importance helps to strengthen this impression of flux and incoherence. Very often they were not strong or self-confident enough to pursue consistent policies and tended to become in effect clients and dependants of some greater power. This exposed them to the temptation to change sides, or threaten to do so, when they felt that such a move might offer greater security or bigger prospective gains. Such a situation explains much of the complexity of the diplomacy of these years. All the other great conflicts of the eighteenth century – the war of the Spanish Succession, the Seven Years War, the war of the American Revolution – had also a complexity and many-sidedness which is oversimplified by their textbook titles. But this is most marked of all where the struggles of the 1740s are concerned.

The most important and lasting results of these struggles came in east-central Europe, in the sudden leap of Brandenburg-Prussia to at least potential great-power status. Yet it was at war for less than three years of the seven and a half during which there was fighting on the continent. The ambitions of Frederick II were, from the widest European perspective, the most important single element in that fighting, and the only genuinely new one. It is from them, and from the reaction to them of the Archduchess Maria Theresa, that

1

much of the drama of the events of these years arises. From this confrontation, even though the king and his great opponent never met face to face, the reader gains a sense of personal conflict, of individuals gambling, sometimes desperately, for the highest stakes, which no other aspect of these years can give. By contrast, much of the fighting in west Germany, the Netherlands or Italy, important as it was and was seen to be, appears almost routine, a continuation of ambitions and antagonisms already visible for generations. Yet here also there were real issues involved with important implications for the future. The emergence from the war of Charles Emmanuel II of Sardinia-Piedmont with significant gains, even though they fell short of what had been hoped for in Turin, underlined the fact that his dominions were now the most ambitious and expansionist of the Italian states. The failure of France to exploit its overwhelmingly strong position in the Low Countries when the war ended was one of the most remarkable renunciations of its kind in the history of modern Europe. The ending in 1748 of the Spanish Bourbon dynastic ambitions in Italy, which had done so much for over a generation to complicate international relations, was a dividing-line in the history of Spain, and a constructive and necessary one. Even the indecisive Anglo-French naval and colonial struggle of 1744–8 strengthened existing antagonisms and hardened in both London and Paris the conviction that a further and conclusive struggle for empire must come soon.

The array of ambitions and fears which underlay the struggle of the 1740s – the desire of Frederick II for reputation and personal achievement; the tradition of French hostility to Habsburg power; the appetite of Charles Emmanuel for any territory he could lay hands on; the eagerness of Elizabeth Farnese and her husband to forward dynastic interests in Italy; the determination of Maria Theresa to preserve the territories she had inherited and the imperial title which was now seen as a Habsburg hereditary possession; the British desire to strike at French trade and colonies and the French one to avert any British maritime and imperial monopoly – all these forces, intertwining and often conflicting, make the story of these years a complicated one. But this does not mean that it was an unimportant one. These struggles were in many respects inconclusive, a prelude to the more decisive ones which were soon to come. In the eyes of posterity they have suffered by comparison with the longer and, for most of the participants, more demanding war over the Spanish Succession which preceded them, and even more because they fall short of the drama of the Seven Years War which followed. The life and death struggle of Prussia in 1756–62 and the sweeping naval and colonial victories of Britain in 1759 and 1762 have an element of the spectacular which the conflicts of the 1740s cannot quite match. But these conflicts were not meaningless. The conventional title 'war of the Austrian Succession' implies that they were inspired, at least in the main, by dynastic considerations. This is only very partially true. Maria Theresa was determined if possible to preserve in its entirety under Habsburg rule her ramshackle inheritance of disparate lands. Elizabeth Farnese's passionate desire to endow her younger son with a substantial principality in Italy irritated many of those who had to cope with its results. But, like the struggle over the Spanish Succession which had preceded it this was essentially a war about power, about territorial ambitions and the European balance, not about the legalities of dynastic rights. These might be used in efforts, often very transparent ones, to justify to the world a course of action inspired by quite different motives. But they were seldom more than camouflage of this kind. Frederick II knew well that the legalistic arguments he put forward to justify his crucial invasion of Silesia in December 1740 were worthless. The Elector Charles Albert of Bavaria had more faith in the claims to much of the Habsburg inheritance which he advanced a few months later; but few contemporaries saw these as much more than a convenient pretext. In this respect the struggles of the 1740s were something of a watershed. They came at a time when dynastic rights and claims of the kind which had so dominated international relations for centuries still had some power to inspire rulers and statesmen and influence state policies. Yet these rights, or alleged rights, were now more that ever before subject to simple considerations of state power. They had become merely one element in a balance whose preservation was now, more than ever before or since, an article of faith for virtually all observers of international relations.

In some ways the war of the Austrian Succession looks back rather than forward. It was the last great Anglo-French struggle, at least before the French Revolution, in which colonial rivalries were clearly subordinate to events in Europe. Much of the fighting was in areas – the southern Netherlands, northern Italy, to a lesser extent the Rhineland – where the great states had already fought out their quarrels for generations, even for centuries. The French attack on Habsburg power in 1741; Saxe's conquest of the Austrian Netherlands in 1744–8; efforts to assert Spanish power in Italy: all these struck chords which had resonated through earlier generations of conflict in Europe, back to the Habsburg–Valois rivalries of the early sixteenth century. Here again, however, forces of change can be seen. The sudden rise of Prussia was a very important element in the eastward movement of the major focus of international relations which was to be so noticeable after 1763, as the questions of Poland and the Ottoman Empire rose to a new level of urgency. The occupation of Prague in 1741–2 was by a considerable margin the furthest penetration eastwards of any west European army before Napoleon's campaigns against Russia in 1807 and 1812.

The war of the Austrian Succession therefore, more than many other great conflicts of its kind, sees the continent in transition, with dynasticism as a guiding principle in the relations between states clearly on the wane, with a great and enduring new rivalry emerging in east-central Europe, with the Bourbon–Habsburg antagonism so long accepted as inevitable now entering its last active phase. But it was more than a mere preface to later and more dramatic changes. It was a great and demanding struggle. It saw military achievements and diplomatic skills which can stand comparison with any during the decades which followed. As such it demands and deserves attention in its own right.

1 EUROPE IN 1740: THE PRAGMATIC SANCTION AND THE ANGLO-SPANISH WAR

FRANCO-HABSBURG RIVALRY

Western and central Europe at the end of the 1730s were at least as much divided by interstate rivalries and jealousies as at any time in modern history. Three sources of division were particularly important and threatening. In the first place, and still bulking largest of all in the minds of most contemporaries, was the traditional rivalry, with roots which went back to the early sixteenth century, between Bourbon and Habsburg. This was a struggle between the rulers of France, who saw themselves as heads of the most powerful of all European ruling families, and those of the Habsburg territories (already conventionally referred to as Austria), the group of provinces in central Europe and outlying possessions in the southern Netherlands and Italy united merely by their common allegiance to the imperial dynasty in Vienna. The sometimes spectacular defeats suffered by Louis XIV in 1703–9 during the war of the Spanish Succession had not shaken the belief of politically conscious Frenchmen that their country was the greatest European power and the focus of European civilisation. But the remarkable successes achieved by the Austrian Habsburgs during the last half-century – the recovery from the Turks of Hungary and part of Serbia; the making of the Hungarian crown hereditary in the Habsburg family and the suppression of a dangerous Hungarian nationalist revolt in 1703–11; the acquisition in 1713–14 of extensive new territories in the southern Netherlands and Italy – had given them an international importance which was not to be surpassed, or indeed equalled, at any time before the collapse of their power in 1918. The mediocre performance of their armies against France in the Rhineland during the war of the Polish Succession in 1733–5 and their downright bad one against the Turks in the disastrous Balkan campaigns of 1737–9 had taken some of the gilt off the gingerbread; and the financial weakness which had always dogged Habsburg government was at the end of the 1730s very serious. None the less, the power of Austria now seemed to many observers more than ever the only effective counterpoise to that of France in continental Europe.

French efforts to check and weaken Habsburg power centred on a line of policy which now had close on two centuries of tradition behind it – that of supporting and strengthening a number of the German states and using them to reduce the still great Habsburg influence in the Holy Roman Empire. Of these states much the most important from this standpoint was the electorate of Bavaria. Its geographical position between the Austrian provinces proper, Bohemia and the Tyrol, meant that it drove a great salient into Habsburg territory and made Bavaria, in spite of its limited economic and military strength, a dangerous weapon in the hands of any enemy of Habsburg power. If, on the other hand, the Habsburgs could acquire the electorate, this would greatly strengthen their own strategic position by rounding out their territories, making their frontiers shorter and more defensible and increasing their influence and prestige in Germany. The dream of adding Bavaria to their dominions was by no means new in the 1730s. Later in the century it was more than once to play a significant role in international relations, most obviously when in 1778–9 it stimulated a short-lived Austro-Prussian war.

The Bavarian Elector Max Emmanuel had thrown his weight on the French side at the outbreak of the war of the Spanish Succession; and a series of agreements made by him and his successor, Charles Albert, notably in 1714 and 1727, promised French support in asserting Bavarian claims to much of the Habsburg territories and the imperial title if the Emperor Charles VI died, as now seemed very likely, without a male heir. These treaties struck notes which were to be heard throughout much of the fighting and the tangled diplomacy of 1741–5 – a heavy French investment in men and money in Bavaria as an anti-Habsburg stalking-horse and a corresponding dependence of its rulers on France and particularly on French subsidies. Yet another agreement of 1733 consolidated this alliance: in Paris it seemed that the electorate might well become the focus of a French-backed anti-Habsburg coalition of German states. The clerical electorates of Cologne, Mainz and Trier might form part of this. More important, Saxony, whose ruler also had dynastic claims against the Habsburg inheritance which he might put forward if the emperor died without a male heir, could well join such an alliance. In July 1732 a

Bavarian-Saxon treaty of friendship supported by France was signed, while the French government supplemented its subsidy agreement with Bavaria by making another with Saxony. The French Foreign Minister, Chauvelin, discussed with Charles Albert the possibility of joint Saxon-Bavarian resistance to any effort by Charles VI, still without a son, to secure before his death the election of a successor of his own choice, and promised if necessary to provide 50,000 men to support such resistance. The great objective which the Marshal de Belleisle pursued so energetically and with such apparent success in 1741,[1] that of building up a union of German states which, with French backing, would reduce or even destroy Habsburg power and make French influence dominant in western Germany, had thus clearly taken shape much earlier. Belleisle's apparently brilliant though only momentary achievement was possible partly because he was pursuing objectives already well-established.

THE PRAGMATIC SANCTION

Charles VI and his ministers were very conscious of the dangers which loomed if he died without a son to inherit his territories; the safeguarding of the succession very soon became the most lasting preoccupation of his reign. His elder brother, the Emperor Joseph I, had left two daughters; and their rights to the Habsburg inheritance had been put aside only by a family arrangement of 1703, the Pactum Mutuae Successionis. If Charles died childless their claim to succeed him would be irresistible. If he left only daughters it would be very strong. In fact a daughter, the Archduchess Maria Theresa, was born in 1717, and another in the following year. For the rest of his life, as it became clear that no son was to be hoped for (one born in 1716 had lived for only a few weeks), Charles's most important objective was to ensure by every possible means that his dominions, so heterogeneous, dispersed and vulnerable, should pass undivided to Maria Theresa when he died. As a woman she could not inherit the imperial title which gave the Habsburgs, in the eyes of many contemporaries, a formal status superior to that of any other ruling dynasty (though it might well be possible to secure the dignity for her eventual husband). But all the Habsburg territories must be hers. Already in April 1713 Charles had issued a formal declaration providing that at his death all his hereditary lands

1 See below, pp. 74–5, 83.

should pass to his male heirs, and in default of these to his daughters and their issue. Only should both these lines of succession fail were collateral branches of the family to have any right to inherit. If this document, the Pragmatic Sanction, were accepted and effectively applied by the different Habsburg territories and the powers of Europe, Maria Theresa would receive the entire Habsburg inheritance.

In 1720 the emperor asked the diets of the various Habsburg provinces for formal confirmation of the Pragmatic Sanction; and this was forthcoming with little difficulty. In particular, the Hungarian diet in 1722–3 agreed to accept Charles's arrangements and the female succession. This was important, since in the kingdom of Hungary the diet was more powerful and had more real independence than similar bodies anywhere else in the Habsburg territories, and since if the Habsburg line were to fail the Hungarians would recover the right to elect their own king. It remained to persuade as many as possible of the states of Europe to recognise and guarantee the right of succession of the young archduchess. In this, over a period of years, Charles VI had considerable apparent success. As part of the complex and often futile diplomacy of the 1720s and 1730s Spain recognised the Pragmatic Sanction in 1725, Russia in 1726, Prussia in 1728, Great Britain in 1731, the imperial diet in 1732, and France in 1735. The next few years were to show how little many of these paper promises were worth. Indeed, most well-informed contemporaries saw clearly in the 1730s that there were threats to the integrity of the Habsburg territories, perhaps even to the continuance of Austria as a great power, which no amount of diplomatic skill could conjure away.

The claims of the daughters of Joseph I were always a potential source of danger. The Pactum Mutuae Successionis had declared itself to be 'irreversible and valid for all time'; but it was possible to argue in divine right terms (as their mother, the Dowager Empress Wilhelmine Amalia seems to have done) that, since their claim to inherit was given by God, no paper renunciation could nullify it.[2] The elder, Maria Josepha, married in 1720 the elector of Saxony; and her younger sister, Maria Amalia, became two years later the wife of the electoral prince of Bavaria. Both husbands formally agreed that the Pragmatic Sanction, and therefore the claims of

2 C. Ingrao, 'Empress Wilhelmine Amalia and the Pragmatic Sanction', *Mitteilungen des Österreichischen Staatsarchivs*, 34 (1981), 337.

Maria Theresa, overrode those of their wives. Yet when in 1732 the imperial diet recognised the Pragmatic Sanction, both Saxony and Bavaria refused to accept this decision; and behind both loomed the power of France. The elector of Bavaria, the pre-eminent French protégé, seemed particularly threatening. 'Europe will never be quiet', wrote the British ambassador to the Dutch Republic in 1734, 'until that Prince is satisfied, and if he can be satisfied it will cut up by the roots all the vast projects of France, upon the death of the Emperor.'[3] The position of France by the middle and later 1730s had indeed become very equivocal. Its guarantee of the Pragmatic Sanction in 1735 could perhaps be reconciled with the promises made to Bavaria in 1727 and 1733; for that guarantee specifically excluded any rights of third parties to the Habsburg inheritance. But a new agreement with Bavaria in May 1738, which confirmed and extended that of 1727, was hard to see as anything but a betrayal of the undertaking given to Charles VI three years earlier. The most effective obstacle to active French intervention as soon as the emperor should die was no paper promise, however solemn, but the attitude and character of the chief French minister, Cardinal Fleury. In power since 1726 and now in his late eighties, he was cautious by nature, and this tendency was strengthened by age. It seemed likely that his death would be followed by a more active and interventionist French policy in Germany. 'The guaranty of peace to the Pragmatick Sanction', wrote the same British diplomat in October 1735, 'is not worth a button after the Cardinal's death.'[4] Events were to show that it was not even necessary for Fleury to die for the ineffectiveness of the efforts of Charles VI and his ministers to be all too clearly displayed.

There was another tangled succession dispute which also gave France opportunities to fish in troubled German waters. This was the question of the Rhenish duchies of Jülich and Berg. Frederick William I of Prussia asserted, against a rival Wittelsbach claimant, that these rightfully reverted to his own Hohenzollern family on the death of their present ruler, the Elector Palatine; and from the 1720s onwards the vindication of this claim became his central objective.[5]

3 J. Black, 'Anglo-Wittelsbach Relations, 1730–42', *Zeitschrift für bayerische Landesgeschichte*, Bd. 55, Heft 2 (1992), 324.
4 Black, 'Anglo-Wittelsbach Relations', 327.
5 A good brief account of the intricacies of this issue can be found in W. Mediger, *Moskaus weg nach Europa: Der Aufstieg Russlands zum europäischen Maachtstaat im Zeitalter Friedrichs des Grossen* (Braunschweig, 1952), pp. 351–4.

Throughout the 1730s, however, it became increasingly clear that Habsburg influence would be used to oppose Prussian aggrandisement of this kind in west Germany. The paranoiac Frederick William developed as a result a deep and partly justified sense of betrayal. Here was another source of anti-Habsburg feeling based on jealously nurtured dynastic claims which France might exploit to reduce the power of its great rival. Its attitude here, however, was even less consistent than where the ambitions of Bavaria were concerned. In January 1739, a secret Austro-French agreement provided for the occupation of both duchies by the prince of Pfalz-Sulzbach, the Wittelsbach claimant, as soon as the old Elector Palatine should die (he did not in fact do so until 1742). But only a few months later secret Franco-Prussian negotiations in The Hague produced a French promise that Prussia should have part of Berg. In this fluid and unsatisfactory situation the question remained during the last days of Frederick William's life. When only a few days before his death in May 1740 he drew up for his son, the future Frederick II, a survey of Prussia's international situation, he urged him to enter into no alliance with France unless he were guaranteed the whole of Berg. In the event the Jülich-Berg issue was very soon to be pushed completely into the background by the spectacular emergence of much greater territorial disputes in eastern Germany and central Europe. But in the 1730s it was one of the more obvious elements of potential conflict in international relations and another indication of the way in which German dynasticism might open the door to French power and influence. 'France hath taken care', wrote an English pamphleteer in 1739, 'to gain over several Princes to the Interest of the House of Sultzbach; by which we see that the two Dutchies in dispute are of no small Importance; and 'tis great chance if, at the Decease of the Elector Palatine, a War will not be inevitable.'[6]

Moreover, if France should attempt actively to weaken the Habsburgs it was likely to find a ready ally in Spain, now also under Bourbon rule. In 1713, at the end of the war of Succession, the Spanish empire in Europe had been destroyed. The Spanish Netherlands, the duchy of Milan, Sardinia and the kingdom of Naples then went to Charles VI, making the territories ruled by the Austrian Habsburgs much more heterogeneous than ever before, while Sicily was taken by the duke of Savoy. (In 1719 he was forced to exchange it with Charles VI for the less valuable Sardinia.) These

6 *The Present State of Politicks in Europe* (London, 1739), pp. 27–8.

catastrophic losses marked the end of Spain's position as the centre of a great multinational European empire. They therefore relieved Spain of military and other burdens which it could not bear and helped it to concentrate on essential administrative reforms and economic growth. In this way they benefited Spain. Yet the losses were deeply resented. The Spanish government in 1713 refused to sign any formal peace with the emperor, while for his part Charles VI stubbornly adhered for a number of years to his claim to be the country's rightful ruler. Moreover, the desire in Madrid to recover lost territories and prestige was sharpened by the ambitions in Italy of Elizabeth Farnese, the second wife of the king, Philip V. Obstinate, domineering, narrow-minded and often stupid, she quickly gained over her husband an ascendancy which lasted until his death in 1746 and which gave her for a generation or more real influence in the affairs of Europe. By his first wife Philip had a son who was likely to survive and succeed him in Spain. To establish her own sons, the Infants Don Carlos and Don Philip, in substantial independent principalities of their own in Italy was therefore the supreme, indeed the only real, objective of the queen's life. Her efforts to achieve this, and to undermine the Habsburg position in the peninsula, underlay much of the convoluted diplomacy of the 1720s and 1730s. By 1735, as a central part of the peace which ended the confused war of the Polish Succession, Don Carlos was established as ruler of Naples and Sicily. This was a handsome endowment and a marked strengthening of Bourbon influence in Italy. But Don Philip, his younger brother, had still to be provided for. Here was yet another dynastic-territorial ambition which threatened the impressive but unstable position of the Austrian Habsburgs. Here again, moreover, the role of France was potentially decisive.

IMPERIAL RIVALRIES AND THE ANGLO-SPANISH WAR

In their rivalry with France the Austrian Habsburgs had usually, since the 1690s, had the support of Great Britain; and by the 1730s the assumption that Austria and Britain were natural allies against French ambitions was deeply rooted in the minds of British statesmen. Some natural law seemed to have decreed that the Habsburgs should counterbalance France in continental Europe while Britain opposed it at sea and in America. Anglo-French naval and colonial rivalries had played a significant role in the great international struggles of 1689–1713, and had remained active during the quarter-century of sometimes uneasy peace between the two countries which followed the Utrecht settlement. By the end of the 1730s they were stronger than ever before: on both sides of the Channel a new and larger-scale conflict of this kind seemed imminent. This readiness for another round in the competition for overseas empire grew out of the Anglo-Spanish war which began in late November 1739.

This conflict, which neither government really wanted and for which neither was well prepared, had several causes. But the fundamental one, from which the others sprang, was the Spanish claim, more and more undermined in practice but still tenaciously clung to, of universal monarchy in Latin America (apart from the Portuguese possession of Brazil with its completely undefined frontiers) and the surrounding seas. Against this the British government, and still more British trading interests, asserted with growing firmness that the high seas were open to the ships of all nations. The Spaniards attempted to make good their pretensions to sovereignty by seizing British ships which they claimed, very often with justification, to be engaged in prohibited trade with the Spanish colonies. Complaints by British merchants and seamen of these 'depredations' began almost at once after the Utrecht settlement; and though their number and intensity fluctuated considerably they were henceforth a constant potential source of trouble between the two countries. The Spanish *guarda-costas* could be brutal in their searches of British ships for suspect goods – indigo, cocoa or Spanish money – and in their interrogation of their crews, while once a ship had been condemned by a Spanish colonial court any appeal against the decision was a slow, difficult and expensive business.

For several years in the early and middle 1730s the number of seizures of this kind, and therefore the amount of conflict over them, was in general small. Moreover, the government in Madrid made some effort to meet British complaints: in 1731 the governors of Puerto Rico and Santo Domingo were recalled, and two years later new regulations made it more difficult for law-abiding British ships to be seized by *guarda-costas*.[7] But in 1737, when eleven British ships were taken, tension began to rise. Britain and Spain had now embarked on a course which was to end in war. There were also territorial disputes between them, though in Britain these

---

7 Jean O. MacLachlan, *Trade and Peace with Old Spain, 1667–1750* (Cambridge, 1940), pp. 90–1.

had much less emotional weight. If Spain were legally sovereign over all central and south America no colonisation there was lawful unless with express Spanish permission. This meant that the small settlements of British logwood-cutters in Campeche and Honduras were illegal, as were the exports of logwood, important in the textile industries, which they provided. The creation of the new British colony of Georgia from 1732 onwards, again, seemed to the Spanish authorities a threat to their tenuous hold on Florida: in the spring of 1738 a substantial expedition (3,000 men to be carried in flat-bottomed boats) was being prepared in Havana to attack the British settlements there.[8]

On neither side was there complete unity or consistency of attitude. On the British one there was a good deal of friction between the South Sea Company, which enjoyed monopoly trading rights with Spanish America given it originally by a Tory government, and the competing private traders, who were generally more aggressive and uncompromising in their demands. It was also frequently claimed in Jamaica, the most important British Caribbean colony, that the company was responsible for pushing up the price of negro slaves there and thus hampering the development of the island. There were allegations, again, that the large-scale smuggling associated with the 'Annual Ship' (the single vessel which, under the Asiento agreement of 1713 with Spain the South Sea Company was entitled to send each year to trade at Porto Bello on the isthmus of Panama) reduced the market for British goods exported legitimately through Cadiz to the Spanish colonies.[9] On the political and parliamentary level there was a marked cleavage between the leading ministers, such as Sir Robert Walpole, First Lord of the Treasury, or the duke of Newcastle, one of the Secretaries of State, who tended to be identified with the great privileged trading companies, and an opposition which stood for the lesser private traders and by the later 1730s was becoming more and more bellicose and unwilling to accept any kind of compromise settlement. On the Spanish side the 1720s and 1730s saw considerable efforts to foster trade with America and the Caribbean; but there were fluctuations in the thoroughness with which the country's claims there were enforced. There was hope in London

---

8 Sir H. W. Richmond, *The Navy in the War of 1739–48* (3 vols, Cambridge, 1920), i, 10.

9 R. Pares, *War and Trade in the West Indies, 1739–1763* (Oxford, 1936), pp. 18–21.

that the death in 1736 of José Patiño, the efficient administrator who had since 1727 been Minister for Marine and the Indies, and his replacement by the less energetic La Quadra, might mean a slackening in this respect, though these were not realised. Underlying the whole situation, however, was an increasing self-confidence in Britain, at least among the 'political nation' and in opinion-forming circles. This bred a strong belief that in a war with Spain Britain was bound to win, and that such a war would be both easy and profitable. Spanish government finances, it was argued, depended very heavily on bullion from America; and Britain's overwhelming naval superiority meant that it could at will cut off its flow with catastrophic results for Spain. If there were a war, argued one pamphleteer just before its outbreak, the Spaniards 'must, at last, be content to agree to such Terms, as we then would be pleas'd to impose, or become bankrupts with other Nations, who are concerned in the Plate Fleet, which it is in the Power of *Great Britain* to keep from ever arriving at *Cadiz*'.[10] History seemed to support such attitudes: in 1657 Blake's destruction of the Spanish treasure-fleet at Tenerife had struck a heavy blow at the already flagging Spanish war effort in Portugal and the Netherlands, while in 1726 a British blockade of Porto Bello, by cutting off supplies of American silver, had helped to prevent Spain from subsidising Charles VI, its very temporary ally, in the international crisis of that year.

The vision of great profits to be made from the capture of Spanish treasure-ships was even more alluring; and though possibilities of this kind were grossly exaggerated they did exist. The taking at Vigo in 1702 of a number of Spanish treasure-galleons seemed an example of what might be achieved; and the war, when it came, produced enough rich prizes to keep hopes of this kind alive. When in March 1739 a member of the House of Lords argued that 'In a War with Spain, if we judge from Experience, we have more to hope than to fear. We may do them great Damage, and gain considerable Advantage to ourselves, even by Privateering, or seizing their Ships at Sea',[11] he spoke for the majority of politically conscious Englishmen. All this reflected the still almost universal assumption that the trade of any state could grow significantly only if that of its competitors declined, that trade between nations was a zero-sum game. War therefore allowed Britain to expand its

---

10 *The Present State of Politicks in Europe*, p. 8.
11 P. Woodfine, 'The Anglo-Spanish War of 1739', in J. Black (ed.), *The Origins of War in Early Modern Europe* (Edinburgh, 1987), p. 189.

commercial life and increase its commercial profits faster than it could in time of peace. By destroying the trade of its rivals Britain would foster its own. War was an opportunity, not a threat. This belligerent attitude, though it reached its climax in the later 1730s, was not new. It had developed to keep pace with the growth of Britain's American and West Indian trade, and had already been summed up in the cumbersome title of a pamphlet published in 1727: 'Britain's Speediest Sinking Fund is a Powerful Maritime War, Rightly Manag'd, and Especially in the West Indies'.

It was very likely that any effort by Spain to resist British expansion would be supported by France. In November 1733 Louis XV and his uncle Philip V, in the treaty usually known as the first Family Compact, had guaranteed each other's territories, colonial as well as European, while Louis had specifically promised to assist Spain if it were attacked and to help it recover Gibraltar. But possibilities of this kind did little to shake the self-confidence of much British opinion. On the contrary; since France was a much greater commercial rival than Spain, there was correspondingly more to be gained, it could be argued, by destroying its trade than by attacking that of Spain. Thus the likelihood of war with France as well as Spain was welcomed rather than feared; from some of the language used by patriotic British pamphleteers and orators it might almost be thought that France, not Spain, had been the real enemy from the beginning. The great West Indian planter William Beckford, who a few years later advocated war with the French because 'our trade will improve by the total extinction of theirs',[12] spoke for a large and noisily vocal body of opinion. This light-hearted view of a struggle with both Bourbon powers was not in 1739 shared by most of those best placed to understand its dangers. The most senior and experienced British naval commander, Sir John Norris, for example, opposed the decision to declare war on Spain. But it was a very widespread attitude.

There was much fruitless negotiation during the 1730s over the points at issue between Spain and Britain, notably in 1737 when for a moment a settlement seemed in sight. Newcastle in that year could even envisage an alliance with Spain which, he thought, 'would not only be for the mutual advantage of both kingdoms, but might also greatly tend to the security of the Balance of Power in Europe'.[13] Finally, in January 1739, Walpole and Geraldino, the Spanish

---

12 *Cambridge Economic History of Europe*, iv (Cambridge, 1967), 561.
13 R. Browning, *The Duke of Newcastle* (New Haven, Conn.–London, 1975), p. 92.

ambassador in London, reached an agreement which was accepted and ratified by Spain. This involved a complicated balancing of claims and counter-claims. On the one side were British demands for compensation for the depredations of the *guarda-costas* and for property of the South Sea Company lost during the brief Anglo-Spanish wars of 1718 and 1727. On the other, the Spaniards claimed money allegedly owed to Philip V by the company as his share in the profits of the Annual Ship (he was entitled to a quarter-share in the cargo and 5 per cent of the profit on the rest) and as duties on the slaves which the Asiento allowed it to sell in Spanish America. The upshot was an agreement by the Spanish government to pay £95,000 by the end of May 1739. This compromise figure was reached only because the British envoy in Madrid, Benjamin Keene, exceeded his instructions and reduced the £140,000 which Britain had originally claimed: Walpole had great difficulty in persuading the Privy Council to accept the lower sum, and some opposition publicists were now claiming that British merchants had lost as much as £500,000. (A pamphlet written to defend the government, on the other hand, calculated the losses caused by Spanish 'depredations' at an annual average of only £5,000 – about $2\frac{1}{2}$ per cent of the whole value of British trade with Spain's West Indian possessions[14] – and it is clear that in directly material terms the issue was a relatively minor one.)

But in any case the Spanish promise was never carried out. In the late spring of 1738 a British squadron had been sent to the Mediterranean in an effort to put increased pressure on Spain. It had been intended to reduce it after the signature of the convention; but towards the end of March its commander, Admiral Haddock, was ordered to keep all his ships with him. By the early summer he was cruising off Cape St Vincent with the obvious intention of cutting Spain's trading links with its American empire; and soon another squadron under Admiral Ogle took up position off the coast of Portugal with the same purpose. The government in Madrid quickly made it clear that so long as this situation continued there was no hope of a settlement. The £95,000 was not paid; and in May the South Sea Company's Asiento was suspended. In taking this line the Spanish ministers may have been influenced by hopes of French support. Certainly, the decision not to weaken Haddock's force was inspired by fears in London of a new Franco-Spanish agreement.

14 Woodfine, 'The Anglo-Spanish War', p. 191.

In London the pressures for war were now rapidly gathering strength. This was not a matter of the relatively trivial £95,000. Walpole's opponents, their appetites sharpened by many years of exclusion from power, now scented an opportunity to bring him down. In the year from March 1738 to March 1739 about fifty memorials, petitions and addresses were sent to Parliament and the Board of Trade by merchant groups protesting against the damage allegedly being done to British trade.[15] The opposition could attack the agreement with Spain, moreover, on at least ostensible grounds of principle. It contained provisions for regulating both the right of search claimed by Spain and the free navigation in American waters demanded by Britain. But, it was argued, to regulate the former was to recognise its legitimacy, something which could be presented as a shameful surrender by Britain, whereas to regulate the latter was to set limits to a natural right which ought to be unbounded.

Much of the outcry raised against the agreement and the government in 1739, however, was at bottom little more than a struggle for office, an effort by one set of politicians to oust another. Walpole's brother, hardly an impartial observer but one with long experience, thought that the whole agitation would die away 'if the Clamour they [the opposition leaders] have raised for a War will but help them to put an End to the present Administration and let in those who have been so long excluded from a share in it'. Two generations later a well-informed historian had no doubt that 'It was the evident purpose of some of those writers [the anti-government pamphleteers] to drive the nation headlong into war, without thinking of any other consequences, than acquiring power, or gratifying spleen'.[16] Nevertheless, in London the agitation was loud and apparently threatening. When the Court of Aldermen rejected as a possible Lord Mayor a known supporter of the government this convinced the always nervous duke of Newcastle that war must be declared before the reassembly of Parliament in November opened the way to possible defeat there. A combination of greed and timidity thus led Britain into a conflict which more statesmanship and stronger nerves could have avoided.

15 Kathleen Wilson, 'Empire, Trade and Popular Politics in Mid-Hanoverian Britain: The Case of Admiral Vernon', *Past and Present*, 121 (Nov. 1988), 78. On the agitation for war with Spain, see in general G. Niedhardt, *Handel und Krieg in der Britischen Weltpolitik, 1738–1763* (Munich, 1979), pp. 73ff.

16 (H. Walpole), *The Grand Question, Whether War, or no War, with Spain* (London, 1739), p. 24; G. Chalmers, *Estimate of the Comparative Strength of Great Britain* (London, 1804), p. 113.

The first weeks of the war saw a success which seemed to bear out the claim that easy and profitable conquests could be made in Spanish America. In November 1739 a force under Admiral Vernon captured Porto Bello. The success was seen in Britain as the first of many to come, and Vernon, an able but impossibly quarrelsome commander, enjoyed extraordinary popularity. He was given the freedom of the City of London and chosen (without his knowledge or any action on his part) as member for three different constituencies in the parliamentary election of 1741, while in 1740–3 over a hundred different medals were struck in his honour, more than for any other figure in eighteenth-century Britain. A leading opposition figure told him in June 1741 that 'You are certainly at this time the most popular and the most loved man in England.' There was even a short-lived newspaper called *The British Champion; Or, Admiral Vernon's Weekly Journal.*[17] But all this flattered to deceive. Though war had become almost certain in May 1739 with the collapse of the agreement reached a few months earlier, the ministers in London wasted a year or more in ineffective discussion of the strategy to be pursued.[18] A large expedition to the Caribbean slowly took shape during 1740; and in London there were even hopes that Cuba, an island much bigger and more valuable than Jamaica, which 'will give us the key to the West Indies', might be taken. Such a success would show the Spaniards that 'they shall in great measure depend upon us, the chief Maritime Power, for the very possession of their Indies'.[19]

Once more, however, these hopes proved ludicrously optimistic. Not until December did the expedition reach the West Indies, and it was poorly organised and ineffectively led. The naval and military commanders involved, Admirals Ogle and Vernon and General Wentworth, found it impossible to work together. Attacks on the important Spanish base of Cartagena in what is now Venezuela in March–April 1741 and on Santiago de Cuba in July–August were humiliating failures. Disease, always the greatest threat to any significant campaigning in the West Indies, carried off appalling

17 Wilson, 'Empire, Trade and Popular Politics', 85–6; *The Vernon Papers*, ed. B. McL. Ranft (Navy Records Society, vol. 99: 1958), p. 240; M. Harris, *London Newspapers in the Age of Walpole* (London–Toronto, 1987), p. 168.

18 Pares, *War and Trade*, pp. 65–77. For a good contemporary statement of British hopes, see *The Present State of the Revenues and Forces . . . of France and Spain, Compar'd with those of Great Britain* (London, 1740), pp. 33, 42.

19 *The Vernon Papers*, pp. 121–2.

numbers of men: of the 10,000 sent there in two separate forces in October 1740 and January 1742 only 2,600 were still alive by October of the latter year. Of the 7,400 who died, only a little more than 600 did so in action: yellow fever and other diseases did for the rest.[20] Moreover, there were soon clear signs that a war even with Spain alone would involve significant commercial as well as human losses. Late in 1741, after a year of ineffective hostilities, a petition signed by over 200 London merchants complained that more than 300 of their ships had been taken by the Spaniards (overwhelmingly by privateers) since the war had begun.[21]

Most serious of all was the danger of French intervention. This was well understood in Whitehall. In August 1739 Newcastle told the earl of Hardwicke, the Lord Chancellor, that 'we take it for granted, that France will join Spain, and that we shall be attacked at home'.[22] Against this threat the obvious strategy was to seek European allies and try to rouse on the continent opposition which would force France to divert its energies to land warfare there. Some efforts in this direction were made; but their failure merely underlined the gravity of the situation and the frivolity of hopes of easy success against both Bourbon powers. 'I think all is at stake', wrote Horatio Walpole in September 1740, 'the whole power of France employed jointly with that of Spain against England without a special Providence will prevail; nothing but a diversion upon the Continent can save us.'[23] Admiral Norris also argued strongly that France and Spain united would be too much for Britain in a naval war; he therefore pressed for military action in Europe to divert French energies away from the conflict at sea and in America. 'I told Sir Robert [Walpole]', he wrote, 'I thought the best way to embarrass France was to endeavour to get four score thousand men into Flanders without reckoning on the Dutch that would then be obliged to come in.' The emperor would join in such a war 'and were I in Sir Robert Walpole's place I would by March have an army of 80 thousand men in Flanders and the Emperor in Naples: [this] would be the greatest hope of success against France'.[24]

20 R. Harding, *Amphibious Warfare in the Eighteenth Century: The British Expedition to the West Indies, 1740–1742* (London, 1991), p. 149.

21 Richmond, *The Navy*, i, 183.

22 J. Black, *Natural and Necessary Enemies: Anglo-French Relations in the Eighteenth Century* (London, 1986), p. 37.

23 Historical Manuscripts Commission, 14th Report (1895), Appendix, Pt ix, C.7882.

24 Richmond, *The Navy*, i, 94–5.

This was a realistic assessment of the situation; and the great diversion of France's attention to its land frontiers was soon to come, though in a quite unforeseen form. But in the first months of the Anglo-Spanish struggle open conflict between Britain and France seemed certain. Almost three months before the opening of formal Anglo-Spanish hostilities a French squadron under the marquis d'Antin had left Brest for the West Indies. D'Antin's instructions meant war with Britain: they envisaged a successful attack on the British squadrons in the Caribbean and on Jamaica. Fleury had now decided that conflict was inevitable. Moreover, Vernon for his part had orders to attack the French if he felt strong enough to do so. By early 1741 there was in the West Indies a concentration of European naval power far greater than any ever seen before; Britain, France and Spain now had there between them more than seventy ships of the line. In European waters also the situation was potentially explosive. At the end of July there was a serious clash between British and French squadrons in the Straits of Gibraltar with loss of life on both sides.

Yet outright conflict between the two great maritime and colonial rivals was to be delayed for several years. In part this was because d'Antin's expedition was a complete fiasco. It was hamstrung by problems of communication and of cooperation with the Spaniards, handicapped by shortage of food and devastated by disease.[25] Like the British expedition of the same year it showed how hard it was to operate efficiently on a large scale in an environment so difficult and in many ways so hostile. But these were merely, in an acute form, the normal difficulties of West Indian campaigning. Much more important, and totally unexpected, was the revolutionary change in international relations which began at the end of 1740. This not merely forced Britain and still more France to concentrate on events much nearer home. It also marked a fundamental rearrangement of the political and military balance of the continent.

---

25 For a detailed account of its tribulations, see Pares, *War and Trade*, pp. 164–77.

2 ARMIES AND NAVIES IN TRANSITION

STATES AND ARMIES: PROVISION AND CONTROL

The ability to wage war successfully was the ultimate test of any state in old-regime Europe. In every major one the government was first and foremost a gigantic war-making machine. The maintenance of adequate and efficient armed forces was in its own eyes, and usually in those of its subjects also, its most fundamental obligation. Tax regimes, administrative mechanisms, even social structures, were powerfully influenced by the need, in a state-system based on conflict and competition, for military strength and efficiency.

In their composition and their relations with the governments and societies which maintained them, armies and to a lesser extent navies were now in a phase of transition. The days of the out-and-out mercenary, the 'military enterpriser' who raised a regiment or sometimes even an army on his own account and made it available for pay to the highest bidder, treating it virtually as a business enterprise, were now in the past.[1] More and more, governments were taking effective control of their armed forces, setting standards, enforcing uniformity, restraining or eliminating private profit as a driving force in military and even more in naval organisation. Yet at the same time relics of the past survived everywhere, sometimes with important effects. In many states the sale of army commissions continued, though governments made increasing efforts to see that this did not interfere, at least to a dangerous extent, with military efficiency. In every army, and to a less extent every navy, noble birth and high social standing continued to be a necessary passport, or at least a very great help, to the achievement of high command. Everywhere government

---

1 The classic treatment of this very important seventeenth-century phenomenon remains F. Redlich, *The German Military Enterpriser and his Workforce* (2 vols, Wiesbaden, 1964–5).

pressures towards central control and direction, economy, standardisation and efficiency continued to meet opposition from deeply-rooted traditional rights and individual and group interests. In Britain, in spite of the lack of a strong military tradition and the popular hostility and suspicion with which the army was regarded, the process of modernisation had gone further in many respects than in most of the great continental states. Efforts to limit the selling of army commissions had begun as early as the 1690s; and both George I and George II disliked the system and wished to end it altogether. This was too drastic a step to be practicable; but in 1720 such sales were regulated by an official tariff of prices (from £9,000 for the colonelcy of a cavalry regiment down to £170–200 for the lowest officer rank in a marching one). Both rulers succeeded in ensuring that colonels, who did more than any other officer to set the tone of the army as a whole, were always competent soldiers with long service.[2] Elsewhere the hold of the past in this respect proved more difficult to shake off. In France regiments and companies remained the undisputed property of the colonels and captains who commanded them, bought and sold like other sorts of property. It was only in 1762, over forty years later than in Britain, that the government laid down a tariff of maximum prices which might be charged for them.

In the Habsburg territories the situation was even more backward-looking and resistant to rationalisation and central control. There the colonel-proprietor (*Inhaber*) of a regiment remained more powerful than anywhere else in Europe. In most regiments he had the power of life and death over the men he commanded. He alone promoted officers and NCOs in it, while no member of it could marry without his permission. He could claim a horse or a money payment from the estate of any officer who died under his command and the entire property of one who died intestate. The way in which the regiment was drilled and the tactics in which it was trained, which had important implications for its behaviour on the battlefield, were entirely under his control. Until at least the middle of the century the Habsburg army was thus in practice little more than a group of loosely associated regiments, each one a kind of little feudal seigneury: this situation, which Maria Theresa recalled with bitteness in later years, does much to explain its lack of success in the 1740s, in spite of its courage in

2 A. J. Guy, *Oeconomy and Discipline: Officership and Administration in the British Army, 1714–1763* (Manchester, 1985), pp. 90–1, 138.

battle, against the much better organised and more integrated one of Frederick II. The chronic poverty of the government in Vienna encouraged this dangerous lack of central control: in the life-and-death struggle which began in 1740 there were Habsburg regiments which could hardly have survived but for the generosity of their wealthy commanders. The failures of these years made modernisation and greater efficiency imperative.[3] In 1748, at the end of the Austrian Succession struggle, the power of the *Inhaber* to impose corporal punishment on the ordinary soldier was limited. From 1749 onwards his freedom of action was cut down by the introduction of a system of tactics which applied to the entire army and by regulations which controlled his management of regimental affairs.[4]

There were a number of ways in which, in the mid-eighteenth century, a regiment or a company in most armies could still yield a substantial profit to its colonel or its captain. A colonel could benefit by the sale of commissions in his regiment, or might gain from private contracts he entered into for the supply of arms or uniforms for it. In the British army 'off-reckonings', the residue of the pay of the rank-and-file soldier after taking account of his subsistence and various deductions, was an important source of income. A captain also might make money from clothing and arming his company, or might extract fees from his men for permission to marry or go on leave. Sometimes, as in the Prussian army, he might pocket during their absence the money allocated for their subsistence. The details, inevitably, varied considerably between different states. But one major theme running through the military history of this period is a growing effort by many governments to restrict such activities, with all the inefficiency and often sharp practice they made possible. Increasingly, they sought to assume many of the powers and functions which had hitherto been in the hands of individual officers. This effort was symbolised by the increasing practice (in the British army from 1713, for example, in the Habsburg one only from 1769) of designating regiments by a number and not, as had hitherto been normal, simply by the name of their colonel. Such a change strongly implied that they were now parts of a much larger whole, centrally organised and controlled,

3 See below, p. 213.
4 C. Duffy, *The Army of Maria Theresa: The Armed Forces of Imperial Austria, 1740–1780* (Vancouver, 1977), pp. 32–3.

and not as in the past essentially the personal fiefs of their commanders.

Of more direct practical importance, governments were now
taking responsibility for the weapons of their armies and beginning
to impose on them uniforms which must conform to official
patterns. More important still, systems of drill and tactics were now
beginning to be standardised: they could no longer be left merely to
the whim of individual commanders.

The functions of the colonel or the captain as an entrepreneur,
an investor who expected to make a profit from the rank he had
purchased as a dealer in arms, uniforms and horses, were thus
becoming less important. For such men war was ceasing to be a
trade and becoming a quasi-profession. Thus in France the
government adopted a single pattern of musket in 1717 and began
to provide arms for its soldiers from 1727 onwards, while at the
same time something was done to standardise uniforms. In Britain
from 1722 onwards colonels, though they still bought arms for their
regiments, had to make sure that these conformed to official
patterns. A generation later, in 1749 and 1751, the British
regulations governing dress became much stricter: deviations from
the official patterns were forbidden, and (a significant breach with
the proprietorial attitudes of the past) colonels were prohibited from
putting their personal arms, crests or parts of their servants' liveries
on their men's uniforms.[5] Almost simultaneously the same process
of change, the replacement of a semi-feudal hierarchy based on
personal relationships by a more rigid, impersonal and bureaucratic
one, was symbolised in France by a change in the way in which
soldiers were referred to in official documents. From 1745 the
formula 'soldat du sieur . . . , capitaine au regiment de . . . ' is
replaced by 'soldat au regiment de . . . , compagnie de . . . ': instead
of belonging in some sense to his captain, the soldier is now seen as
a member of a larger and less personal unit.[6]

Whether this taking-over by governments of many of the
functions hitherto carried out by colonels or captains always led to
greater efficiency, at least in the short run, is open to question. It
may have reduced the incentive for these officers to look after their
men as carefully as in the past.[7] Certainly it is striking that the

---

5 Guy, *Oeconomy and Discipline*, p. 149.

6 A. Corvisier, *L'Armée française de la fin du XVIIe siècle au ministère de
Choiseul: Le soldat* (Paris, 1964), ii, 850.

7 C. Duffy, *The Military Experience in the Age of Reason* (London–New York,
1987), pp. 68–9.

Prussian army, the most successful of the age, was also the one in which the powers and responsibilities of the captain in the supplying and general running of his company (*Kompagniewirtschaft*) were least touched by the intrusion of any central authority and the one in which opportunities to make substantial profits in this way were most marked. In the 1740s and 1750s it was reckoned that a captain in a Prussian infantry regiment could normally make 3,000 thalers a year, and one in a cavalry regiment more: the weapons of the company, for example, were considered his private property, so that when he retired or was promoted he could demand payment, normally 800 thalers, for them from his successor. Frederick II, who himself became colonel-proprietor of a regiment in 1732, claimed that one of his generals, starting with nothing, had amassed merely through military service a fortune of 150,000 thalers.[8]

Uniformity in drill and tactics was an essential step towards greater military efficiency, since on the battlefield regiments moved, deployed and fired as far as possible as they had been taught to do on the parade-ground. Differences in drill and tactics might therefore make it very difficult for different regiments to work together effectively in face of an enemy. In 1727 the later Marshal de Belleisle, who was to be the most important single influence on French policy in the crucial year 1741, complained that it was impossible 'to make several [French] regiments drill together, there being not one (*sic*) who does it in a uniform manner', since each colonel preferred his own movements and words of command. Some years later the Marshal de Saxe, the most successful French commander in the Austrian Succession struggle, made the same point. 'I have seen troops belonging to the same government', he wrote, 'when assembled after a long peace, differ to such an extent in their manoeuvres and formation of their regiments that one would have taken them for a collection from several different nations'.[9] One of the reasons for the formidable and unexpected effectiveness shown by the Prussian army in the 1740s was the fact that it had a uniform drill-code as early as 1714, before any other major state; and it was Prussia's achievements in the struggles of 1740–63 which, more than anything else, impressed on the rest of

8 O. Busch, *Militärsystem und Sozialleben im alten Preussen, 1713–1807* (Berlin, 1962), p. 133; C. Duffy, *The Army of Frederick the Great* (Newton Abbot–London–Vancouver, 1974), p. 32.

9 R. Butler, *Choiseul*, i, *Father and Son, 1719–1754* (Oxford, 1980), 278: *Roots of Strategy: A Collection of Military Classics*, ed. T. R. Phillips (London, 1943), p. 113.

Europe the need to move in this direction. Austria, which had borne the brunt of Prussian military efficiency during the 1740s, did so after 1748; but other states were slower to respond. Drill in the Russian army, for example, was standardised only in 1763, and in France in the following year.

Increased efficiency, greater professionalism, tighter control by central governments – all this accelerated the development of a distinctively military society with its own rules and values, one which was more clearly separated from the civilian life around it than ever before. This growing cleavage took concrete and visible form in the quartering of soldiers in peacetime in purpose-built barracks. More and more they were no longer billeted on the civilian population in the way which had been normal for generations, but physically segregated from it. This had important psychological implications. Barracks made possible a discipline which was stricter because more continuous and unremitting. They also helped to generate among the soldiers who lived in them a stronger *esprit de corps* and therefore a greater sense of separation from civilian society (something to which growing government control over the feeding, clothing and arming of the soldier also contributed). The states of Europe provided barracks for their armies at widely differing rates and times. In France a decree of 1719 ordered their building in all towns on major roads along which soldiers were likely to pass; and by 1742 over 300 French towns possessed them.[10] Elsewhere the process was much slower: cost alone made it difficult for the poorer states of central and eastern Europe to indulge in large-scale building of this kind. In the Habsburg territories, where one of the main motives of the military reforms set in motion after 1748 was to make the army more professional and efficient by separating it more completely from civilian society, an increasing proportion of it was housed in this way during the second half of the century. In Prussia, however, it was only in the decade or so before the death of Frederick II in 1786 that barracks began to be provided even in all the major towns; and in Russia to the end of the century they existed only in Moscow, St Petersburg and one or two provincial cities.

10 C. Jones, 'The Military Revolution and the Professionalisation of the French Army under the Ancien Regime', in *The Military Revolution and the State*, ed. M. Duffy (Exeter, 1980), p. 42. On barrack-building in France, see *Histoire militaire de la France*, ii, *1715–1871*, ed. J. Delmas (Paris, 1992), 47–8, and on its wider significance Corvisier, *L'Armée française*, i, 138.

ARMIES: THE HOLD OF THE PAST

In several ways, therefore, armies by the 1740s were clearly becoming more modern. Yet they also retained characteristics which were deeply rooted in the past. This is perhaps most noticeable in the extent to which they were still officered and led by aristocrats and ruled by aristocratic values. The Prussian army, the most strikingly successful of the period, was the one in which the officer corps was most completely dominated by a traditional landed ruling class. In 1739, on the eve of the Austrian Succession war, all its thirty-four generals were noble and of its 211 staff officers only eleven were commoners.[11] But everywhere aristocratic influences in military affairs remained very powerful. Indeed, growing government control and provision may well have made it more difficult for the poor officer with no personal fortune to have a satisfactory military career. By stripping away the opportunities for personal profit which officers had hitherto enjoyed in the clothing and arming of their men, without giving them any compensating increase in pay, these changes probably sometimes made an officer corps more aristocratic and snobbish. It is at least arguable that this happened in the British army.[12]

Snobbery and class-consciousness did not necessarily mean inefficiency, as the Prussian example showed. There was still a very widespread feeling that a member of a noble family, inheriting a tradition of military service and imbued with family pride, made a better officer than a commoner who was more likely to think primarily of material advantage and personal safety. Of this attitude the most uncompromising spokesman was Frederick II of Prussia. He fought throughout his life to safeguard the social and economic position of the Prussian *Junkers*, since 'they with their sons in wartime give the greatest service and have to defend the country' and 'the deserving nobility has sacrificed blood and goods in the service of the state'. The small and weak Prussian middle class, on the other hand, had little or no military value in his eyes, since 'most of them think meanly and make bad officers'.[13] But even if it did not impair efficiency in any serious way, the legacy of aristocratic attitudes and assumptions which the armies of this period had inherited was still very visible. It showed itself very

11 Busch, *Militärsystem und Sozialleben*, p. 93.
12 Guy, *Oeconomy and Discipline*, pp. 165–6.
13 Busch, *Militärsystem und Sozialleben*, pp. 103–4.

obviously in a continuing feeling, which was to persist for generations to come, that cavalry regiments, the traditionally aristocratic arm, were somehow superior to infantry ones, with the humble and almost artisan artillery and engineers at the bottom of the military social scale. Sometimes snobberies of this kind could be very complex. In the French army the twelve oldest regiments, which traced their history back to the sixteenth or early seventeenth century, formed an elite, the *vieux corps*, which was further subdivided into the *vieux* and *petits vieux* regiments. Officers in these enjoyed a range of privileges – special allowances in addition to their pay, first choice of billets when on campaign, and even the right to choose the position of their regiment on the battlefield.

A similar adherence to the values of a feudal past can be seen in a feeling that high-ranking officers should not be subjected to the full rigours of warfare. When in 1743 the Marshal de Noailles, the commander of the French army in west Germany, learned that the earl of Stair, then commanding the British forces which formed part of the army opposing him, had had a French bullet through his hat, he described this as something 'which I cannot approve; for I think it very indecent to fire upon a general'. In a somewhat similar way in September 1744, before beginning the bombardment of the fortified town of Coni in northern Italy, the French commander sent a flag of truce to ask the Austrian officer commanding the garrison to identify his own house so that the French artillery might try to spare it.[14] The same quasi-feudal heritage and resulting willingness to sacrifice efficiency to tradition and social status shows itself in the way in which officers, especially high-ranking ones, still very often took with them on campaign quantities of baggage which could seriously impede the movement of armies. At the highest level this could reach remarkable proportions. George II in the Dettingen campaign of 1743 had a personal baggage train of 660 horses, thirteen berlins (a type of coach), thirty-five wagons and fifty-four carts. His son, the duke of Cumberland, as commander of the allied forces in the Netherlands two years later, planned to bring with him on campaign 140 tons of baggage, while Louis XV, when he joined the French army there in the same year, came with an enormous retinue which included even the royal clock-winders.[15]

14 Butler, *Choiseul*, i, 413, 533.
15 R. Whitworth, *Field-Marshal Lord Ligonier: A Story of the British Army, 1702–1770* (Oxford, 1958), p. 94; J. M. White, *Marshal of France: The Life and Times of Maurice, Comte de Saxe* (London, 1962), p. 151.

The armies which fought the war of the Austrian Succession therefore combined, more than in most periods of European history, conflicting forces and tendencies. In them drives towards modernity, towards rationalisation and efficiency to be achieved through more effective control by central governments, coexisted with a large and still important residue of tradition.

ARMIES: RECRUITING

These armies were in many cases strikingly non-national, remarkably varied in their origins and linguistic make-up. The day when 'the nation in arms' would be an ideal, at least for some enthusiasts, was still far in the future. As yet no government hesitated to employ large numbers of foreigners in its army. Some tried hard to do so if this meant that useful tax-paying citizens could be left in their civilian employment and the economic strength of the state thus protected. Of all the combatants in the 1740s Prussia strove hardest to recruit outside its own frontiers. Even under Frederick William I only two-thirds of the army had consisted of native Prussians; and Frederick II tried to reduce this proportion to a third. He did not quite achieve this; but in his *Political Testament* of 1752 he made it clear that he wished to have an army at least half of which was not Prussian by origin.[16] Much of the Prussian army was recruited, mainly in the smaller German states, by methods which became notorious even in an age not very scrupulous in such matters. Men might be decoyed by promises of civilian employment and then, once on Prussian soil, find themselves enlisted willy-nilly. Thus an unfortunate but not untypical young Swiss, one of the few such recruits who has left an account of his experiences, after being engaged as personal servant to a Prussian recruiting officer, found himself when he got to Berlin forced into Frederick II's army.[17] Sometimes recruits were obtained from neighbouring states by what was in effect kidnapping. In 1729 Prussia and Hanover were for a moment not very far from war over the use of arbitrary methods of this sort; while some German rulers forbade Prussian recruiters (who were sometimes attacked by mobs in areas in which they appeared) to enter their territory.

16 Busch, *Militärsystem und Sozialleben*, p. 30.
17 U. Braker, *The Life Story and Real Adventures of the Poor Man of Toggenburg*, ed. D. Bowman (Edinburgh, 1970), pp. 119–21.

Soldiers obtained by such methods were particularly likely to desert at the first opportunity (as the Swiss mentioned above did); and guarding against desertion was throughout his reign the most enduring military preoccupation of Frederick II. The instructions for his generals which he drew up in 1747, the first document of this kind which he produced, begin depressingly but typically with elaborate advice on minimising desertion: armies should not camp near dense woods in which deserters could hide; they should not move by night unless this was unavoidable; soldiers were to be under guard when detached in small parties to collect water or forage; the flanks and rear of an army on the march must be covered by cavalry (with a much smaller foreign element and therefore less likely to desert than the infantry) in 'order to prevent escapes. Similar preoccupations, in a less extreme form, affected many European armies.[18]

Prussia, in fact, was merely an extreme example of a very widespread tendency. France had a long tradition of employing foreigners in its army: Swiss, Irish and, in particular, Germans still made up a very significant fraction of it, while France acquired a regiment of Corsicans in 1739 (thirty years before the island became French territory) and had earlier even recruited in Hungary. Something approaching a quarter of its army in the Austrian Succession struggle was made up of foreigners: by one calculation it was employing 52,000 such when it ended.[19] The Habsburgs recruited extensively from some of the states of the Holy Roman Empire, though after 1741, with Bavaria and for a time Saxony ranked among Maria Theresa's enemies, this source of manpower was considerably reduced. None the less, in 1744 nearly a fifth of all recruits for the Austrian army were from outside the Habsburg territories. Moreover, the character of the lands ruled from Vienna, with their complex mixture of ethnic and linguistic groups, meant that the Habsburg army was the most cosmopolitan of all: for generations ambitious foreign officers, from Germany, Italy, Lorraine, the southern Netherlands, even Ireland and Scotland, had sought to make careers in it.[20] It was only in 1905 that the

18 *Die Instruction Friedrichs des Grossen für seine Generale von 1747*, ed. R. Fester (Berlin, 1936), pp. 2–4.

19 P. Losch, *Soldatenhandel* (Kassel, 1933), p. 17.

20 Duffy, *The Army of Maria Theresa*, p. 47; on the very mixed geographical origins and linguistic character of the Habsburg officer corps, see T. M. Barker, *Army, Aristocracy, Monarchy: Essays on War, Society and Government in Austria, 1618–1780* (Boulder, Col., 1982), pp. 138–42.

Habsburg government ended the custom by which foreign officers could serve in its army without giving up their native citizenship. Elsewhere a willingness, even eagerness, to make use of foreigners is very clearly visible. In Spain (where there had been an effort to introduce a limited form of conscription in 1704 and the prestige of the army was relatively low) there was a proposal in 1751 to recruit twenty new battalions in Italy and the German states, though this was not followed up. This was at a time when twenty-eight of the existing 133 Spanish infantry battalions were already made up of foreigners. Even a relatively small and poor state such as Sardinia-Piedmont had a considerable number of Germans in its army, while in Russia, though it never recruited its rank and file abroad, in 1740 the forty-six generals who were natives of the country were supplemented by thirty-three who were not.[21] It was quite possible for a state to recruit in wartime even from the subjects of an enemy one: in 1745, when Britain and France were at war, a Jacobite clan chief was hard at work finding recruits in Scotland for the French regiment of which he was colonel.[22]

The fact that armies were so often a mixture of nationalities and languages made it possible for many officers to have remarkably cosmopolitan careers, moving easily from the service of one state to that of another as inclination impelled or opportunity offered. Perhaps the most striking example is the Danish comte de Lowendahl, who in the last months of the Austrian Succession war was to become Saxe's second-in-command in the Netherlands. He served first in the Polish army (at the age of thirteen) and then successively in those of Denmark, the Habsburgs, Poland once more, Prussia, Saxony and Russia, before entering French service in 1747 with the rank of lieutenant-general and becoming a marshal of France four years later. This cosmopolitanism and ease of movement meant that there were fairly numerous instances of members of the same family serving simultaneously in the armies of opposing states, sometimes even on the same battlefield. In the 1740s, for example, the future duc de Choiseul, a Lorrainer by birth, served in the French army while his younger brother was an officer in the Austrian one.[23]

21 G. Desdevises du Dézert, *L'Espagne de l'ancien régime*, ii (Paris, 1899), 218–19; A. de Saluces, *Histoire militaire du Piémont* (Turin, 1818), i, 362–5; A. T. Baranovich *et al.*, eds, *Ocherki Istorii CCCP XVIIIv.; vtoraya chetvert* (Moscow, 1957), p. 302.

22 B. Lenman, *The Jacobite Clans of the Great Glen, 1650–1784* (London, 1984), p. 153.

23 Butler, *Choiseul*, i, 401.

Apart from the direct employment of foreign mercenaries, many of the European states were able also to increase their military strength by hiring substantial auxiliary forces from other states. Many of the smaller German rulers found raising regiments for use in this way by larger and wealthier states a convenient method of keeping armies larger than their own territories could support. They might well also profit financially by what sometimes amounted to the sale of their own male subjects. Hesse-Kassel, a relatively poor area, was particularly prominent in this way: from the 1670s to the end of the Napoleonic Wars its rulers signed at least thirty-seven treaties for the hire of troops to other states.[24] Such arrangements were particularly useful to Great Britain, which had a markedly unmilitary population together with the resources of hard cash which the hiring of foreign auxiliaries in this way called for. Thus in 1741 the Danish and Hessian regiments then in its pay were a significant factor in the diplomacy of that crucial year, while in 1747–8 those hired in Russia seemed for a time a possibly decisive factor in the unsuccessful military struggle with France.[25]

Mercenaries and auxiliaries obtained from relatively poor areas – Switzerland, parts of Germany, even Russia – were important to wealthier western states such as France or Britain because it was often difficult for them to persuade adequate numbers of their own subjects to enlist. In both, the persisting strength of quasi-feudal ties meant that a local notable, an aristocrat or squire who was himself an officer, could often bring with him to the army a following of men who felt for him some personal loyalty or sense of obligation. Captains recruiting for their companies used to the full any local or family connections which might be useful in this way: this meant that a high proportion of the strength of many companies was often drawn from their commander's home area. Recruitment of this kind, based largely on personal relationships, was still significant over much of western Europe. But as armies became bigger and their organisation more impersonal and professional, it gave way more and more to other methods. Increasingly, particularly in towns, the officer or NCO who set up his table outside some inn and tried by beat of drum, by promises of adventure and opportunity, or even by printed leaflets, to persuade young men to enlist, was now the most important recruiting agent.

---

24 These agreements are listed in Losch, *Soldatenhandel*, pp. 7–15.
25 See below, pp. 78 and 174–6.

Positive motives might impel a man to become a soldier – a desire for change, for a new environment and a glimpse of a wider world – and clearly military service did sometimes offer escape from stultifying routine and monotonous drudgery. But to a very large extent voluntary or quasi-voluntary recruiting drew only on the poorest, the most marginal, the least economically valuable elements in society, on men who became soldiers because they had little or no choice, because the available alternatives were even less preferable. Men for whom society had no use continued, as for generations past, to make up a large fraction of the British and French armies. In the central European territories of the Habsburgs the situation was sometimes not greatly different. 'If we take the trouble to investigate the most important impulses which bring the lads to the free recruiting table', wrote an observer there in mid-century, 'we shall find they are things like drunkenness, a frenzy of passions, love of idleness, a horror of any useful trade, a wish to escape from parental discipline, inclination towards debauchery, an imaginary hope of untrammelled freedom, sheer desperation, the fear of punishment after some sordid crime, or however else you care to define the motives of worthless people like these.'[26]

Governments were only too glad to see such undesirables removed from civilian life and sent to fight for a society to which they could make no other positive contribution. In Britain there was no compunction, when it seemed necessary, about forcing such individuals into the ranks. Press Acts for the compulsory recruitment of criminals, debtors and vagrants, a kind of limited and class-based conscription, had been in force during the war of the Spanish Succession and reappeared in 1745–6 as the demands of the Austrian Succession struggle bit more deeply. In France also, an element of compulsion crept into army recruiting as the war went on. This took the form, again one well-established during the Spanish Succession struggle, of drafting considerable numbers of militiamen for service with the regular army. In 1741–4 almost 47,000 men were obtained for regular regiments in this way, and over the whole course of the war the total may have rached 80,000, perhaps some 30 per cent of all those who served.[27] In England this expedient could not be used. Any effort to do so would have aroused enormous opposition from Parliament and public opinion; and in any case the militia there now existed in form rather than as

26 Duffy, *The Army of Maria Theresa*, p. 48.
27 Corvisier, *L'Armée française*, i, 245; *Histoire militaire de la France*, ii, 20.

an effective force. The Jacobite rebellion of 1745–6 stimulated active discussion of the need to reform and strengthen it;[28] but nothing was done until the following decade. However militias, or even *ad hoc* forces of armed or partly armed peasants, could sometimes supplement effectively the operations of regular armies and become a significant factor in their own right. In 1741 such a peasant force offered considerable opposition to the Prussian invasion of Moravia, while in 1744 resistance of this kind did a good deal to hinder the operations of the French and Spanish armies in northern Italy.[29]

But of all the combatant states in the 1740s it was Prussia which, in spite of the desire of Frederick II for a high proportion of foreigners in his army, made the most effective military use of its limited manpower. Here peasant conscripts figured more prominently than in any other state except Russia.

In 1713–14 Frederick William I had enunciated more clearly than any of his predecessors the principle that the peasant was under a lifelong obligation to perform military service. In 1733 three cabinet orders, the culmination of a process which had been going on for decades, established the cantonal system, which became the most important single foundation of the Prussian army and was extended in the 1740s to the conquered areas of Silesia. This divided Brandenburg-Prussia into 'cantons' of about 5,000 households. Each was to produce recruits for a particular regiment, which was normally stationed in the area in time of peace. The poverty of a backward agrarian state such as Prussia, however, meant that the demands of the army, whatever the military ambitions of its rulers, could not be allowed to override completely the needs of agriculture: already in 1721–2 Frederick William had been forced to set limits to the burdens which recruiting placed on the peasant, since if these became impossibly heavy the position of the *Junker* landowner, the essential source of officers and officials, would also be fatally weakened. The result was that the men raised under the cantonal system, after a training period of eighteen months or two years, normally served in peacetime for only two or three months in each year and were otherwise free to work on the land or elsewhere. Even with this limitation the system, coupled with the taxes and other army-orientated obligations of the peasant (he often had to

28 J. R. Western, *The English Militia in the Eighteenth Century* (London–Toronto, 1965), pp. 105–17.

29 S. Wilkinson, *The Defence of Piedmont, 1742–8: A Prelude to the Study of Napoleon* (Oxford, 1927), pp. 162–4, 208.

provide forage for cavalry horses at fixed prices or help maintain those of the artillery train), was a heavy burden.

Nevertheless it was a regulated system, and as such preferable to the arbitrariness which had marked much earlier recruiting in Prussia. It had also considerable military advantages: these explain the adoption of a similar system, after several earlier suggestions, in the Habsburg provinces in 1781. It ensured a steady flow of recruits from the dispersed territories of the Prussian monarchy. Moreover, in an army in which there was a very large number of foreigners of diverse origins the *Kantonists* acted as a stabilising force and provided an important element of cohesion. The cantonal system also meant that the recruit was likely to find himself in a regiment and even a company where he was among men from his own immediate area, some of whom he might well already know or even be related to. This probably had important though unquantifiable effects on morale. In every old-regime army nothing placed the young peasant recruit, accustomed to a small and tightly knit village society, under greater psychological strain than to find himself thrust suddenly into a strange new environment in which he knew no one and had no one to whom he could look for support.

ARMIES IN ACTION

Commanders in the eighteenth century seldom thought in terms of fighting great battles and winning decisive victories. Such battles were inevitably risky: the objective was rather to outwit and outmanoeuvre the enemy, to force him into difficult and costly retreats (the situation in which he was most likely to lose men by desertion), to occupy his territory and draw food and other supplies from it, thus destroying his resources while economising one's own. Campaigning of this kind could sometimes be very effective, as the Austrian Marshal Traun showed when he forced Frederick II into a disastrous retreat from Bohemia in the last months of 1744.[30] The king of Prussia may well have had this experience in mind when, only a year or two later, he declared that without adequate supplies 'no army is brave, and a great general who is hungry does not remain a hero for long', while 'the greatest secret of war and the masterpiece of an able general is to make his enemy go hungry'. It is clear that he wished his generals to accept battle only with great

30 See below, pp. 134–5.

caution and when they felt in an obviously favourable position to do so.[31] Saxe, who was in most ways a radical military thinker, believed that a good commander might make war all his life without fighting a battle, while in 1752 the Saxon *Dienstreglament*, reflecting the received opinion of the age, declared that 'a battle is at once the most important and the most dangerous operation of war. A great general shows his mastery by attaining the object of his campaign by sagacious and sure manoeuvres, without incurring any risk.'

Moreover, even when a battle had been fought and won, the victors hardly ever pressed home their success in Napoleonic style. Frederick II again spoke for his age when he stressed the need for caution even in pursuit of a defeated enemy. Victory, he insisted, must not lead to the taking of any risk; so that after it had been won the successful commander must make sure that his army camped in the regular and approved manner and not throw away through carelessness the advantage he had gained.[32]

Even had commanders wanted to pursue highly aggressive strategies, to move swiftly over long distances, take the enemy by surprise, force battle upon him and then crush him, this was usually a physical impossibility. Rapid movement was difficult for an army of any size. Roads were always more or less bad and very easily damaged by having to carry much heavy traffic. 'A little rainy weather and a hundred or so wagons', complained Saxe, 'are enough to destroy a good road and make it impassable.'[33] This meant that the ability to move its equipment and supplies on a navigable river was one of the greatest advantages any army could enjoy. Frederick II in 1740, for example, commandeered boats on the river Oder to help his attack on Silesia. But such good luck was the exception rather than the rule. Guns and wagons were heavy and cumbersome (the 12-pounder field-gun, the heaviest in general use, weighed about 1½ tons) and needed large numbers of horses, or sometimes oxen, to pull them. These demanded large quantities of forage, which in its turn might have to be transported with much cost and difficulty. Feeding draft animals and cavalry horses, therefore, was often more difficult than feeding men. It was calculated that an army of 60,000 (a very large one) needed 40,000

---

31 *Die Instruction Friedrichs des Grossen*, pp. 8, 14, 112.
32 *Die Instruction Friedrichs des Grossen*, p. 110.
33 Phillips, ed., *Roots of Strategy*, p. 131; *Die Instruction Friedrichs des Grossen*, pp. 20, 24.

horses, and that in summer these needed 500 tons of fodder every day.[34] Given all the problems involved, the armies of the 1740s often moved as fast as could have been reasonably expected. Certainly those of Frederick II were usually more mobile than the Austrian ones which faced them; this was one of his major advantages, for at a pinch his army could march a dozen miles a day for two or three weeks at a stretch. But really quick movement, at least for large forces, was never easy.

Swift advances and daring, aggressive strategies were also often stultified by the continuing importance of fortresses and sieges. Saxe, when he condemned 'that rage for sieges which prevails at present', exaggerated somewhat. The days when an entire series of campaigns extending over many years might well consist of little more than a continuous chain of sieges (the classic example is the Spanish military effort in the Netherlands in 1621–48) were now in the past. But a commander had still often to capture a fortress which barred his advance or whose garrison, if he bypassed it, might seriously threaten his communications. Moreover, to take one which was well designed and resolutely defended a considerable number of heavy siege-guns (24-pounders weighing $2\frac{1}{2}$ tons each) was needed. To transport these, and the powder and shot for them, could add considerably to already substantial difficulties of movement; while to feed a besieging army, forced to remain for weeks stationary within a very limited area whose own resources were soon eaten up, might well not be easy. Prolonged resistance by a single fortress could therefore still powerfully influence or even decide an entire campaign. The fact that Neisse, alone of the Austrian strongholds in Silesia, resisted the Prussian invasion of 1741 became a fact of political as well as military importance, while in 1744 the operations of the French and Spanish forces in northern Italy were greatly hampered by the resistance of the relatively minor fortress of Coni.[35] There were still some areas, notably the Netherlands, where it was impossible to win any solid success without besieging and taking a considerable number of great fortress-cities. What allowed Saxe to achieve so much there in 1744–8 was not merely his hard-won victories on the battlefield, but at least as much the feebleness with which many of these towns

34 J. Keegan and R. Holmes, *Soldiers: A History of Men in Battle* (London, 1985), p. 225.
35 See below, p. 137.

were defended and the ease and speed with which he was able to capture them.

Even when two opposing forces found themselves face to face it was far from certain that there would be serious fighting. Armies moved in columns; but they fought in lines. To change from one formation to the other was a complex and usually very slow manoeuvre: the relative speed with which the well-trained Prussian army could manage it was another of its advantages, as Frederick II was well aware.[36] Even if one army wished to fight, therefore, the other could often retreat safely while its would-be assailant was getting into line. Like the difficulties of movement and the enduring significance of fortresses, eighteenth-century tactics helped to encourage cautious and defensive attitudes and an unwillingness to take risks.

Battles nevertheless were fought; and when they took place they could be very bloody. The muzzle-loading flintlock muskets with which infantrymen were armed were very inaccurate; and, since they had no sights, aiming in any effective sense was hardly possible. Their weight and clumsiness (the French musket, a typical one, weighed 9 pounds and was well over 5 feet long, while the Austrian one weighed over 11 pounds) helped still further to make accurate fire very difficult. A Prussian experiment towards the end of the century, in which a battalion of infantry fired at a target 100 feet long by 6 feet high representing an enemy unit, showed that they scored only 60 per cent hits even at so short a range as 75 yards.[37] In battle conditions the percentage of hits would certainly have been lower; and the Prussian army for most of the century was the only one in which there was any effort to give the soldier real musketry instruction. The ideal was fire which was rapid and sustained rather than accurate: on the parade-ground a rate of five rounds a minute could be achieved, though on the battlefield this fell to two or less. Most fighting was at very short range, however, and the heavy and soft lead bullets, fired with low muzzle velocities, could inflict very serious wounds as they spread on impact. Moreover, these wounds, in an age which knew nothing of antiseptics, very often became infected with devastating results.

Tactics on the battlefield were rigid and stereotyped. The infantry were drawn up normally in four ranks; but when Frederick II changed to a three-rank line in 1742 this was copied by the

36 *Die Instruction Friedrichs des Grossen*, p. 104.
37 Keegan and Holmes, *Soldiers*, p. 66.

French army in 1754 and by the Austrian one three years later – a sign of the new military prestige of Prussia and the growing tendency to imitate Prussian methods. The cavalry was usually stationed on the wings, while the lighter and more mobile field-guns were placed in the line of infantry, and advanced and if possible retreated with it. Such tactics stressed above all rigid discipline, the discipline which might enable men to withstand potentially murderous enemy fire. They had much less place for flexibility, improvisation or rapid adaptation to changing circumstances. They helped to ensure that battle casualties, in spite of the relatively primitive weapons, were often heavy.[38]

NAVIES: THE PROBLEM OF MANNING

In some aspects of naval warfare private enterprise remained important long after it had lost much of its significance on land. In wartime every belligerent at sea still sanctioned, indeed encouraged, the activities of privateers, privately owned vessels licensed by governments, usually fairly small and often very small, which preyed on the shipping of enemy states. The greatest age of this form of warfare was now in the past. The achievement of French privateers in the war of 1689–97 in taking over 4,000 English and Dutch prizes was not approached in the 1740s. But it was still very significant. If Dunkirk as a French privateering base had now lost its former importance St Malo had replaced it, while Spanish privateers sailing from the ports of the Basque provinces and Asturias during the war of the Austrian Succession did much damage to British trade: one of the ships had taken 120 prizes by the time she was herself captured. As early as 1742 the merchants of London presented petitions to both houses of Parliament complaining of the number of ships they were losing to Spanish privateers and of the failure of the Admiralty to protect them; this was followed by similar complaints from many of the outports.[39] On the British side there was much privateering all along the south coast of England, while the Channel Islands remained, as in the past, a nest of such activity.

38 On such issues generally, see B. Nosworthy, *The Anatomy of Victory; Battle Tactics, 1689–1763* (New York, 1990).

39 R. Beatson, *Naval and Military Memoirs of Great Britain from 1727 to 1783* (London, 1804), i, 123–4.

But the essential struggle at sea was between navies; and here all the belligerents had to face the same fundamental problem – that of manning their fleets. Finding enough experienced seamen – and when they had been found, preventing them from deserting – was a difficulty which none of them ever completely overcame. Navies were expensive. Men-of-war had very large crews (a first-rate ship of the line, mounting 100 guns, might have one of over 1,000), and these had to be paid, however inadequately. Ships were costly to maintain, especially if they were kept at sea for long periods. Every government, therefore, at the end of a war laid up much of its navy, keeping a small proportion of it active but most of its ships in harbour in varying states of preparedness. Officers were expected to be ready to serve as soon as called upon. In the British navy from the beginning of the century the system of half-pay had ensured the existence of a reserve of this kind; and in France, though the years 1715–40 saw the fleet in general suffer from a good deal of neglect, care was taken to keep the officer corps intact.[40] But in every navy, with the coming of peace the great majority of ordinary sailors returned to civilian life. Thus, though the British navy had serving in it during the war of the Austrian Succession an annual average of 50,000 or more men, this number fell very sharply to 10,000 or fewer with the coming of peace in 1748. When each new war broke out men had therefore to be recruited hastily and in large numbers. This, coupled with the fact that many of the ships needed much work before they were ready for sea, meant that no navy could reach its full strength until at least several months had passed.

In this process of mobilisation France had, at least in theory, some advantage over Britain. The French system of *inscription maritime*, which had been codified in 1689 and remained unchanged in essentials until the end of the old regime, was based on the drawing up of lists of seamen available for service in all the seaward areas of the country. This should have made it relatively easy to provide quickly most of the men needed for the navy in time of war; and the French system was admired and copied in several parts of Europe. Yet it was always very unpopular with those subject to it. To avoid service, French seamen often posed as foreigners, took service on foreign merchant ships, or simply left the area in which they were registered. In Spain, where a similar system was attempted from 1737 onwards, there were similar difficulties.[41] In Britain no

40 *Histoire militaire de la France*, ii, 175.
41 Desdevises du Dézert, *L'Espagne de l'ancien régime*, ii, 306–12.

official register of this kind was ever introduced, though proposals for one were debated in Parliament in 1720, 1740 and 1744.

Merchant interests which, as less effectively in France and Spain, claimed that conscription of large numbers of men for the navy seriously damaged the country's foreign trade, strongly opposed anything of the kind. More important, such proposals were widely and fiercely resisted as a gross infringement of individual liberty and a French-style tyranny. One of the parliamentary opponents of the proposal in 1740 claimed that 'if the bill should pass, a sailor and a slave would become terms of the same signification'.[42] Even in 1749, after the struggle with France and Spain had shown how acute these manning difficulties could be, a modest proposal for the creation of a small naval reserve (3,000 men, each of whom would be paid £10 a year to hold himself in readiness for service in case of war) had to be abandoned in the face of opposition of this kind.

Voluntary enlistment was not unimportant. In the British navy, at least, a captain was sometimes able to attract to his ship, through ties of personal and family loyalty, men from his own locality, just as in many armies a captain might attract men to his company. Again sailors, like soldiers, might be tempted by the offer of a premium, a lump sum which they received on enlistment. But such methods by themselves could never provide all the men needed.

The central difficulty was money. Every great war at sea, by increasing sharply the demand for seamen, raised the wages paid on merchant ships. At the same time service on a privateer offered a sailor the prospect of a sudden windfall if his ship were lucky enough to take some worthwhile prizes. With such inducements it was difficult for any navy, with its stricter discipline and poor wages, to compete. The leading historian of the subject in the British navy during this period makes the essential point with brutal clarity: 'The men recognized the king's service for what it was; they refused to enter it willingly and deserted it whenever opportunity offered.'[43] No government ever thought seriously of easing the problem of recruitment by paying its sailors better. The British navy therefore continued to rely heavily on the impressment of seamen, the seizing by force of men in seaports, either by the navy itself or by

42 Beatson, *Naval and Military Memoirs*, i, 55.

43 D. A. Baugh, *British Naval Administration in the Age of Walpole* (Princeton, 1965), p. 500. Chap. 4 of this book is the best account of the problems of manning the British fleet in this period.

41

press-gangs, which were private business ventures financed by the navy.

No one doubted that this was a bad system. The men it produced were often of poor quality and understandably ready to desert as soon as they could. Yet at the same time hardly anyone believed that the press-gang could be dispensed with, for national security demanded that the navy have the men it needed. This imperative overrode any consideration of personal freedom. Even with such methods the Admiralty often had great difficulty in manning its ships. When the navy was mobilised in 1739–40 the crews of the Channel fleet could be brought up to strength only by using considerable numbers of soldiers as substitutes for the missing seamen.[44] Even some years later, when in 1744 Commodore Anson was sent to attack Spanish shipping and settlements in the Pacific, the crews of his little squadron, as it prepared for this exceptionally testing voyage, were provided in part by a draft of 500 out-pensioners of Chelsea Hospital. Half of these deserted at once; and of those who remained most were over sixty years old and a good many over seventy. The impressment of men for the navy was even more unpopular in the American colonies than in Britain itself. In 1747 there was a serious riot in Boston when sailors were taken from merchant ships there; and powerful colonial trading interests, which emphasised the need not to weaken the crews of merchantmen in this way, were always opposed to such methods. In 1708 and again in 1746 impressment in American waters was banned by Act of Parliament, though the Admiralty was able to have the second Act modified to apply only to the West Indies, where such commercial pressures were stronger than in the mainland colonies.[45]

Yet in spite of all these difficulties Britain enjoyed throughout the eighteenth century one fundamental advantage over its great rival France. Its seaborne trade, whether coastal, with other European states or transoceanic, was larger than that of France. Both were growing, and at times (notably during the 1720s and 1730s) that of France was growing the more rapidly of the two. Yet Britain never lost its advantage in this repect; and its greater maritime trade meant a larger pool of experienced sailors on which to draw, however arbitrarily and inefficiently, in time of war. France built excellent warships. Many contemporaries thought them

---

44 Baugh, *British Naval Administration,* pp. 150–62, 187–8, 190.
45 Baugh, *British Naval Administration,* pp. 218–21.

superior to those produced in British dockyards. But it never had at
its disposal enough seamen to allow it to meet the British navy on
equal terms. Their number during the century never rose above
60,000, whereas in its later years the corresponding figure for
Britain was over 100,000.[46] The same weakness affected Spain even
more markedly. Ensenada, when as the new chief minister in
Madrid he urged Ferdinand VI in 1746 to strengthen his navy,[47]
explicitly recognised that the lack of seamen would make it
impossible for Spain ever to equal Britain as a naval power.

At sea decisive battles were even rarer than on land. During the
Austrian Succession struggle that between the British and French
fleets off Toulon in February 1744 was a victory for neither side;
and not until 1747 did Britain win clear and undeniable successes of
this kind.[48] For this situation there are several explanations. It was
inherently even more difficult at sea than on land to force an
unwilling opponent to accept battle. It was also often a good deal
harder, if the opposing fleets were more or less evenly matched, to
press home any advantage gained in a naval battle than in one on
land. It was more difficult for an admiral to control a fleet and
make it work as an effective unit than for a general to do the same
with an army: naval signalling was still primitive, and a signal might
be misunderstood or, in the smoke and noise of battle, not even
seen at all. Naval operations in the sailing-ship age were at the
mercy of the weather, and especially of the wind, to a far greater
extent than any on land.

Also the prevailing climate of ideas was unfavourable, in naval
at least as much as land warfare, to the taking of unnecessary risks
and to the attitudes which Nelson most of all later came to typify.
Neither the French nor the Spanish navy was willing to think in
terms of an aggressive strategy; in both there was an unwillingness
to risk battle except in the most favourable circumstances. The
general rigidity of eighteenth-century naval tactics, again, tended to
damp down, particularly in the fleets of the two Bourbon powers,
individual initiative and aggressive spirit on the part of both
commanders and individual captains. To see this, as has been
done,[49] as an aspect of an alleged general decadence and frivolity of
the age is certainly unjustified. In every navy of the period can be

46 On this very important point, see *Histoire militaire de la France*, ii, 151–2.

47 See below, p. 219.

48 See below, pp. 138, 188.

49 R. Castex, *Les Idées militaires de la marine du XVIIIe siècle: De Ruyter à
Suffren* (Paris, 1911), pp. 74–5.

found striking examples of courage and self-sacrifice, of ships stoutly defended against heavy odds. But the dominant attitudes did not encourage the taking of risks, even to gain important objectives. This situation bred a good deal of cynicism about the very possibility of winning genuine victories at sea. 'Do you know what a naval battle is?' asked Maurepas, who as French Secretary of State for the Navy during the Austrian Succession war was well placed to judge. 'I will tell you: the fleets manoeuvre, come to grips, fire a few shots, and then each retreats . . . and the sea remains as salt as it was before.'[50]

Finally, it must be remembered that all the great maritime powers of western Europe saw their navies as existing primarily to protect their own seaborne trade in wartime and to harass and if possible destroy that of their opponents. This was very clearly true of the Austrian Succession struggle. Very soon after war was finally declared by France on Britain, in March 1744, this became from the French point of view a war of convoys, one in which the navy struggled to defend France's transatlantic trade against British attack. It was the interception of two of these convoys by British squadrons, and the willingness of their French escorts to sacrifice themselves in their defence, which produced in 1747 the only decisive naval battles of the war.[51]

50 J. Tramond, *Manuel d'histoire maritime de la France* (2nd edn, Paris, 1927), p. 459.
51 See below, p. 188.

3 WAR AND SOCIETY

Different parts of Europe were affected by war in the eighteenth century to widely differing extents and in widely differing ways. On the one hand there were large areas of the continent which, though they might in wartime have to face increased taxation and heavier demands for recruits, were largely or wholly immune from invasion and from the potentially crippling destruction and loss it might bring. During the war of the Austrian Succession France saw hostile armies on its territory only in 1744, when Austrian forces invaded Alsace, and in 1747-8, when Austrian and Piedmontese ones were in occupation of part of Provence. Neither invasion touched more than a small and peripheral part of the country; and neither lasted for long. The Dutch Republic, though afflicted from 1744 onwards by justified fears of French invasion, did not have to face this until the very last stages of the war, and then only to a very limited extent. Britain, though the Jacobite rising of 1745-6 produced widespread and serious alarm, was never invaded; and even in 1744, in spite of the French hopes and preparations of that year,[1] was never in serious danger of invasion. Spain was never touched by such fears throughout the struggle. Side by side with these, however, were other states which, because they were small and militarily weak, or because they had exposed and vulnerable frontiers, were very much open to invasion by stronger neighbours. Even the qualities and achievements of the Prussian army could not protect Frederick II in 1745 from fears of this kind; while Sardinia-Piedmont, militarily much the strongest of the Italian states, nevertheless during the war saw much of its territory more than once overrun by French and Spanish forces. Smaller and weaker principalities in Germany and Italy could not possibly protect

1 See below, p. 131.

themselves by their own efforts against the armies of any of the greater states. This situation, that of a frame of major powers – France, Britain and Spain in the west, Russia, to some extent the Habsburg territories and now potentially Prussia in the east – enclosing a great belt of political division and military weakness which stretched from the north German coast to Sicily, was now well established. It would persist for generations to come.

Every state, great or small, was profoundly influenced by international conflict. In an age when governments were primarily war-making machines, and when the inevitability of struggle between them was a deeply rooted assumption, it could not have been otherwise. Yet to determine with any accuracy how and how much any one of them was affected is extremely difficult. Any reliable estimate of the social and economic effects of war has to be largely quantitative; and the figures available in this period are usually limited to particular areas or short spans of time, or are unreliable and difficult to interpret. Also any calculation of this kind is complicated by the fact that, although war undoubtedly meant loss and suffering, it could also mean opportunity and growth. Material destruction, loss of life and waste of resources were to some extent counterbalanced by positive stimuli which war created and which would have been weaker, or would not have existed, without it. Any discussion of the question, therefore, especially one which attempts to cover even very briefly struggles as complex as those of the 1740s, must inevitably be largely impressionistic and conjectural.

WASTE AND LOSS

In the seventeenth and early eighteenth centuries wars had usually meant, at least indirectly, heavy losses of population by disease and general disruption of normal life. An obvious example is the great outbreak of plague which began in Poland in 1708 and was spread by the Swedish and Russian armies during the next five years until it affected the whole Baltic area, with devastating results. The 1740s, however, saw no such outbreak on anything like this scale. This does not mean that the war of the Austrian Succession had no demographic effects at all. There is evidence from the southern Netherlands, the only area of conflict for which the question has been explored in detail, of loss of civilian life through dysentery and other diseases brought, as had been the case all over Europe for generations, by the movement of armies.[2] Less obvious, though often more important, was the way in which the demands of an army for food, especially if these were concentrated in a relatively small area and continued for a number of years, could produce shortages and high prices which led to marriages being postponed, and hence the fertility of married women and the number of births being reduced. Again the southern Netherlands produce some evidence for this chain of cause and effect, though here the loss of population, which came after thirty years of peace, was quickly made good.[3] It seems very likely that something similar must have happened elsewhere – for example, in some parts of northern Italy – though detailed evidence is lacking. But by the standards of earlier comparable struggles in Europe such demographic repercussions were in the 1740s mild and limited.

The clearest and most direct, though not necessarily the most important, indicator of the human cost of any war is the casualties suffered by the armies and navies involved. (Predominantly these came in this age through disease rather than losses in battle, especially where navies were concerned.) Here again reliable figures, especially if they attempt to cover all the belligerents, are hard to obtain. In this way also, however, the fighting of the 1740s was not particularly destructive when set against comparable struggles which preceded and followed it. The most recent effort at such a global calculation suggests that total losses of this sort during the war of the Austrian Succession may have been about 450,000; but this contrasts with a much higher figure of 700,000 for the Spanish Succession struggle and a considerably greater one of 550,000 for the Seven Years War.[4]

Physical loss – the destruction of towns and villages, the killing of livestock, the commandeering of stocks of food – was by the mid-eighteenth century often at least as obvious and important to contemporaries as loss of life. In this respect also the war of the Austrian Succession compared favourably with its predecessors. During it there was nothing comparable to the deliberate devastation of the Rhenish Palatinate by the French army in 1674 and 1689, or to the ravaging of much of Bavaria in 1704 by the English and Austrian forces under Marlborough and Prince Eugene.

2 M. P. Gutmann, *War and Rural Life in the Early Modern Low Countries* (Princeton, 1980), p. 165.

3 Gutmann, *War and Rural Life*, pp. 148, 159, 189.

4 B. Ts. Urlanis, *Voiny i narodonaselenie Evropy. Lyudskie poteri vooruzhennykh sil evropeiskikh stran v voinykh XVII–XVIIIvv.* (Moscow, 1960), pp. 335–7.

This does not mean that the presence anywhere of a foreign army was not a burden, often a heavy one. There was certainly much less random pillaging and ill-treatment of civilians than in earlier generations: this stricter discipline was an important aspect of the increasingly tight control of their armed forces which governments were now exerting. It was now normal, at least in western Europe, for invading armies to agree with local authorities on a sum of money which the latter should pay for the maintenance of the soldiers so long as they remained in the area concerned: this avoided the arbitrary violence which was inevitably involved if, as in the past, raiding parties went from village to village demanding contributions in cash or kind. But armies still made heavy demands on the civilian populations among which they fought. In the Netherlands, for example, the very small town of Dalhem, during the siege of Maastricht in the spring of 1748, had to pay in a month 2,500 florins, mostly to supply the besieging French soldiers with food, at a time when its total tax payment for the entire year was only 1,000.[5] On the other hand, occasionally at least, civilians were able to recover from a belligerent government some compensation for such losses. At the end of the Austrian Succession war the French government reimbursed in this way the little principality of Liège, paying it $2\frac{1}{2}$ million florins in 1746–55. Though this represented only two-fifths of the total claimed, it was none the less a striking illustration of how warfare, at least in western Europe, was now becoming milder and more influenced by humanitarian considerations.[6]

War slowed economic growth by diverting to completely or relatively unproductive uses labour and capital which might have been otherwise more constructively employed. So far as the men who did the fighting were concerned, this was a less important consideration than their mere numbers might suggest. Since armies (and to a notably less extent navies) were recruited to a large extent from the least productive and economically valuable parts of society,[7] their demands in terms of human resources were less than appears at first sight. Many of the vagrants, debtors and criminals who became soldiers, willingly or otherwise, would not have contributed much to society had they remained civilians. As a later British analyst pointed out, 'the sword had not been put into *useful*

5 Gutmann, *War and Rural Life*, p. 39.
6 Gutmann, *War and Rural Life*, p. 66.
7 See p. 33 above.

hands'.[8] Moreover, many of the armies which fought in the 1740s were smaller than those which had been seen at the beginning of the century. Even in 1748 the British army totalled on paper only about 88,000 (including the separate Irish Establishment of 12,000 and 11,500 marines under War Office control).[9] This was less than it had numbered in the days of Marlborough, while the French army fell well short of the 380,000 whom Louis XIV had mobilised at the height of the Spanish Succession struggle.

The misuse of capital resources which were still scarce almost everywhere in Europe was probably more serious from an economic point of view. An army, even when it was operating in enemy territory, usually drew a large part of its supplies from magazines replenished from its homeland; and these supplies might have to be carried over long distances. A large army therefore made heavy demands on still relatively primitive transport facilities. A commissariat official estimated in 1744 that merely to carry bread to Italy for the 70,000 French soldiers there demanded 2,500 mules, while for the same purpose the 100,000 men in the Netherlands would need 2,800 horses. The supply of this one basic foodstuff also required very large numbers of sacks and baskets, a great quantity of firewood and many of the portable mills and ovens which all armies used in the field.[10] The continuing importance of sieges also did much to make land warfare expensive, for it was costly both to build and maintain a first-class fortress and to capture it. The great age of fortress-building was now in the past. The mid-eighteenth century saw no parallel to Vauban and Coehoorn, the great French and Dutch military engineers who had so influenced the wars of three generations earlier. But to take a major fortress was still a very expensive undertaking if it were resolutely defended, one which made great material demands. One French calculation was that an army of 60,000 men (an unusually large one) would need, for a siege lasting forty days, 3,300,000 rations for the soldiers, 730,000 issues of forage for the horses, 56,000 rounds of shot for its heavy guns with which to make a practicable breach in the walls, almost a million pounds weight of gunpowder

8 G. Chalmers, *Estimate of the Comparative Strength of Great Britain* (London, 1804), p. 138.

9 A. J. Guy, *Oeconomy and Discipline: Officership and Administration in the British Army, 1714–1763* (Manchester, 1985), pp. 9–10; cf. J. Brewer, *The Sinews of Power: War, Money and the English State, 1688–1783* (London, 1989), p. 30.

10 *Histoire militaire de la France*, ii, 40.

and 550,000 cubic feet of timber for gun-platforms and shoring up trenches, as well as tools and many other things.[11]

In material and financial terms, however, navies in proportion to their size made far greater demands than armies. Poor states such as Prussia or Piedmont might, by the effective exploitation of limited resources, maintain disproportionately large armies; but even if the crucial difficulty of an adequate supply of trained seamen could be surmounted, only the wealthiest states could afford large navies. Warships were expensive to build: in Britain even the smaller ones each cost more than most factories. They also made heavy demands in terms of maintenance: in the first half of the eighteenth century such costs represented about 4 per cent of the national income in Britain.[12] They carried huge numbers of guns, 100 or even more in a first-class ship of the line: this in itself made them very costly. They had very large crews: in Britain, the extreme case, the 40,000 or more men who served on them in time of war meant a shipboard population greater than that of any town apart from London itself.[13] A navy also needed a very complex and expensive infrastructure of dockyards and naval stores, which contrasted strikingly with the much simpler needs of an army in this respect. All this meant in Britain that a sailor cost more than twice as much as a soldier; and it is likely that the ratio was, if anything, greater in the French and Spanish cases.

In wartime, even more than in time of peace, the cost of the armed forces dominated government expenditure in every state. In Britain during the Austrian Succession war, 64 per cent of all the money the government spent went to meet the cost of the war; but this was by no means an intolerable burden. The percentage had been slightly higher during the Spanish Succession conflict at 66 per cent, and was to be higher again in the Seven Years War, at 71 per cent. It is striking, moreover, that in the 1740s the most important single source of tax revenue, the excise duty on beer and porter, which was raised during every other major war fought by Britain between the 1690s and the 1780s, remained unchanged. This is the most convincing indication that the financial demands made on the country by the fighting of 1739–48 were relatively modest: during the great conflict with France of 1755–63 average annual

---

11 D. Chandler, *The Art of Warfare in the Age of Marlborough* (London, 1976), p. 241.

12 Brewer, *The Sinews of Power*, pp. 34–5.

13 Brewer, *The Sinews of Power*, p. 36.

government expenditure was to be more than twice that during the Austrian Succession struggle.[14] But Britain was wealthy and industrialised, with a large and profitable colonial trade and the best system of public finance of all the major states of Europe. A war which it could pay for with relative ease might very well inflict severe hardship on poorer states. Prussia, though there are no reliable figures, probably spent a considerably higher proportion of its national income on war costs during the years (1740–2, 1744–5) when it was a belligerent. Piedmont-Sardinia, whose military effort and organisation have attracted much less attention from historians, may very well have made the greatest relative effort of all the states at war in the 1740s. In 1745 it was maintaining an army of more than 50,000 men,[15] not a very great deal less than the average of 62,000 which Britain, with a much larger territory and population and enormously greater national wealth, supported in 1739–48. Certainly, Piedmont was helped by British subsidies and had no expensive navy to pay for; but its military effort during these years was, none the less, impressive.

STIMULUS AND OPPORTUNITY

Clearly, then, war could make for loss and waste of resources which was sometimes heavy. Yet it could also stimulate constructive change and create new opportunities. Very often it showed both faces simultaneously, inflicting damage on some parts of society and at the same time benefiting others. Very often also it was for individuals a matter of mere luck whether they gained or lost by it.

It meant a sharp increase in the demand for supplies of all kinds – arms, ships, food, uniforms – for the armies and navies concerned; and this meant increased production, employment and profits for those who supplied these things. One of the clearest illustrations of this is the stream of contracts for ships for the British navy from which privately owned shipyards benefited in 1739–48. The outbreak of war with Spain created an immediate demand from the Admiralty for many more of the smaller vessels, frigates and sloops, which were essential for the protection of commerce and of which the navy tended to be chronically short. By the end of 1739, therefore, the Navy Board, which controlled the building and

---

14 Brewer, *The Sinews of Power*, pp. 40–1, 176, 214.
15 N. Brancaccio, *L'Esercito del vecchio Piemonte* (Rome, 1923–5), Pt i, p. 255.

maintenance of British warships, had already contracted for twelve new 24-gun ships and five of 44 guns to be built in this way.[16] This was the beginning of a long series of such contracts, which provided work for many shipwrights and carpenters and profits for their employers. During the war almost all new British frigates and sloops, as well as a number of ships of the line of 50–60 guns, were built in private yards; these therefore made an essential contribution to the country's naval strength. Their importance meant that during the short-lived Jacobite invasion of England in late 1745 the government took special measures to protect against rebel attack the ships then being built in this way in Liverpool and Hull; while in the following year the Admiralty, in the teeth of opposition from the Navy Board, tried hard to develop such building in North America (though there was never any possibility of a British transatlantic rival to the great Spanish dockyard at Havana). By October 1746 the Navy Board calculated that more than 130 warships had been built in merchant yards since the beginning of the war.[17] The majority of ships for the navy, however (though only a small majority), were still produced by royal naval dockyards; and here also, inevitably, the war brought an upsurge of activity. The workforce in the Plymouth yard, for example, doubled in 1739–48.[18] Moreover, there was a consistent tendency during the first half of the century for ships officially of the same 'rate' to become perceptibly larger and therefore more expensive to build. One of 50 guns, the smallest which could be considered a 'ship of the line', for example, was 38 per cent bigger in 1741 than it had been in 1706.[19] This meant that the demands of the navy in this respect were constantly becoming heavier in terms of materials and labour and thus economically more important.

This pattern of war-generated demand and the opportunities to which it gave rise can also be seen where the other needs of the fighting services were concerned. It seems likely that in the southern Netherlands, at least, the substantial farmer who produced for the market profited from the higher prices produced by the presence of

16 D. A. Baugh, *British Naval Administration in the Age of Walpole* (Princeton, 1965), p. 254; B. Pool, *Navy Board Contracts, 1660–1832* (London, 1966), p. 80; Brewer, *The Sinews of Power*, p. 19.

17 Pool, *Navy Board Contracts*, pp. 83–5.

18 M. Duffy, 'The Establishment of the Western Squadron as the Linchpin of British Naval Strategy', in *Parameters of British Naval Power, 1650–1850*, ed. M. Duffy (Exeter, 1992), p. 72.

19 Baugh, *British Naval Administration*, p. 485.

a large French army in 1744–8 and its need for food. He might also benefit if his cart and the horses which drew it were hired by the invaders; while even the poor peasant might earn a little welcome cash if he were paid to dig trenches or for some similar work: in 1748 the French paid a florin a day to labourers engaged for the siege of Maastricht.[20] (Much depended on the timing of such demands, however; if they fell during the harvest season or at some other difficult moment they could be extremely burdensome.) Certainly, Adam Smith himself believed that international conflict could sometimes be beneficial: some years later he asserted confidently that

> war is so far from being a disadvantage in a well-cultivated country, that many get rich by it. When the Netherlands is the seat of war, all the peasants grow rich, for they pay no rent when the enemy is in the country, and provisions sell at a high rate.[21]

The experience of a peasant in Bohemia or Moravia at the hands of the invading Prussian army, and still more that of his Bavarian counterpart when exposed to the ravages of the Croat and Hungarian irregulars of the Habsburg one, was often very different. In this respect, as in many others, there was a tendency for observance of the niceties and conventions of warfare to erode as the seat of the fighting moved east from the Rhine. But there is good reason to believe that at least in some parts of Europe and in some circumstances the presence of a foreign army was not an unmitigated disaster.

It must also be remembered that the effects of war, both good and bad, were often short-lived. A moderate amount of material destruction and some loss of population might be made good fairly easily by a few years of peace and reasonable harvests: in the same way the increased demand and the spur to greater production generated by conflict frequently disappeared the moment the fighting ended. Wartime needs were often acute while they lasted, but also irregular and temporary. Thus in 1748 the workshops of Charleville in north-eastern France, a centre of small-arms production, were still at the end of the war so pressed to meet orders for muskets for the French army that skilled workmen were imported from Liège for the purpose (as had been done in Prussia

---

20 Gutmann, *War and Rural Life*, pp. 40, 130.
21 *Lectures on Justice, Police, Revenue and Arms* (London, 1896), p. 273.

also a year or two earlier); but by 1750, with wartime demand a thing of the past, they could not employ even the local workforce.[22] Sometimes the demands of the armed forces had constructive results of a more permanent kind. In particular, the need of navies for guns and anchors, the largest metal artefacts of the age, did something to stimulate progress in metallurgy and metals production. In Britain the wars of the first half of the century helped the spread of new techniques in the metal industries, such as the use of the reverberatory furnace and of coal in iron-smelting. In Spain too, the iron industry of the Basque provinces in such places as Santander, Lierganes and La Cavada was stimulated by the demands of the navy for cannon, as it was rebuilt by Patino in the 1720s and 1730s.[23] In the same way later in the century the demand for arms generated by the war of American Independence did much to foster the growing iron industry in south Wales.[24] Such demands were certainly big enough to be a considerable stimulus: in 1741, when it was still at a rather low ebb, the ships of the French navy mounted, at least on paper, over 1,600 guns of the heaviest types – 18-, 24- and 36-pounders.[25] No army needed artillery on this scale; but even in fighting on land, and especially in fortress warfare, considerable quantities were called for. The Prussians had 82 guns on the battlefield at Chotusitz in 1742, and the Austrian army in Bohemia in 1745 was equipped with 94 field-pieces. Saxe, when he opened the campaign of 1745 in the Netherlands, had at his disposal 336 cannon of all kinds, including 87 heavy siege guns; and when the great Dutch fortress of Bergen-op-Zoom was taken by the French in 1747, 238 guns were part of the spoils.[26] Prussia was a far poorer state than France, and with a smaller army, but even she produced 444 guns of various calibres in the war years 1741–5.[27]

22 *Histoire militaire de la France*, ii, 16.

23 A. H. John, 'War and the English Economy, 1700–1763', *Economic History Review*, 2nd ser., vii (1954–5), 330–1; J. Lynch, *Bourbon Spain, 1700–1808* (Oxford, 1989), pp. 119–20.

24 A. H. John, *The Industrial Development of South Wales, 1750–1850* (Cardiff, 1950), pp. 24–5, 99–100.

25 J. Boudriot, 'France 17e–18e siècles: artillerie et vaisseaux royaux', in Martine Acerra and others, eds. *Les Marines de guerre européennes, XVIIe–XVIIIe siècles* (Paris, 1985), p. 10.

26 C. Duffy, *The Army of Maria Theresa* (London, 1977), pp. 105, 107; F. Hulot *Le Maréchal de Saxe* (Paris, 1989), pp. 157, 229.

27 C. Duffy, *The Army of Frederick the Great* (Newton Abbot, 1974), p. 132.

War demands could also have results which were qualitative as well as quantitative. This can be seen in the way in which they fostered the growth of productive units which were bigger and more complex than any others of the age. These called for their efficient working for qualities of foresight, administrative skill and ability to plan on a large scale in a way which no other enterprise – no factory, mine, estate or bank – did. The most convincing illustration of this is the great naval dockyards. These were by far the biggest employers of the age. At the peak of the war of 1739–48 there were 8,500 men at work in British ones; and for France the figure was much higher, though it probably includes men working in the royal yards but employed by private contractors.[28] In the second half of the century that at Brest, the biggest in France, gave work to 10,000 men, though not all of these worked in the dockyard itself; and around the coasts of western Europe, at Rochefort, Toulon, Coruna, Cartagena, St Petersburg, Plymouth, Chatham and Ports- mouth, there were yards with work-forces far larger than any civilian enterprise could boast.

Moreover, they were not merely very large organisations but also very complex ones. In them a whole series of different skills, those of shipwrights, carpenters, smiths, ropemakers, caulkers and sailmakers, had to be brought together to create the biggest, most expensive and most complex material product of the age – the sailing man-of-war. They incorporated a whole range of facilities ancillary to the building of ships but essential to it – mast-ponds, ropewalks and forges. The royal dockyard at Deptford, for example, by no means the largest in Britain, gave work in 1748 to more than 1,500 men who were classified in thirty-one different trades. The men they employed were skilled, very conscious of traditional rights and craft customs, and often very ready to resist anything which seemed to threaten these. The war of the Austrian Succession saw strikes in British dockyards in 1739, 1742, 1743 and 1744. This combination of scale and complexity could not be matched, or even approached, in any other productive enterprise of the age. Here, it can be argued, and on a smaller scale in such enterprises as cannon-foundries, the demands of war and preparations for war forced the eighteenth century to develop organisational and administrative techniques which would otherwise have been learned more slowly.

28 R. J. B. Knight, 'The Building and Maintenance of the British Fleet during the Anglo-French Wars, 1688–1815', in *Les Marines de guerre européennes*, p. 38.

Even the feeding of armed forces had the same effect. Here again navies were particularly difficult and important. An army might live to some extent on the resources of the area in which it fought, at least until those became exhausted by a period of occupation and its cumulative effects. But this was not possible for a fleet. Everything which it consumed had to be supplied by the state which it served. Even when it was in home waters this involved careful planning and a very large infrastructure of bakehouses, slaughterhouses, breweries and storage facilities. A first-class navy therefore placed and had to supervise huge contracts with its suppliers.[29] In Britain, even a fleet in which only 40,000 men were serving (this was the artificially low figure used for formal 'Declarations of Victuals') needed each year 12,000 head of cattle and 40,000 hogs to satisfy its demand for meat alone.[30]

When a large fleet was in distant waters the problems were greater and the need for efficient planning and administration even more pressing. In this as in other respects the West Indies was the most difficult area of all. Normally nine months elapsed between stores being ordered from England or Ireland and their arrival in the Caribbean; and the long (and moreover *unpredictably* long) sea journey greatly increased the difficulty of planning and risk of spoilage *en route*. Food and other stores were also obtained, of course, from the North American colonies; but here too delay and spoilage were serious considerations. Also there was the important complication that ships tried to avoid either arriving in or sailing from the West Indies during the hurricane season of August to October.[31] The fact that during the first stages of the Austrian Succession war a high proportion of Britain's naval and military strength was concentrated in the Caribbean (20,000 soldiers and at least 10,000 sailors in 1741) made these problems particularly acute. That during these years none of these men went short of food or essential supplies was a very considerable administrative achievement, one which has until recently had less attention from historians than it deserves. The Mediterranean, closer to home and with the possibility of drawing supplies from parts of Italy or even North Africa, did not pose quite the same problems. But even here

29 See the detailed account of British arrangements of this kind in Baugh, *British Naval Administration*, pp. 432–40.

30 Baugh, *British Naval Administration*, p. 407.

31 On these supply problems, see D. Crewe, *Yellow Jack and the Worm: British Naval Administration in the West Indies, 1739–1748* (Liverpool, 1993), pp. 7 and 147 and chap. 4 *passim*.

they were considerable. In 1742 and 1743, when there were about 18,000 British seamen serving there (two-fifths of the entire navy), supply convoys had to be sent out every six months or so.

The maintenance and supply of effective armed forces therefore presented administrative problems whose scale and urgency were unparalleled in any other aspect of eighteenth-century government. This made war a school in which the techniques of large-scale administration could be learned and perfected. More realistic planning, more effective collection of information (the Victualling Commissioners in Britain, for example, now demanded regular reports which would enable them to detect developing shortages in time to deal effectively with them);[32] more careful supervision – all these were real advances over anything known in the past. During most of the seventeenth century the military and naval operations of all states had often been seriously hampered by supply problems. This happened very seldom in the war of the Austrian Succession. Conflict between states was therefore a force making for rising standards of administration in general. The outstanding illustration of this is the growth in Prussia under Frederick William I of an administrative system which was geared entirely to meeting the needs of a great army and which, however demanding and even brutal in its impact on those subject to it, was by the standards of that age remarkably efficient. The benefits which Europe derived from this goading of governments into greater effectiveness do not always leap to the eye and are impossible to quantify; but they were none the less real.

THE DIFFICULT BALANCE

To strike a clear balance between the positive and negative effects of war in the first half of the eighteenth century is impossible. There are too many unquantifiable and imponderable elements on both sides. Yet it is hard not to feel that almost invariably, and even in the Austrian Succession struggle, which was less demanding and destructive than the great wars which preceded and followed it, the negative ones were the more important. Certainly individuals, groups, particular industries or geographical areas might gain, at least in the short term, from wartime stresses and demands. A manufacturer or even an artisan could well profit from a wartime

---

32 Baugh, *British Naval Administration*, pp. 449–50.

demand for arms or uniforms. A seaman, if he escaped the press-gang, would almost certainly be able to demand higher wages. A farmer might sometimes benefit by selling his produce to an army in the field. A merchant might reap a windfall gain from the opportune arrival of a convoy from America or the West Indies. Perhaps entire branches of a national economy might gain in a more permanent way. It may be true that Britain's foreign trade grew more rapidly during the eighteenth century than it would otherwise have done because of the wars it fought, since its naval strength allowed it to protect its own shipping, attack that of its opponents, develop its carrying trade and supplant that of its enemies in neutral markets.[33] But it seems very unlikely that its economy as a whole gained from these wars. Conflict, after all, greatly increased many economic uncertainties in a world in which, even in peacetime, they bulked far larger than they do today. 'If there had been no wars', one of the greatest authorities on the subject has argued, 'the English people would have been better fed, better clad, certainly better housed than they were. War deflected energies from the course along which – so it seems in retrospect – the permanent interests of England lay.'[34] And yet Britain made fewer sacrifices in wartime than any other major state. It was never invaded by a foreign enemy. It suffered virtually no physical damage on its own territory. Though its navy lost very heavily through disease, its army was relatively small and its losses on the battlefield were correspondingly light. Undoubtedly, it was heavily taxed, in peace as well as in war.[35] But its tax system was efficient and equitable by comparison with that of any other great state; and its growing wealth made the fiscal burden quite bearable. If with all these advantages it still lost, in economic and social terms, from the wars it fought, then the other belligerents of the 1740s must have lost still more.

33 See, e.g., John, 'War and the English Economy', 337–8; W. W. Rostow, *The Process of Economic Growth* (Oxford, 1953), pp. 159–60. The impact of the Austrian Succession struggle on British trade is discussed briefly on pp. 190–1 below.

34 T. S. Ashton, *Economic Fluctuations in England, 1700–1800* (Oxford, 1959), p. 83.

35 Brewer, *The Sinews of Power*, p. 91.

4 THE PRUSSIAN INVASION OF SILESIA AND THE CRISIS OF HABSBURG POWER, 1740–41

FREDERICK II INVADES SILESIA

The Emperor Charles VI died on 19 October 1740. Two months later, on 16 December, the Prussian army invaded Silesia, the richest of all the central European lands of the Habsburgs. This at once made Brandenburg-Prussia and its young king, Frederick II, who had ruled in Berlin for only five months, leading actors on the European stage. It began a long process of Austro-Prussian and Habsburg-Hohenzollern rivalry in the German world which was to last until the final Prussian victory in 1866. It confronted the European powers with new and unexpected challenges and opportunities.

There were Prussian legalistic claims to Silesia; but they were weak ones. In 1686 the Great Elector Frederick William of Brandenburg had renounced the rights he claimed over the province in return for the cession to him of a small part of it; but eight years later his son, the later King Frederick I, agreed in a secret treaty with the Emperor Leopold I to return this territory in return for a money indemnity. Frederick II argued both that the Great Elector had had no power to surrender his claims in perpetuity and that they could therefore be revived at any time by his successors, and that the agreement with his son had been obtained by deceit and threats and was therefore invalid.[1] But assertions of this kind were no more than a fig-leaf to cover an act of blatant aggression, and indeed were never seen by Frederick himself as more than that. The idea of a Prussian conquest of Silesia was not new: the invasion of 1740 made some use of plans for such an attack drawn up sixty

---

1 The complexities and essential weakness of the Prussian claims are discussed in more detail in C. T. Atkinson, *A History of Germany, 1715–1815* (London, 1908), pp. 112–14, which is still probably the best treatment of the subject in English.

years earlier.[2] What brought it now suddenly to fruition was the character and ambitions of the new ruler in Berlin. The young Frederick (he was twenty-eight years old) had for years been thinking in terms of territorial expansion, an expansion to be achieved by force, by the use of the fine army and large reserve of money built up over the years by his father. In 1731, in his earliest significant comment on international affairs, he had envisaged the possible seizure of Polish Prussia (achieved in 1772) and Swedish Pomerania (which became Prussian only in 1815).

In the later 1730s it was the question of Jülich and Berg which most preoccupied him; and here his attitude was uncompromising. When early in 1739 the representatives in Berlin of France, Austria, Great Britain and the Dutch Republic presented identical notes asking for the Jülich-Berg dispute to be submitted to the decision of a conference of the four powers, Frederick was scathing in his comments on what seemed to him the weakness of his father's response. Soon afterwards he was hoping for the death of the Elector Palatine, which he thought would be followed by a decisive struggle on the lower Rhine for the territories claimed by Prussia.[3] Only a few weeks after his accession he demanded as the price for alliance with France a guarantee by Louis XV that Prussia should obtain Berg, and in particular Düsseldorf, its main city. He made no effort to hide his contempt both for what remained of imperial institutions and for the emperor himself. He refused, as a king, to submit to the judgement of the Reichskammergericht, the supreme law-court of the Holy Roman Empire, in a trivial dispute with the bishop of Liège over the tiny territory of Herstal, and spoke of Charles VI as 'a broken-down emperor, whose death will throw Europe into bloody conflict'.[4] He was also intensely anxious to cut a figure in the affairs of Europe, to show that he was a force to be reckoned with and to achieve an international reputation, most of all a military one. In 1736 the Austrian minister in Berlin had reported, with considerable penetration, that the crown prince wanted no 'mean agreement' over Jülich and Berg but rather to begin his reign with 'a startling stroke'.[5] In Paris also Frederick's character and its potentialities were correctly interpreted almost as

2 A. Berney, *Friedrich der Grosse: Entwicklungsgeschichte eines Staatsmannes* (Tübingen, 1934) p. 129.

3 Berney, *Friedrich*, pp. 106–7.

4 Berney, *Friedrich*, pp. 113–15.

5 Berney, *Friedrich*, p. 75.

soon as his reign had begun. 'The late king of Prussia', wrote the French Foreign Minister at the end of July 1740, 'was an indecisive prince whose natural timidity made him little to be feared. The prince who has succeeded him already shows that he is quite different. He makes it clear that he is ambitious for glory, confident of the solidity of his rights, conscious of his strength, and no more obvious and natural object for his ambition can be seen than the Berg-Jülich succession.'[6] Certainly the young king was determined from the start to take his his own decisions and not to depend on, or even be much influenced by, any minister; this determination was to permeate his entire reign. When the die was cast and the invasion of Silesia decided on, Frederick spoke of himself as having 'a rendezvous with Fame' and insisted that he alone was responsible for the decision and entitled to credit for any success it achieved. 'I reserve this expedition to myself alone', he told Prince Leopold of Anhalt-Dessau, one of the creators of the Prussian army, on 2 December, 'so that the world does not believe that the king of Prussia takes the field with a tutor.'[7]

The attack on Silesia, however, had a more solid basis than the personal ambitions of the young king. Frederick had at his disposal an army ready for immediate use which was enormous (about 80,000 men) in terms of the size and resources of his territories; and its quality, which the caution of Frederick William I had hitherto kept hidden from the eyes of the world, was soon to become apparent. Almost equally important, Frederick had a large reserve of hard cash, the 8 million thalers which his father had accumulated over many years. By comparison Maria Theresa was in a critically weak position. The Habsburg armies had performed very poorly in the war of 1737–9 with the Turks. The Habsburg finances, always weak even by the undemanding standards of that age, were in an appalling condition. The ministers in office in Vienna were mostly mediocrities, and many of them, and of the Habsburg generals, were too old to face effectively the crisis which now loomed. Count Philipp Sinzendorf, the Austrian Chancellor and the minister most concerned with foreign policy, for example, was almost seventy, while count Gundaker Starhemberg, who had played an important role in financial affairs, was close to eighty (he was born in 1663),

---

6 M. Sautai, *Les Préliminaires de la Guerre de la Succession d'Autriche* (Paris, 1907), p. 174.

7 *Politische Correspondenz Friedrichs des Grossen* ed. J. G. Droysen *et al.*, (46 vols, Berlin, 1879–1939), i, 177.

and count Johann Franz Dietrichstein, the president of the Hofkammer Council and the nearest approach to a minister of finance, was sixty-eight. Maria Theresa's husband, Francis Stephen, the former duke of Lorraine, whom she had married in 1736 and to whom she was devoted, was to show considerable ability in improving the financial position of the Habsburg family; but he was not a soldier, and his wife, in spite of her feeling for him, was never willing to give him a leading role in government.

Frederick was well aware of these weaknesses. In his correspondence with Prussian diplomats, notably with Borcke, his minister in Vienna, he stressed increasingly the terrible position of the Habsburgs and their complete inability to maintain themselves in their hereditary possessions unless they could draw on outside help.[8] By the beginning of November 1740 he was hinting ominously that if they did not call on Prussia for that help, as Borcke for a moment hoped they would, then 'other measures' would have to be used.[9] His low opinion of the ability of the Habsburg territories to defend themselves was all too well founded. Shortage of money meant that the Austrian army was not strengthened as it ought to have been after the disastrous Turkish war. In spite of its paper strength of 160,000, it numbered in reality barely half that figure. Its morale was low in the aftermath of humiliating defeats. Hungary still seemed a seedbed of possible revolt: there was significant unrest there in 1735, while the distrust of the Magyars which was all too visible in Vienna increased their discontent.[10] In the last days of Charles VI gloom and pessimism pervaded his regime. To the Austrian ministers, reported Thomas Robinson, the British minister in Vienna, three days after the emperor died,

> The Turks seemed . . . already in Hungary; the Hungarians themselves in arms; the Saxons in Bohemia; the Bavarians at the gates of Vienna, and France the soul of the whole. I not only saw them in despair; but that very despair was not capable of rendering them truly desperate.[11]

8 *Pol. Corr.*, i, 7–8, 36, 63.

9 *Pol. Corr.*, i, 36, 63, 88–9.

10 A. von Arneth, *Geschichte Maria Theresias* (10 vols, Vienna, 1863–79), i, 58–60.

11 W. Coxe, *History of the House of Austria, from the Foundation of the Monarchy by Rodolphe of Hapsburgh to the Death of Leopold II*, 3rd edn (London, 1847), iii, 242.

These forebodings were only too well justified; but the real threat was to come not from Saxony or Bavaria, whose territorial ambitions were well known, or even from France, but from the still largely unconsidered new ruler in Berlin.

In a struggle with Maria Theresa, Frederick was likely to have yet other advantages. He might reasonably expect the help of other anti-Austrian powers; and this meant first and foremost France. From the moment of his accession he was anxious for alliance with France, promising that he could render it services more important than those of Gustavus Adolphus in the 1630s and stressing that he had turned a deaf ear to British efforts to draw him into the anti-French camp. If France supported him, he promised effusively, 'I shall be her most faithful, most zealous and most grateful ally in the world.'[12] When he wrote these words it was still of Jülich and Berg that he was thinking; and it was there if anywhere that observers expected him to act. Indeed, if Charles VI had lived even a few months longer it is very likely that Frederick would have launched his 'startling stroke' on the lower Rhine and not in Silesia: in that case the history of Germany and Europe would have been very different. But a Prussian challenge to Habsburg power in central Europe served France's traditional ambitions as a dynastic struggle on the lower Rhine could not. Once the invasion of Silesia had begun, powerful forces in Paris would certainly press for advantage to be taken of this opportunity to weaken the old enemy; and these pressures a chief minister almost ninety years old might well find it impossible to resist.

Against this had to be set the possibility that Russia, traditionally friendly to the Habsburgs, might intervene to help Maria Theresa. Frederick William I, deeply impressed by the rise of a great new power and by the vulnerability of his dispersed territories, most of all the kingdom of East Prussia, to possible attack from the east, had shown throughout his reign a healthy respect for Russia. This feeling his son fully shared. In 1726 Austria and Russia had signed a treaty of alliance, one which proved remarkably durable by the standards of that age of diplomatic instability. It lasted because it was based on genuine mutual interests – the maintenance of the dominant influence of the two empires in Poland and their shared hostility to the Turks. In 1737–9 they had been allies, however unsuccessfully, against the Ottoman Empire. Possible Russian support for the Habsburgs was therefore a factor

12 *Pol. Corr.*, i, 4, 25, 27, 28.

in the equation which could not be ignored, above all because of the sheer military strength of Russia. Respect for its army, and particularly for the Cossack and Kalmuck irregulars who could rapidly devastate any territory they overran, was a feeling which influenced Frederick throughout his entire reign.[13] Foreign diplomats in years to come were frequently struck by the fear of Russia which he showed and which they often saw as the most important restraint on his ambitions.

In the first few months after his accession he hoped for a Russian alliance which would protect his eastern frontiers in case of a war over Jülich and Berg. Early in August 1740 he sent a draft Russo-Prussian treaty to baron von Mardefeld, his able minister in St Petersburg, and for a moment even hoped for Russian military backing in such a war and for a Russian guarantee of his succession to the disputed duchies.[14] Once his ambitions had changed their focus to Silesia they were clearly directed against the Habsburgs and not merely against the Wittelsbach claimant to two small west German territories. In such an enterprise there was no hope of active support from Russia. But there seemed good reason to believe that it could at least be kept neutral. By the autumn of 1740 it was clear that the Empress Anna was unlikely to live much longer; and her death would almost certainly lead to a period of factional struggle in St Petersburg which would make difficult any strong and consistent line in foreign policy. Frederick therefore looked forward eagerly to Anna's disappearance from the scene. 'The Empress of Russia is about to die', he wrote on 9 November to his chief minister, count Podewils, 'God favours us and destiny seconds us.' In fact she had already died, on 28 October: this, Frederick claimed in the account he wrote of these events more than thirty years later, with how liberal a use of hindsight it is impossible to say, was the deciding factor in his resolve to attack Silesia.[15] The death of the empress was at once followed by the fall of her favourite, Ernst Johann Biren (Bühren), a Courlander of German origins who had dominated her court during the 1730s and was bitterly disliked by almost all the Russian nobility. He was succeeded as the controlling

---

13 For French comments to this effect see Sautai, *Préliminaires*, pp. 206, 253. Frederick's view of the Russians as still barbarians in spite of the civilising efforts of Peter I is brought out in W. Mediger, 'Friedrich der Grosse und Russland', in O. Hauser, ed., *Friedrich der Grosse in seiner Zeit* (Cologne–Vienna, 1987), pp. 109–10.

14 *Pol. Corr.*, i, 6, 29–31, 41–2, 47, 64–6.

15 *Histoire de mon temps* (Berlin, 1846), i, 56.

personality in St Petersburg by Burkhard Christoph von Münnich, a German soldier who had entered the Russian army in 1716 and become its commander-in-chief. Münnich's hold on power, however, was short-lived: after only a few weeks he was overthrown by a conspiracy led by the Vice-Chancellor, count A. I. Ostermann, yet another German who had been a very important figure in the government of Russia for well over a decade. He in his turn was driven from power in November 1741.

Frederick thus saw in Russia precisely the instability he so much wished for. Moreover, ruling circles there were notoriously corruptible. Even a relatively stable regime might therefore, he hoped, be influenced in his favour by judicious bribery. While Biren was still in power Frederick had hoped to win his support by the offer of a Prussian guarantee that the duchy of Courland should become a hereditary possession of his family. Also Biren owned estates in Silesia; and his desire to protect them might well lead him to favour Prussia if it invaded the province. The seizure of power by Münnich, whose pro-Prussian tendencies Frederick overestimated, led at once to an offer to him of extensive estates in Silesia in return for his support of a Prussian invasion.[16] Frederick therefore believed by the autumn of 1740 that in one way or another Russian power could and would be nullified and that he could attack Silesia with little danger of finding himself threatened from the east. When in February 1741 Guy Dickens, the British minister in Berlin, warned him that Prussia, because of its geographically dispersed territories, was particularly vulnerable to outside attack, Frederick replied that he was now sure of Russia and therefore of the safety of his frontiers.[17]

By comparison, Great Britain and the Dutch Republic, the traditional allies of the Habsburgs, did not seem to him very formidable opponents. Neither was a great military power. In both there was powerful resistance, popular as well as governmental, to involvement in European conflicts. To neither was the fate of Silesia in itself of much importance.

The invasion of Silesia was therefore a risk, but one not taken blindly. It was very much Frederick's personal decision. Almost as soon as news of the death of Charles VI reached him he had a long

16 *Pol. Corr.*, i, 31, 91, 127.

17 J. Black, 'Mid-Eighteenth Century Conflict with Particular Reference to the Wars of the Polish and Austrian Successions', in J. Black, ed., *The Origins of War in Early Modern Europe* (Edinburgh, 1987), p. 227.

series of meetings with Podewils and his most senior military commander, Field-Marshal count Schwerin. For four days the three men discussed Prussia's best course of action in the new situation. Neither Schwerin nor Podewils liked the idea of an attack on Silesia. In so far as there was any traditional Prussian foreign policy it was still one of cooperation with the Habsburgs and with the maritime powers, Britain and the Dutch. Podewils wished to adhere to this. He disliked in particular any possibility of an alliance with France, which he thought likely to lead to a general war in Europe. If Prussia remained faithful to the old system of alliances this might avert such a war, or at least mean that if it came it would be fought in circumstances favourable to it. In a long joint memorandum he, and more particularly perhaps Schwerin, put forcibly the case for avoiding conflict with the Habsburgs. That the acquisition of Silesia was highly desirable was not disputed. But the best and safest way of achieving this was by agreement with Maria Theresa. She could be promised, in return for the cession of the province, Prussian support for the election as emperor of her husband. (Paving the way for this had been a major preoccupation of Charles VI in his last years and it was certain to be an even more central one of his successor.) She could also be offered Prussian help in defending all her other territories in Germany and the Netherlands against attack, the cession of all Prussian rights in Jülich and Berg, and, if unavoidable, a large sum of money (this, it was argued, would be the most potent inducement of all, given the desperate state of the Austrian finances). It must be impressed on the ministers in Vienna that acceptance of these proposals was the only means of saving Habsburg power from ruin, preventing the dismemberment of Maria Theresa's territories and ensuring the continuance of the imperial title in the Habsburg family. To this end Prussia would work in concert with the maritime powers, Russia and as many as possible of the imperial electors. An alliance of this kind would be able to defeat any effort by France to support the Bavarian claim to the Habsburg inheritance and prevent the Prussian acquisition of Silesia. Clearly Schwerin and Podewils still thought in traditional terms of France rather than Austria as the most important obstacle in the way of Prussian ambitions. The memorandum did envisage the possibility that Maria Theresa and her advisers would stand firm and refuse any concession to Prussia. In that case quite different policies would be called for: cooperation with Bavaria and Saxony to partition the Habsburg inheritance; some kind of alliance with France to discourage the maritime powers from any attempt to help

Maria Theresa; alliance with Sweden, Denmark and if necessary even the Turks to make sure that Russia did nothing to assist her; and measures to secure the imperial title for Charles Albert of Bavaria. But, it was emphasised, the peaceful course was much the better of the two and the alternative much more risky and uncertain.[18]

Frederick was unimpressed by these arguments. The death of Charles VI had transferred his ambitions from Jülich and Berg to the much greater prize to be gained in Silesia. This change was remarkably rapid. It may not be true, as the French minister in Berlin reported a few weeks later, that the invasion of Silesia was decided on in two days; but the decision was taken with what to Frederick's advisers seemed disconcerting speed.[19] He was now thinking in military at least as much as political or diplomatic terms; and Podewils, for all his diplomatic experience, played no role in decision-making. When Frederick put his ideas on paper on 6 or 7 November he began by stressing that the strength of its army and the speed with which it could be set in motion gave Prussia an enormous advantage over all its neighbours. Prompt action would prevent Saxony from aggrandising itself at Habsburg expense, something it was essential to avoid. Britain was certain to oppose any French intervention in German affairs of a kind which might hamper Prussia. Russia, the only power which could effectively oppose Frederick, would be nullified by internal problems if the empress died, by lavish bribery in St Petersburg if she did not, and perhaps by a new struggle with Sweden. It was essential, he concluded, to seize Silesia immediately. Once in possession of it he could negotiate from strength with Maria Theresa or anyone else.[20] Simultaneously he sent Podewils an uncompromising rejection of his arguments for caution and avoidance of conflict. Here the stress on ruthless use of military strength was heavy. The conquest of Silesia, and if necessary also of Saxony, which could be easily crushed, would provide him with money (a remark which anticipates Frederick's unsparing exploitation of these areas during the Seven Years War). A Russian attack, even if it came, could be met by devastating Courland and enforcing a scorched-earth policy throughout a 20-league belt along the Prussian frontiers. He ended by announcing that he had just given his regiments their marching

18 The memorandum is printed in *Pol. Corr.*, i, 74–8.
19 Berney, *Friedrich*, pp. 121–2.
20 *Pol. Corr.*, i, 90–1.

orders and that they would be in motion by the beginning of December.[21]

The die was now cast. Frederick's desire for a 'rendezvous with fame' had launched Prussia on a path which seemed to his ministers dangerously risky and was to almost all contemporary observers startlingly unexpected. It could be justified in at least quasi-rational terms; but the driving force behind it was simply the personal ambition of one man. Few events in history show more clearly the way in which its course can be changed by the arbitrary and unpredictable effects of an individual personality.

EUROPE REACTS TO THE INVASION

Within six weeks of crossing the frontier the Prussian army had overrun Silesia virtually without resistance. The Austrian defences were pathetically weak. For many years the attention of the government in Vienna had been concentrated on Hungary, and on the Italian possessions, which seemed in much greater danger of attack. No work had been done on the fortifications of Brieg, one of the main Silesia fortresses, for almost a century. A month before the Prussian attack there were in the whole province a mere 3,000 infantry and 600 cavalry available for its defence (against a theoretical peacetime establishment of 13,000 men). As rumours of the impending invasion became more threatening count Wallis, the military governor, and his second-in-command, General Browne, had managed to increase these to a total of about 7,800; but this was still less than a third of the numbers which Frederick had immediately available. It was impossible to place a garrison in Breslau, the largest Silesian town, or to improve its defences, since it claimed to be a free imperial city and as such to have the right to garrison itself; moreover, Protestant influences and therefore sympathy for Prussia were strong there. In fact, the city surrendered to the invaders on 2 January 1741 without a shot being fired. By the end of that month the whole province, apart from the fortresses of Brieg, Glogau and Neisse, was under Frederick's control. In a letter of 17 January he claimed that the conquest had so far cost him only twenty men and two officers, while Prussian cavalry was able to raid as far as the Bisamberg, high ground north of Vienna within sight of the Austrian capital.

21 *Pol. Corr.*, i, 91–3.

Greedy as he was for military glory, a long war was the last thing Frederick wanted. He hoped that Maria Theresa would reconcile herself to a *fait accompli* and cede Silesia, or most of it, in return for pledges of Prussian support against the other enemies who were now certain to challenge her. To achieve this he made considerable diplomatic efforts. Already on 15 November he had stressed to Borcke that allowing him to take the province was the only way in which she could preserve the 'melancholy wreck' of Habsburg power. In return for Silesia he would guarantee all her other German possessions, forming for this purpose a close alliance of Austria, Prussia, Russia and the maritime powers, and pay her 2 or perhaps even 3 million florins. This was in fact very much the policy which Podewils and Schwerin had urged less than a month earlier, but backed by the military force from which they had recoiled. The queen of Hungary (the title by which Maria Theresa was now generally known) was in a position, Frederick argued, from which she could not escape without substantial sacrifices. Even if in desperation she made an alliance with France (an interesting anticipation of the 'diplomatic revolution' of 1755–6), this might well lead only to her complete destruction.[22] On 7 December, little more than a week before his regiments crossed the frontier, he followed this up by ordering Borcke to offer the Austrian Grand Chancellor, count Philipp Ludwig von Sinzendorf, a bribe of up to 200,000 crowns, as well as up to 100,000 to the secretary of Francis Stephen, if they would persuade the Habsburg court to accept the offer he was about to make over Silesia. The following day, in instructions drawn up for count von Gotter, his Marshal of the Court, who was being sent on a special mission to Vienna, Frederick put forward once more essentially the same arguments. Habsburg power was on the point of collapse; he was willing to save it; but he must have compensation in the form of Silesia for the risks this would involve, especially the danger of his incurring the hostility of France. (He also stressed his legal claims to Silesia; but this was no more than a face-saving afterthought. In the confidential discussions with his ministers which followed the death of Charles VI these, significantly, were never mentioned.)[23] On 9 December, as the moment for action drew closer, the king had an interview with the marquis Botta d'Adorno, the Austrian minister in Berlin. Once more he stressed his essential goodwill towards Maria Theresa. But

22 *Pol. Corr.*, i, 102–5.
23 *Pol. Corr.*, i, 131–4.

he could not be expected to protect her against the enemies who now threatened her – Bavaria and Saxony and, looming behind them, France – without the reward of Silesia. This would allow him to ensure that she held her other territories and to help secure the imperial crown for Francis Stephen. As the interview went on it became clear to Botta that Frederick's mind was now made up and could not be changed. He left the king with a plea merely to take no action until he had heard the result of Gotter's negotiations; but he immediately warned Maria Theresa that the Prussian attack would probably not be confined to Silesia but would extend also to Moravia and the Austrian provinces proper.[24]

Frederick knew that his proposals must arouse deep-seated resistance in Vienna. This might be overcome, however, not merely by his own diplomacy and military strength but also by the action of Austria's only important potential allies, Great Britain and Russia. Their mediation might bring him the territorial gain he was determined to have. On 4 December, therefore, he wrote a personal letter to George II. In this he claimed that he had been forced to invade Silesia to forestall the plans to do so of other (unspecified) states, and because Maria Theresa was about to throw herself into the arms of France. 'My intention in this', he insisted, 'has no other aim but the conservation and the real welfare of the house of Austria,' A week later, quite typically, he tried to reinforce these protestations by straightforward bribery. If George II could obtain for him the peaceful cession of Silesia, he told count Truchsess von Waldburg, his new minister in London, then he would be rewarded by some minor concessions in Mecklenburg and by the secularisation of the bishopric of Osnabrück, which would become a hereditary possession of the house of Hanover.[25] A month later, as the invasion of Silesia proceeded, Mardefeld in St Petersburg was told that if the Russian government could gain acceptance in Vienna of Frederick's proposals it would receive in return Prussian backing for any action it took in the duchy of Courland (still formally a part of the Polish Republic but in fact virtually a Russian possession). Here again bribery was to play its part; Mardefeld was empowered to spend up to 100,000 crowns in winning over Münnich and other people of influence. A few days later the king stressed to Podewils that it was essential to make every effort to use British and Russian mediation to secure at least a large part of Silesia in return for a

---

24 Arneth, *Geschichte*, i, 114–16.
25 *Pol. Corr.*, i, 121–3, 140–1.

money payment; and at the end of January 1741, with the province at least for the time being in his hands, he wrote once more to George II and also to Münnich. With the king he now played the religious card, presenting himself as the only protector of the persecuted Protestants of Silesia and stressing (very unconvincingly, since George intensely disliked him) all that the two rulers had in common – 'our interests, our religion, our blood is the same'. To the Russian minister he emphasised once more the complete reasonableness of his demands.[26]

This flurry of diplomacy reflects the tension which filled Frederick's mind during these weeks. But it was completely unsuccessful. In Vienna during the last days of 1740 warnings of Prussian military movements at first aroused little alarm: these might well be directed towards Jülich and Berg. Even when their objective became clearer there was a willingness to believe that, like his father, Frederick might be making threatening gestures without intending effective action. As the attack on Silesia developed, some Austrian ministers became willing to contemplate concessions. Sinzendorf, old and pessimistic, suggested that in the appalling situation in which the Habsburg monarchy was now placed some loss of territory to Frederick might be unavoidable. But the dominant tone was one of outraged resistance. Francis Stephen, when he first met Gotter and was told by him that Prussian troops had already crossed the frontier, said defiantly,

> Then go back to your master and tell him that so long as a single man remains in Silesia we would rather face ruin than have dealings with him. I for my part would not give up any right of the queen or a handsbreadth of her lawfully inherited lands for the imperial throne, or for the whole world.[27]

In a second and stormy interview he completely rejected Gotter's offer of compensation in money for the loss of most of the province.[28]

Johann Christoph Bartenstein, the secretary to the Geheime Conferenz, the council of great officials which advised the Habsburg rulers, now emerged, as he was to remain in the years to come, as the most bitter opponent of any concession. To accept Frederick's proposals, he argued at the meeting of the Conferenz on 18

26 *Pol. Corr.*, i, 186, 187.
27 Arneth, *Geschichte*, i, 130–1, 121.
28 C. Grünhagen, *Geschichte der ersten Schlesischen Krieges* (Gotha, 1881), i, 92ff.

December, would merely expose the Habsburg monarchy to other territorial demands, including perhaps new ones from Frederick himself. Also, could the young king of Prussia, even if he were given all he asked in Silesia, be relied on to provide the support he promised against any further threat?[29] Bartenstein's influence was considerable, especially as he was supported by count Philipp Kinsky, the Chancellor of Bohemia. Most important of all, Maria Theresa herself refused absolutely and indignantly to buy off her faithless neighbour. Faced by such determined hostility, Frederick somewhat reduced his demands. By early January Gotter and Borcke were asking for only a 'good part' of Silesia, while the king told Podewils that he would be satisfied with lower Silesia only, and if necessary even with slightly less than that.[30] But such concessions made no difference. To give way to Frederick would not merely set off a whole series of other claims to Habsburg territory: the abandonment of Silesia would infringe the Pragmatic Sanction and its central provision of the indivisibility of the entire Habsburg inheritance, which was an essential legal and moral support to Maria Theresa. This was another argument put to the Conferenz by Bartenstein on 18 December and clearly a weighty one.

Maria Theresa's first reaction to Frederick's attack was to try to unite the other German princes so far as possible against him. The Austrian representative at the imperial diet was ordered to bring officially to its notice the gross illegality of his actions and to stress the need for the states of the Holy Roman Empire to combine to restrain him. Augustus of Saxony was reminded that, as hereditary Imperial Vicar, he had a duty to act against the lawbreaker, and also that by a treaty of 1733 he was obliged to provide Maria Theresa with an auxiliary corps to help in her resistance to Prussia. The ruler of Hesse-Kassel was asked in the same way for the 3,200 men stipulated in a treaty signed with Charles VI, while George II was faced with a request for the Hessian and Danish troops then in his pay to be made available for use against Frederick. But none of this could prevent the position of the Habsburg monarchy becoming rapidly more difficult. Now its very survival seemed threatened.

---

29 A. von Arneth, 'Johann Christof Bartenstein und seine Zeit', *Archiv für Österreichische Geschichtsforschung*, 46 (1871), 37. An interesting character sketch from the Prussian point of view of this able but obstinate man can be found in O. C. von Podewils, *Friedrich der Grosse und Maria Theresa. Diplomatische Berichte von Otto Christoph von Podewils* (Berlin, 1937), pp. 92–3.

30 Arneth, *Geschichte*, i, 128; *Pol. Corr.*, i, 157, 179.

Charles Albert of Bavaria was determined to assert his claim to all its hereditary lands. He had already, as soon as he heard of the death of Charles VI, ordered his minister in Vienna to protest against the recognition of Maria Theresa as her father's heir. The Bavarian claim turned out, however, to be much weaker than he contended. It rested on an agreement made in 1546, when duke Albrecht V of Bavaria had married the eldest daughter of the Archduke Ferdinand (who in 1556 became the Emperor Ferdinand I), on Ferdinand's earlier will of 1543 and on a codicil to it of 1547. The Bavarian argument was that under their provisions the inheritance passed to the descendants of Ferdinand's daughter if the *male* Habsburg line died out, as had now happened. However, on 3 and 4 November 1740, Sinzendorf showed to the representatives in Vienna of a number of states, including Bavaria, the originals of the will and its codicil (there was no reliable copy of the latter in Munich). These showed that the Bavarian pretensions were valid only if the Habsburg line produced no *legitimate* heirs of either sex.

But this did not end the matter. Charles Albert refused to admit that the documents barred his claim; and there were discrepancies˙ between the marriage agreement of 1546 and the codicil of the following year as well as legal arguments about the precise meaning of the latter's wording. Moreover, there was considerable support for him in the Austrian provinces, where Francis Stephen was unpopular and seen as a Frenchman rather than a German. Clearly, the elector would not abandon the ambitions he had cherished for so long. Frederick II was well aware that these Bavarian claims might be a useful weapon in forcing Maria Theresa to give way. Even before his forces had crossed the Silesian frontier he had ordered his minister in Munich secretly to urge Charles Albert to attack her (at a moment when he was assuring her of his desire to protect her against such an attack). By the beginning of March, when it was clear that Silesia would have to be fought for, he was egging on the elector to make a close alliance with France, assert his claims and then secure his own election as emperor.[31] By itself, however, Bavaria could achieve little against Maria Theresa even in her now extremely difficult situation. At the end of 1740 the whole army of Charles Albert amounted to only 10,000 men; and he could never by himself be a serious military force. To make good his claims he must have the active support of some major power. In effect, this meant France.

31 *Pol. Corr.*, i, 138–9, 200.

The death of Charles VI did not at first seem in Paris to threaten a great political upheaval. Louis XV on hearing of it said he would 'stay with his hands in his pockets' unless there were a move to elect a Protestant as emperor. When late in October Charles Albert wrote to Fleury and the king asking for support for his claims, the letters had no effect.[32] On 12 April 1741, the elector made a more specific appeal; a French army of 40,000 was needed to support the attack he hoped to make on the Habsburg lands. Long before this, however, Fleury had begun to consider giving support to Bavaria. On 4 January he sent to Berlin the text of a proposed defensive alliance with Prussia; in one of its three secret articles France agreed to provide Charles Albert as soon as possible with the subsidies which would allow him to take the field against Maria Theresa.[33] Frederick refused to commit himself. He still had hopes of gaining what he wanted through British mediation and was uneasy about the possible Russian reaction if he united with the traditional enemy of the Habsburgs. He therefore demanded a French guarantee of his possession of Silesia and, almost as important, a promise that France's influence would be used in Sweden, and perhaps also in Denmark, to threaten Russia and make sure that it did not intervene in German affairs.[34] It was only on 21 May that he told Podewils, still attached to Prussia's traditional system in foreign policy, that 'you will be forced to agree with me that the only good course of action to take is that of alliance with France'.[35]

On the French side also there was hesitation and uncertainty. But the long tradition of rivalry with the Habsburgs told heavily in favour of an interventionist policy in Germany which, it seemed, might quickly and easily deal a death-blow to the hereditary enemy. Pressures of this kind crystallised around a soldier, Charles Fouquet, duc de Belleisle. In January he strongly urged Fleury to give Charles Albert immediate help in the form of a French army of 35,000 men. Simultaneously, the forces of the Elector Palatine and the elector of Cologne should counterbalance those of Hanover and the Dutch on the lower Rhine and make sure they did not intervene on the side of Maria Theresa, while French officers might be sent to Stockholm and Constantinople to stir up anti-Russian feeling there and thus

32 Sautai, *Préliminaires*, pp. 109, 118.
33 Sautai, *Préliminaires*, p. 191.
34 Sautai, *Préliminaires*, pp. 209–10, 226–7.
35 *Pol. Corr.*, i, 245.

nullify any Russian action in Germany.[36] At the beginning of March, Belleisle left Paris on a special mission to a number of German rulers to gain their support for the election as emperor of Charles Albert. This, if it could be achieved, would be a great blow to Habsburg prestige and a corresponding moral victory for France. Belleisle was, in particular, to have discussions with Frederick II: he was promoted to the rank of marshal to increase his standing in these. On 29 April he had a long interview with the king, who complained that when he invaded Silesia he had done so in anticipation of French support which had been denied him. Now, he claimed, he was in imminent danger of attack by Russia, Hanover and Saxony, supported by Hessian and Danish auxiliaries hired by Britain, not to speak of Austria. France could transform this situation by putting two armies in the field, one in Bavaria and the other on the lower Rhine. By the end of May, Frederick had finally plumped for an alliance with France. 'I doubt at present,' he wrote fulsomely to Fleury, 'whether you are a better Frenchman than I am,' while on the same day he promised Belleisle to be 'faithful to France as none of her allies ever has been'.[37] Events were soon to show what these assurances were worth. On 4 June Podewils and the comte de Valory, the French minister in Berlin, signed at Breslau a treaty of defensive alliance. By this Louis XV undertook, in a number of secret articles, to send adequate military help to Charles Albert, to guarantee Frederick's possession of lower Silesia with Breslau and to persuade Sweden to break off relations with Russia. In return, Frederick abandoned his claim to Berg and promised his vote to Charles Albert when the imperial election took place. Maria Theresa was now more seriously threatened than ever; and Frederick began at once to press for the French to act swiftly and decisively in Germany, a note which he was to strike repeatedly in the following months.

He had been driven into alliance with France by Maria Theresa's continuing refusal to give way over Silesia. As her difficulties multiplied, feeling in the Conferenz grew in favour of concessions to Prussia. Sinzendorf was now joined in favouring such a policy by Starhemberg, the Finance Minister, and others; and even Francis Stephen inclined in that direction. Almost alone Bartenstein steadily supported his mistress in uncompromising resistance. On 11 April an alliance with Saxony was signed; but its terms showed how

36 Sautai, *Préliminaires*, pp. 200–3.
37 *Pol. Corr.*, i, 251–2.

desperate Maria Theresa's need for help now was. The Elector Augustus agreed to support Francis Stephen in the imperial election and to try to induce the other electors to do the same. He would also cease to oppose Maria Theresa's claim to cast the Bohemian vote in the election. But he was to be paid, for joining in the struggle with Prussia, a very large subsidy. He was also to make territorial gains at Prussia's expense if the war were successful; these were to include a narrow strip of Silesian territory which would join his German territories to Poland (of which since 1733 he had been king). In addition, he was to be given help, should Francis Stephen become emperor, in raising his electorate to the status of a kingdom.[38] Saxony was an ally worth having: its army was estimated by a French observer at 37,000 men. But Augustus was a very uncertain support. He had no intention of running any genuine risk merely to help Maria Theresa; and Frederick had wanted French backing partly as a means of frightening him into neutrality.

Moreover, the day before this treaty was signed the first battle of the war had been fought, at Mollwitz a few miles from the fortress of Brieg; and the Austrians had lost. It was far from an overwhelming defeat. The Austrian cavalry regiments drove the Prussian ones from the field; and Frederick himself took to flight, believing the battle lost. Only the steadiness and fire-discipline of the Prussian infantry under Marshal Schwerin saved the day. The Austrian losses were not much more than those of their opponents and the Prussians made no attempt to pursue the retreating enemy. But the moral impact was considerable. There had been high hopes in Vienna that Marshal Neipperg, the Austrian commander, would defeat without too much difficulty the upstart king of Prussia; and it was easy to underestimate the Prussian army which had seen no real fighting for a quarter of a century. Now its quality had been at least partially revealed and the vulnerability of the Habsburg territories yet more heavily underlined. The appetites of Maria Theresa's enemies, Spain in Italy, Bavaria and perhaps also Saxony in Germany, had been whetted. On 28 May, Spain signed with Bavaria the treaty of Nymphenburg. This promised Charles Albert a down-payment which would allow him to strengthen his army by 5,000 infantry and 1,000 cavalry, as well as a substantial annual subsidy. The elector had hoped for much more. He was already suffering from the chronic shortage of money which was to afflict him for the rest of his reign; and it was largely pressure from

---

38 Arneth, *Geschichte,* i, 206–8.

Belleisle which led him to accept these terms.[39] But the treaty made clear Spain's emergence as yet another active claimant to Habsburg territory.

As soon as news of the death of Charles VI reached Madrid Elizabeth Farnese began to urge immediate action by the Bourbon powers, saying that 'the time has come when France and Spain must unite more closely than ever for each to profit from so great an event; the Spaniards should enter Italy without delay and the French take possession of the Low Countries'.[40] Fleury had no sympathy with this attitude. For him the area of importance was Germany; and there he was interested in securing the election of Charles Albert as emperor and thus dealing a crushing blow to Habsburg prestige, not in territorial changes. In his eyes the queen of Spain's maternal solicitude for her younger son was merely an irritating complication. To the intense annoyance of the Spanish court, therefore, he remained cautious and essentially non-committal in his attitude to Elizabeth's Italian ambitions. It was only in November 1741 that a Spanish army, evading the British squadron in the western Mediterranean, landed at Orbetello in Tuscany. But this meant that Maria Theresa's very limited resources were now to be stretched still further by the need to defend the Habsburg position in Italy.

Moreover, her one important ally, Great Britain, was proving a disappointment. George II's personal hostility to Frederick II was intense (and fully reciprocated). In Hanover there were real fears of Prussian expansionism; and George, who was sincerely anxious to protect and if possible enlarge his electorate, shared these to the full. The king of Prussia was driven merely by ambition and the desire to enlarge his dominions, he told the Saxon minister in London on 16 December 1740, and mocked all observance of treaty obligations. No German ruler could now feel safe, for Frederick was 'a prince without loyalty or faith'. If he were not restrained he would soon have 150–200,000 men under arms: his wings must be clipped.[41] Moreover these personal feelings were by no means a negligible factor in the situation. In Britain there was a deep-seated distrust of possible Hanoverian influences on the country's foreign policy; but

39 Sautai, *Préliminaires*, pp. 282–4.

40 A. Baudrillart, *Philippe V et la Cour de France* (5 vols, Paris, 1890–1902), v, 1–2.

41 Grünhagen, *Geschichte*, i, 275–6; W. Mediger, *Moskaus Weg nach Europa: Der Aufstieg Russlands zum europäischen Machtstaat im Zeitalter Friedrichs des Grossen*, (Braunschweig, 1952) p. 362.

the king might well be able to give it a clear anti-Prussian slant. Early in 1741 George even drew up plans for a great concentric attack on Prussia by Hanover, Saxony, Britain, the Dutch Republic and, if possible, also Russia, and dreamed of a partition of Frederick's territories in which Hanover and Saxony would make substantial gains.[42] He also made it clear that he was willing to use the Danish and Hessian forces then in British pay, as well as Hanoverian troops, in support of Austria, and asked that Ostein, the Habsburg minister in London, be given full powers to conclude an Austro-British alliance. A draft treaty was in fact sent from Vienna on 13 March, while in the following month Parliament voted £300,000 to be used in supporting Maria Theresa.[43] A Hanoverian general was sent to Dresden to concert operations with Saxony against Frederick.

All this stiffened Maria Theresa's resolve to make no concessions. But she failed to realise that George's dislike of the king of Prussia was shared by neither public opinion nor politicians in London; and the hopes which had been placed in British support were soon to be followed by complaints and acrimony. On 24 June a secret subsidy treaty provided for the payment by Britain of £300,000 a year in quarterly instalments: Maria Theresa undertook that this money should be used only to strengthen her army or to pay for the hire of foreign auxiliaries. At the same time she was promised the help of the British-paid Danish and Hessian regiments, 12,000 men in all, while George II, as elector of Hanover, promised in a separate agreement to provide 13,000 of his own troops: in return he was to have two-thirds of the British subsidy of £300,000. A second separate agreement provided that this composite force of 25,000 men was to be ready to march within a month. This complex arrangement, quite typical of the period, therefore offered Maria Theresa substantial help; but it soon proved a house of cards. The landgrave of Hesse was unwilling to provide his 6,000 men if they were to be used against Prussia. The Danes refused to go on supplying their contingent after their existing subsidy treaty with Britain expired in November. The loyalty of Saxony, which it had been hoped would join this anti-Prussian coalition, was clearly very doubtful. News of the Franco-Prussian alliance of 4 June

42 U. Dann, *Hanover and Great Britain, 1740–1760* (Leicester–London, 1991), p. 27; W. Mediger, *Moskaus Weg nach Europa*, p. 371.
43 *Österreichische Staatsverträge: England*, i, *1526–1748*, ed. A. Pribram (Innsbruck, 1907), 556–67.

disconcerted George II; and Münchausen, the most important of his Hanoverian ministers, was strongly opposed to any military action against Frederick. On 22 July, therefore, the king refused to ratify the agreements he had entered into as elector, on the pretext that Augustus of Saxony had not himself ratified his treaty of 11 April with Maria Theresa.

More important, it became clear that the British government cared very little about the fate of Silesia. Its attention (apart from the disappointing and now increasingly secondary war with Spain) was now focused entirely on France, the traditional enemy, in British eyes the only enemy which really mattered. It wanted a settlement between Frederick and Maria Theresa, which could now be achieved only by the sacrifice of at least part of Silesia. With peace once made, Habsburg resources could then be used, in the tradition of William III and Marlborough, to resist jointly with the British and Dutch, and perhaps also with Prussia itself, any effort at French expansion in Germany or the Low Countries. Austria must be supported, but only as an essential safeguard against the growth of French power. It was, as a government speaker put it in the House of Commons debate of 13 April, 'the bulwark of Great Britain which, if it be thrown down, leaves us naked and defenceless'.[44] But neither politicians nor public in Britain had much interest in weakening Frederick II. Both Lord Hyndford, the new minister to Berlin, and Robinson in Vienna were therefore ordered to work for an agreement which would end the Prusso-Austrian struggle. To Maria Theresa the enemy was now Prussia; to the British, as always, France. The two powers were irremediably at cross-purposes: from this they were never to escape.

The isolation of Maria Theresa was accentuated when in July Sweden went to war with Russia. The struggle which followed was humiliatingly unsuccessful for the Swedes. Popular hostility to Russia and the hope of recovering the Baltic possessions lost to it in the great Northern War of 1700–21 provided the driving force on their side. The Hat party, which had gained control of the Swedish diet in the elections of 1738, was strongly pro-French and anti-Russian. Moreover, a secret agreement had been made with the Tsarina Elizabeth which provided that if, helped by the diversion created by the Swedish attack, she became empress (as she did in November 1741) the lost Baltic provinces would be restored. But

---

44 M. Schlenke, *England und das friderizianische Preussen, 1740–1763* (Munich, 1963), p. 120.

Elizabeth was unable or unwilling to carry out her part of the bargain. In 1742 Swedish-held Finland was overrun by the Russian army: Helsingfors (Helsinki) fell in August of that year. When peace was made at Abo in August 1743 only a strip of southern Finland was ceded to Russia: but the Swedes had to accept the stationing on their territory of 12,000 Russian troops as a guarantee of the succession to the throne of a Russian-backed candidate, Adolphus Frederick of Holstein-Gottorp. For the time being at least the country was almost a Russian protectorate.

None the less, the outbreak of the war, which Belleisle had hoped for and which was largely the result of French influence in Stockholm, helped to free Frederick II from his greatest anxiety, that of Russian intervention in support of the Habsburgs.[45] Though the invasion of Silesia had come as an unwelcome surprise in St Petersburg, divisions and uncertainties there had prevented any strong Russian reaction. The war with Sweden ruled one out completely. It was impossible, reported the British envoy to Russia at the beginning of June 1741, to bring the court to any decision to act in Germany, for 'they are entirely taken up with the Swedes, and have more at heart to secure the assistance of others for themselves, than to furnish any to the house of Austria'.[46] The Russo-Swedish war therefore had a very important indirect influence on events in the German world, and one which was clearly unfavourable to the beleaguered government in Vienna.

THE HABSBURG MONARCHY SURVIVES

As the summer of 1741 wore on the position of Maria Theresa became desperate. Never until the final collapse of 1918 was Habsburg power to be under such threat as during these months. Frederick was now urging Charles Albert to march at once directly on Vienna, and threatening not to support him as a candidate for the imperial title until he had committed himself in this way. At the same time he stressed to Fleury that France had now an un-repeatable opportunity to strike at its great rival: it must seize it by acting swiftly and decisively in Germany.[47] In spite of his military success in Silesia, the king of Prussia was uneasy and

45 *Histoire de mon temps*, i, 85–6.

46 *Sbornik Imperatorskogo Russkogo Istoricheskogo Obshchestva* (St Petersburg, 1867–1916), xci, 131, 289.

47 *Pol. Corr.*, i, 265, 266–7, 276, 281, 285.

anxious to end the war as soon as the government in Vienna could be forced to accept his conquest of the province. He feared, or claimed to fear, that unless there were decisive action by France he would soon be attacked by Hanover and Saxony, since George II and the Elector Augustus were envious of his success; but in the meantime he tied down in Silesia the bulk of Maria Theresa's inadequate forces. In Vienna the efforts of Robinson to persuade her to concede the greater part at least of what he was demanding were still fruitless. If Frederick were left in control of Silesia, it was argued, he could attack Bohemia or Moravia as soon as his unpredictable ambitions drove him to do so. So serious was the situation, however, that some effort must be made to buy off the Prussian threat and free resources to face the apparently inevitable Franco-Bavarian onslaught. Even Bartenstein was now willing to contemplate ceding territory in Silesia if this would restore the old Austro-Prussian alliance against France.[48] Maria Theresa was therefore forced to offer Frederick the province of Gelderland in the Austrian Netherlands, part of which had already been acquired by Prussia in 1713; and to this she reluctantly agreed to add the second province of Limburg. She would also abandon her claim to compensation for the losses caused her by the Prussian invasion of Silesia and pay Frederick 2 million thalers. Loss of territory in the Netherlands, distant and hard to defend, could be contemplated. Of concessions in Silesia, however, she would not hear. She would show herself, she told Robinson at the end of July, 'as yielding on the side of the Netherlands as firm and unshakeable on that of Silesia'.[49]

But no compensation in the Low Countries, detached from the main body of his dominions and likely to arouse Dutch suspicions of so formidable a neighbour, could distract Frederick from Silesia. When on 7 August Robinson, who had come on a special mission from Vienna to put the proposal to him, met him in his camp at Strehlen, the king rejected the suggestion with contempt. 'Have I occasion for peace?' he said. 'Let those who want peace give me what I want; or let them fight me again and be beaten.' It was insulting to be offered money as Maria Theresa proposed; and it would be fatal to his honour to give up his Silesian claims and abandon to renewed Catholic rule the Protestants there who had received him with open arms. He would die in the province rather

48 Arneth, 'Johann Christof Bartenstein', 39.
49 Arneth, *Geschichte*, i, 235, 394.

than give it up; and the threat to the European balance of power and the imperial constitution if Habsburg power were destroyed (the main argument used by Robinson) was purely the result of Maria Theresa's obstinacy.[50] No compromise with Prussia could therefore be hoped for in Vienna; and Maria Theresa still did not really want one. When Robinson warned her that Frederick would refuse to be fobbed off with territory in the Netherlands, she replied that she hoped this would indeed be so. Instead, she played in July 1741 with a series of what the British diplomat called 'wild plans', talking of winning over Augustus of Saxony by holding out to him the hope of gains in Lusatia and Crossen, of persuading Charles Albert to exchange his Bavarian electorate for the grand duchy of Tuscany (ruled by Francis Stephen) and the Habsburg duchy of Milan, and of throwing herself as a last resort into the arms of France.[51] But all this was merely a desperate clutching at straws. At the end of July the threat not merely to the integrity but to the very existence of the Habsburg monarchy became acute. On the last day of the month a Franco-Bavarian force occupied the independent bishopric of Passau, crossed the Austrian frontier and began to advance on Vienna.

However, the formidable array of enemies which now faced the Habsburgs was from the beginning weakened by the divisions and mutual mistrust of its members. Frederick II was effusive in his protestations of loyalty to his allies. He was, he told Charles Albert, the most faithful friend the elector had in the world. To Fleury he gave 'assurances of the most unbreakable fidelity to my promises', and said that he was 'overcome with joy to have taken on such obligations' as those laid down in the treaty of 4 June.[52] But by now no one trusted him. The attack on Silesia had made him overnight a figure of international importance as no previous ruler of Brandenburg-Prussia had been. It had also, however, marked him as completely untrustworthy in the pursuit of his own objectives; and this mark he was never to the end of his long reign to lose. Fleury deeply distrusted him. 'Good faith and sincerity are not his favourite virtues', he told Belleisle on 17 June, 'he is false in everything, even in his efforts to please. I doubt whether he is a reliable ally, for his only principle is his own interest. He wants to rule and have his own way without any concerted action with us, and all Europe

50 Coxe, *History of the House of Austria*, iii, 258–9; *Pol. Corr.*, i, 297–301.

51 E. Guglia, *Maria Theresia: Ihre Leben und ihre Regierung* (2 vols, Munich–Berlin, 1917), i, 84–5.

52 *Pol. Corr.*, i, 309, 310, 314.

detests him.'[53] Frederick for his part had already made it clear to Valory that he could not be relied on as an ally unless France acted quickly and effectively in Germany, while he made no secret of his determination to ensure that Saxony, Prussia's most obvious rival among the German states, gained as little as possible from any share it took in the attack on Maria Theresa.[54]

Fleury's distrust, allied to his age and inherent caution, had important results. They made French policy more hesitant and less effective than it might otherwise have been. In May and June there was a long conflict between the old minister and Belleisle over the size of the French force to be used in support of Charles Albert, with Belleisle asking for 43,000 men and Fleury refusing to provide more than the 35,000 he had already reluctantly agreed to. It was only after the marshal returned to Versailles on 10 July from his German mission that he was able, using his now great personal prestige, to force agreement on his plan of operations. By 15 August 15,000 French soldiers were to join Charles Albert on the Danube. In September 25,000 more were to invade Bohemia by way of the upper Palatinate. Another army of 40,000 was to take up winter quarters in Westphalia and thus hold Hanover in check.[55] France was now committed to a demanding and expensive war from which it could hope for little material gain. To secure the election as emperor of Charles Albert and thus break the centuries-old Habsburg hold on the imperial title would be for France a great prestige victory. But though Prussia, Bavaria, Saxony and Don Philip in his Italian ambitions might benefit in material terms from the destruction of Habsburg power, France had little or nothing of this kind to hope for. Moreover, it would be fighting with allies most of whom were highly unreliable and many of whom were likely to be a drain on its strength as much as an addition to it.

The odds against Maria Theresa holding any of her German-speaking territories seemed in the autumn of 1741 ominously great. Belleisle looked forward to her early and complete defeat. Maurice de Saxe, the illegitimate half-brother of the Elector Augustus, who was a general in the French army and soon to become its outstanding commander of the war, thought that the concerted attack on her would 'resemble an occupation rather than

---

53 Sautai, *Préliminaires*, p. 327.

54 *Pol. Corr.*, i, 315, 337–8.

55 Vicomte de Boislecomte, 'Le Maréchal de Belle-Isle pendant la Guerre de la Succession d'Autriche', *Revue des Questions Historiques*, 65 (1899), 193–4.

a war'. On 6 September he assured Augustus that the anti-Habsburg allies would be in Vienna before the end of the month. A well-informed observer in Paris thought it impossible for her to resist the forces arrayed against her and that the French and Bavarians could not be prevented from reaching Vienna.[56] At first, events seemed to bear out these predictions. On 15 August the French forces destined to support Charles Albert began to cross the Rhine; and as the Franco-Bavarian army advanced on Vienna the electors of Saxony and Bavaria concluded on 19 September, under Belleisle's influence, an agreement to divide between them the whole western half of the Habsburg lands in central Europe. Moravia, upper Silesia and part of lower Austria were to go to Augustus, while Bohemia, upper Austria and the Tyrol would fall to Charles Albert.

During September and October, as the enemy drew nearer, hasty preparations for a siege were made in Vienna. Building materials were assembled to strengthen the fortifications, stores of food were laid in and each household was obliged to provide a man to work on the defences.[57] But the need to buy off some, at least, of the enemies who now surrounded Maria Theresa grew more and more urgent. At a ministerial conference on 18 August a majority favoured concessions to Frederick II in Silesia; but a minority argued that it would be better to come to an agreement with France than with the new and more dangerous Prussian foe. Maria Theresa had already had some fruitless contacts with the French government through Wasner, the representative in Paris of her husband in his capacity as grand duke of Tuscany; and on 24 August she authorised him to offer Fleury the duchy of Luxemburg in return for a French abandonment of the Prussian alliance. A few days later she had an interview with the Dowager Empress Wilhelmine Amalia, the mother-in-law of Charles Albert, and through her tried to persuade him to accept territory in Italy or the Netherlands, perhaps with a royal title attached, instead of pressing his claims against the main body of the Habsburg territories.[58] Some tentative approaches were also made to him through the papal nuncio in Munich. But nothing came of all this, while it became increasingly clear that Austria had nothing to hope from its only significant ally. On 27 September

56 J-P. Bois, *Maurice de Saxe* (Paris, 1992), p. 284; *Chronique de la Régence et du Règne de Louis XV (1718–1763) ou Journal de Barbier* (Paris, 1885), iii, 291, 301.

57 Arneth, *Geschichte*, i, 326.

58 Guglia, *Maria Theresia*, i, 93–4.

George II, deeply alarmed for his electorate, now threatened by a French army and the hostile attitude of Frederick II, made an agreement with France. By this he promised to observe a strict neutrality, to give no help to Maria Theresa and not to impede the military operations of Frederick, Charles Albert and the other allies of Louis XV. He would also not oppose the candidacy of Charles Albert in the approaching imperial election. In return, the French forces were to remain at least 3 leagues from the frontier of Hanover and France was to use its good offices to free George from any threat of Prussian attack. He made this agreement only as elector, not as ruler of Great Britain. Nevertheless, the threat to the Habsburg lands was becoming more and more alarming. On 21 October the Franco-Bavarian army, after wasting precious time inactive in Linz, reached St Polten, only 60 kilometres from Vienna. The supreme crisis seemed to have come.

The threat was not pressed home. An attack on Vienna, which Frederick II was urging, would probably have succeeded; and there were clear indications that the Bavarian elector was by no means unwelcome as ruler to many of his potential subjects. The death of Charles VI had been followed by signs of popular sympathy for Charles Albert in Vienna, while when he captured Linz in September 1741 the estates of upper Austria assembled there had made no difficulties about taking an oath of allegiance to him. Yet after much hesitation he failed to advance on the Habsburg capital. Instead, the Franco-Bavarian forces turned northwards and marched into Bohemia. Charles Albert may have been influenced in this change of plan by the fact that he lacked the heavy artillery needed for a siege. Belleisle had earlier been unfavourably impressed by the weakness of the Bavarian army in this respect and complained to the war ministry in Paris of Charles Albert's rashness in advancing so far against Vienna.[59] It may also be true that his French allies feared that by taking the city and then gaining the imperial title the elector might become too powerful to be easily controlled by them.[60] But the main reason for his decision was the fear that, unless he were on the spot in force, his claim to Bohemia, recognised by his agreement of 19 September with Augustus of Saxony, would be ignored by his allies. With good reason, he trusted neither

59 Sautai, *Préliminaires*, pp. 307–8; P. C. Hartmann, *Karl Albrecht – Karl VII: glücklicher Kurfürst, unglücklicher Kaiser* (Regensburg, 1985), p. 192.
60 Hartmann, *Karl Albrecht*, p. 179.

Augustus nor Frederick II. Maria Theresa's capital was saved by the deep-seated lack of unity among her enemies.

She was also now encouraged by the prospect of help from Hungary, hitherto seen in Vienna as the most potentially disloyal of all her territories. Already late in January, Field-Marshal Count Palffy, the Iudex Curiae (chairman of the upper house of the Hungarian diet) had appealed with some effect for the raising of forces to defend the kingdom against possible Prussian attack. On 25 June, Maria Theresa was crowned as ruler of Hungary in Pressburg (the present-day Bratislava) with unprecedented pomp. On 7 September, with the Bavarians about to take Linz and the French approaching the Danube, she had a meeting with the leading Hungarian magnates, the true rulers of the country: at this they agreed to provide an army of 40,000 men and asked her, if her position became completely desperate, to choose the Hungarian fortress of Raab as a refuge and place herself and her children under their protection. On the same day Robinson returned from a second completely unsuccessful effort to persuade Frederick II to agree to peace terms: the king now refused even to give him an audience. Four days later the new queen made a dramatic appeal to the diet, asking it for help for herself and her children in this hour of extreme need. This display of emotion on her part (when she spoke of her children she shed genuine tears and wiped her eyes with a handkerchief) was greeted with an outburst of enthusiastic sympathy by her audience, which burst into cries of 'We dedicate our lives and blood' (or perhaps merely 'Lives and blood'). Francis Stephen, to the great pleasure of his wife, was accepted as co-ruler of Hungary; and it was agreed that a substantial military force should be provided. On 21 September, when her husband took the oath of office as joint ruler, Maria Theresa appeared before the Hungarian nobles with her infant son, the future Emperor Joseph II, in her arms, and provoked another outburst of enthusiasm.

All this was a personal triumph for the queen, but its effective results were somewhat limited. Though in the first flush of enthusiasm there had been talk of raising a Hungarian army of 100,000 men, in fact fewer than 22,000 infantry and a little more than 14,000 cavalry were voted; and the total effective force made available in the following year was only 20,600. Moreover, for them Maria Theresa had to give a substantial quid pro quo. The control of taxation in Hungary by the diet, and therefore the exemption from it of the nobility, was confirmed. Hungarian affairs, inside and outside the kingdom, were to be handled only by native

Hungarians. The main Hungarian administrative institutions were to be independent of their counterparts in Vienna. The queen's German ministers continued to be distrustful: one of them said that she 'should trust the devil rather than the Hungarians'. None the less, though the help she received was less than had at first seemed likely, help was given and, even more important, was given when it was most urgently needed. She did not forget this display of loyalty. Thirty years later she told her daughter-in-law that 'I feel so deeply indebted to the Hungarian nation that I cannot recommend it to you strongly enough.'[61]

Yet in the later months of 1741 the difficulties of the queen of Hungary still seemed almost overwhelming. On 20 November a Saxon army of 20,000 men joined the French and Bavarians before Prague. Five days later the city fell, to a daring surprise attack led by Saxe. On 7 December Charles Albert was crowned there as king of Bohemia. Members of many of the greatest noble families of the kingdom – Kinsky, Gallas, Königsegg, Kolowrat – took part in the ceremony; and twelve days later he convoked a meeting of the Bohemian estates to display his assumption of sovereignty. The new ruler also seemed to many of his humbler Bohemian subjects to hold out the promise of some improvement in their condition: as early as August it was reported that 'the peasants drink openly to the health of the elector'.[62] To Maria Theresa the loss of Bohemia was the most bitter of a whole series of blows: she burst into tears when told of the surrender of Prague. Almost simultaneously she heard of the beginning of hostilities against her by the Spaniards in Italy; and she was now pregnant with her fifth child.

Nevertheless, she still enjoyed the great negative resource of which no military or diplomatic failure could deprive her – the disunity and mutual disloyalty of her opponents. Frederick understood the deep hostility which he had aroused in Vienna. But the most immediate threat, in his eyes, was the possibility that Saxony might make large territorial gains of the kind envisaged in the agreement of 19 September with Charles Albert. Such success would make her a neighbour who could compete with Prussia on at least equal terms. He was therefore willing, with Silesia now in his hands apart from the fortress of Neisse which was still holding out,

---

61 Guglia, *Maria Theresia*, i, 100–16; the preceding paragraphs are largely based on this account. Arneth, *Geschichte*, i, 298–302 gives the speech to the Hungarian parliament.

62 Hartmann, *Karl Albrecht*, p. 204.

to relax the pressure on Maria Theresa, at least for a time, and thus allow her to resist her other enemies more effectively. Also his military position, though strong, was not impregnable. The siege of Neisse was dragging on and Marshal Neipperg was advancing to relieve it. Frederick may also have wished to avert too great a growth of French influence in the German world and therefore have been willing to give Maria Theresa some breathing-space so that Habsburg power could survive in a form which would still counterbalance that of France. This at least was the retrospective excuse for his conduct which he gave many years later.[63] There was much to be said, therefore, for at least some temporary agreement with the queen of Hungary.

At the end of September Colonel von Goltz, one of Frederick's aides-de-camp, told Lord Hyndford, the British envoy who had arrived in Berlin five months earlier, that the king could make no formal treaty with Maria Theresa because of his commitment to France. He was, however, willing to give a secret undertaking that if he were left in possession of lower Silesia and Neisse he would take no action against the queen or her allies. 'We are willing to stop making war', said Goltz with undiplomatic frankness, 'but we do not want to appear to have stopped making it.' He suggested a secret armistice; but one which was well camouflaged. Austrian hussars would make some very minor demonstrations of activity, while the Prussians on their side would put on an equally meaningless show.[64] Maria Theresa still bitterly resented the need to make any concessions at all. But there was an overwhelming need to free the army in Silesia for use against the French and Bavarians. For the time being at least they were a more serious threat than Prussia. It was therefore worth while, with almost all Silesia in Frederick's hands, to buy time by surrendering Neisse to him if by doing this Bohemia could be saved. The result was a convention mediated by Hyndford, and signed by him as a guarantee of its genuineness in the castle of Klein-Schnellendorff on 9 October.

This agreement is notorious as an example of the shallow artifice which marked so much eighteenth-century diplomacy. Neisse was to be surrendered to the Prussians after a sham siege lasting a fortnight; and Frederick would demand from Maria Theresa nothing more than lower Silesia, including the fortress. Efforts were to be made to agree a definitive peace-treaty by the end of December; and

---

63 *Histoire de mon temps*, i, 93–4.
64 *Pol. Corr.*, i, 356, 359–60.

when it was made these gains would be formally ceded to him. Some ostensible hostilities would continue, to hoodwink the outside world; and if no peace treaty were signed there would be agreement during the winter as to what was to happen in the spring, when the new campaigning season began. Finally, at the request of Frederick, the agreement was to be kept strictly secret.[65] Certainly he did his best to keep his allies in the dark as to what was going on. Only a week before the convention was agreed he assured Belleisle that he would do everything he could to drive the Austrians back into Moravia, and perhaps even further; while after it had been made he repeatedly wrote both to him and to Charles Albert in terms which clearly implied that he was actively continuing the war.[66] He took elaborate precautions to prevent Hyndford's visit to Klein-Schnellendorff arousing French suspicions; and at the end of October he explicitly denied, in a letter to Fleury, that he had embarked on any negotiations at all with the Austrians. He even had the effrontery to reproach him for having allowed Wasner and the Marquis de Stainville, as representatives of the Grand Duke Francis Stephen, to remain in Paris, since this was likely to arouse the suspicion that Franco-Austrian contacts were being maintained.[67]

The convention of Klein-Schnellendorff, born in duplicity, was to have a brief and inglorious existence. Nevertheless it was important. Neipperg's army was now available for use in Bohemia, though he moved too slowly (a besetting sin of Habsburg armies throughout the war) to prevent the fall of Prague six weeks later. The disunity of Maria Theresa's enemies, and in particular the selfishness and unreliability of Frederick, were once more underlined. As the winter of 1741–2 began, her position was still fraught with difficulties. But the worst was now over. Bitter disappointments were still to come; but the extreme and imminent danger of the summer and autumn would not recur. The Habsburg monarchy, battered and even mutilated, had survived and was to emerge strengthened from the trial.

---

65 *Pol. Corr.*, i, 371–2.
66 *Pol. Corr.*, i, 362, 377, 383–4, 384–5, 388–9.
67 *Pol. Corr.*, i, 392–3.

5 FROM KLEIN-SCHNELLENDORFF TO BRESLAU, 1741-2

THE IMPERIAL ELECTION AND THE HABSBURG CONQUEST OF BAVARIA

The Klein-Schnellendorff agreement had never been meant to last: in fact, it endured for only a few weeks. Frederick looked on it as little more than a scrap of paper: only a month after it had been made he signed with Saxony and Bavaria a treaty for the partition of Maria Theresa's territories. Lower Silesia, with Breslau, was to remain Prussian, while upper Silesia and Moravia were to go to Augustus and upper and lower Austria, Bohemia and the Tyrol fell to Charles Albert. This was a flagrant breach of the Klein-Schnellendorff understanding; and clearly it was only a matter of time before there was fresh fighting between the Prussian and Austrian armies. It was not until 16 December that the king admitted to Hyndford, whom he had been carefully avoiding for some weeks, that he had decided to abandon the agreement, giving as his justification that the Austrians had not kept it secret as they had promised. There was some substance in this charge: it would have taken great self-restraint in Vienna not to exploit this chance to show the French how they had been deceived by their ally. However, the mere fact that Neipperg could now move his army without opposition to Bohemia in itself created a strong presumption that some at least temporary understanding had been reached. Certainly the Austrian government was not ready for a renewal of the struggle. It sent a plenipotentiary, Freiherr von Gillen, to Silesia to negotiate a durable peace with Prussia as agreed at Klein-Schnellendorff; and when on 24 December Hyndford told him of Frederick's decision, the news caused consternation in Vienna, where an imminent Prussian advance on the city was feared.

Frederick's position was, moreover, strengthened by an important slice of luck which he had not foreseen. On the night of 23-4 November a *coup d'état* in St Petersburg overthrew the infant tsar, Ivan VI, and replaced him by Elizabeth, the daughter of Peter the Great. The coup was inspired by the French ambassador, the Marquis de la Chétardie, who had been sent to Russia in 1739 with the task of reversing the pro-Habsburg orientation of the country's foreign policy. In this he now seemed to have been spectacularly successful. Ivan's parents, Prince Anton Ulrich of Brunswick and Anna Leopoldovna, were under arrest. So were Münnich and Ostermann. German influences, so long dominant in Russian ruling circles, had now apparently been replaced by more authentically national Russian ones and the chance of any action to help Maria Theresa greatly reduced. These appearances were deceptive. Count A. P. Bestuzhev-Ryumin, who now became the leading influence in the making of Russian foreign policy, was at least as sympathetic to the Habsburgs as his predecessors. But Frederick, when he had news of the coup, was understandably encouraged by the belief that it reduced the likelihood of his great antagonist receiving any aid from the east,[1] while the same news produced a corresponding gloom in Vienna.

It was also clear by the end of 1741 that Maria Theresa must prepare herself for a greater and more public setback – the failure of her efforts to have her husband elected to the imperial throne. To achieve this, and therefore retain the title of Holy Roman Emperor in the Habsburg family even though not in the direct male line, had been a major ambition of Charles VI. In 1732 he had made an arrangement with the archbishop of Mainz by which the latter promised his electoral vote for Francis Stephen, while similar promises were extracted from the other ecclesiastical electors, the archbishops of Cologne and Trier. Also it had been agreed, when the rulers of Hanover were given electoral rank in 1692, that in future imperial elections they would always vote for the Habsburg candidate (though it was realised in the 1730s that George II might feel himself released from this undertaking by the failure of the male line). Maria Theresa was determined to see her husband chosen. She truly loved him; her affection for this very mediocre man is one of her most attractive personal characteristics. But quite apart from this, very important political considerations were involved. For three centuries there had been an unbroken succession of Habsburg emperors. Possession of the title made the head of the Habsburg family formally the greatest secular ruler in Europe (the assumption

---

1 *Politische Correspondenz, Friedrichs des Grossen*, ed. J. G. Droyson *et al.* (46 vols, Berlin, 1879–1939) i, 438–40.

of an imperial title by Peter the Great in 1721 could be seen as a threat to this status, but Russia's position as a true part of Europe was still open to question). It was important in strengthening Habsburg claims to the support of the lesser German rulers, many of whom still felt a genuine sense of loyalty to the emperor, even though his overlordship had long been hardly more than a fiction. Personal feeling and family ambition were thus joined with political advantage in calling for every possible effort to secure the imperial dignity for Francis Stephen.

Ensuring her husband's election was thus one of the first preoccupations of Maria Theresa when she succeeded her father. Active canvassing for electoral votes was begun. Count Rudolf Colloredo was sent for this purpose to Mainz, Cologne and Trier, while count Joseph Khevenhuller went to Dresden and Botta d'Adorno to Berlin. Ostein was ordered to hasten his journey to London, where he had already been appointed as minister, to solicit the vote of George II as elector of Hanover. But Maria Theresa knew that she faced considerable difficulties. The house of Lorraine, to which Francis Stephen belonged, was not popular in Germany; and it could be argued that since he had no German territory of his own (apart from the little principality of Teschen given him by Charles VI) he was hardly a German prince at all. Also he would face serious rivals in any effort to become emperor. In particular, Augustus of Saxony had ambitions of his own for the imperial title, for which he sought French and Spanish backing: to reinforce his arguments against the election of Francis Stephen he once confronted count Wratislaw, the Austrian ambassador to Poland, carrying in his hands a copy of the Golden Bull, the document of 1356 on which the electoral procedure was based.[2]

There was also a more specific problem which Maria Theresa had to confront. One of the nine imperial electors was the ruler of Bohemia, in other words herself. As a woman she could not vote in the election: but could she transfer to her husband her right to vote? She claimed that she could. On 21 November 1740, some weeks before the whole situation was transformed by the Prussian invasion of Silesia, she formally entrusted Francis Stephen with the Bohemian vote; and in February 1741 Freiherr von Brandau was sent to Frankfurt, the free city in which imperial elections took place, as the representative there of the Bohemian crown. But there was

---

2 A. von Arneth, *Geschichte Maria Theresias* (10 vols, Vienna, 1863–79), i, 175–6, 196.

widespread resistance to the Bohemian vote being used in this way. In the early months of 1741 even George II, Maria Theresa's ally, made difficulties. More fundamental was the inevitable tendency among the electors, as the Habsburg position became more and more difficult, to abandon an apparently sinking ship; and this was reinforced by the use of French influence and money to ensure that the long Habsburg tenure of the imperial title was at last broken. The nephew of the elector of Mainz, for example, who was known to have much influence over his uncle, was promised 200,000 francs as soon as an emperor acceptable to France had been chosen, as well as an abbey worth 15–20,000 livres a year. At the same time Belleisle promised 80,000 livres to one of the elector's councillors and a pension of 6,000 to his vice-chancellor.[3] The autumn and early winter of 1741 therefore saw a steady erosion of the Habsburg position in this as in other respects. Charles Albert of Bavaria as a candidate for the imperial title could count on the votes of the three Wittelsbach electors (himself and the electors of Cologne and Mainz). When at the end of August Frederick II let it be known in Frankfurt that he also would support the Bavarian candidacy, this gave him four out of a total of nine (or eight if the Bohemian vote were disregarded). On 7 September, the elector of Trier, of the Schönborn family which was traditionally pro-Habsburg, agreed to back Charles Albert, saying that he 'must swim with the current'; and a week later George II wrote to the Bavarian elector promising him his vote. Finally on the 19th Augustus of Saxony abandoned his claim to the imperial title. Charles Albert was now certain of success: hopes of a new Habsburg emperor had collapsed. The weakness of Maria Theresa's position can be seen in the fact that her name-day (15 October) was not recognised at all at the court of the elector of Mainz, whereas that of Louis XV (25 August) had been celebrated there like that of the ruler himself.[4] The election, when it took place on 24 January 1742, was therefore a complete victory for the anti-Habsburg forces: Charles Albert was chosen unanimously and crowned on 12 February. Most of all this was a victory for France and seen as such. 'It is certainly a glorious achievement for the king', Fleury wrote to his ambassador in Madrid a few days later, 'the transfer of the empire to another

---

3 M. Sautai, *Les Préliminaires de la Guerre de la Succession d'Autriche* (Paris, 1907), i, 277–8.

4 E. Guglia, *Maria Theresia: Ihre Leben und ihre Regierung* (2 vols, Munich–Berlin, 1917), i, 143–4.

house than what remains of that of Austria, and to have made it pass to a prince who is so faithful an ally of France.' It was, however, a success which brought prestige rather than any tangible benefit, as he went on to admit in the same despatch. 'So far', he wrote, 'this event is rather like a fine tree covered with beautiful and very green leaves and with no fruit. We must hope that we shall gather it later.'[5] None the less, French influence in Germany was now running very high. It can be seen in the fact that in the promises (*Wahlkapitulation*) which, in the usual way, the new emperor made at his accession to the German princes, the hitherto customary article in which he undertook to seek the liberation of Alsace from French rule did not appear.

But if Maria Theresa had been politically defeated in Frankfurt she had had striking military success elsewhere. On 28 October count Ludwig Andreas von Khevenhuller, a veteran soldier with experience going back to the Spanish Succession war, had sent to her at Pressburg a plan of campaign for the recovery of the occupied Austrian provinces and an invasion of Bavaria. Almost a month later, on 22 November, he was appointed to command the army which had been collected for this purpose. On the last day of the year he began his advance up the Danube valley, while a second force under General Barenklau moved through the Tyrol towards Munich. The weeks which followed saw the most striking series of military victories hitherto achieved by any of the combatants. Upper Austria was rapidly reconquered. A Bavarian army was defeated at Scharding on 17 January 1742. Ten thousand French soldiers were surrounded and forced to surrender at Linz a week later. The day of Charles Albert's coronation as emperor in Frankfurt, 12 February, saw the surrender of his capital. Apart from one or two fortresses, notably Ingolstadt, Bavaria was now in Austrian hands. The military and political situation had been transformed. Charles Albert had always been heavily dependent on French backing, for Bavaria was not a wealthy state. In 1740–41 he had managed, by levying extraordinary taxation, mainly on the church, to raise 1.5 million gulden; but this was not enough to maintain an army adequate to the tasks he imposed on it. He had probably only 10–12,000 men available for the advance towards Vienna in 1741: the Bavarians, by one estimate, made up only a fifth of the infantry and a seventh of the more expensive cavalry in the invasion force. Now, with his

5 A. Baudrillart, *Philippe V et la Cour de France* (5 vols, Paris, 1890–1902), v, 81.

electorate in enemy hands, he was more than ever a client of France and helpless without its support. He was able to obtain from the Elector Palatine Charles Philip an auxiliary corps which eventually amounted to 4,600 men, while the landgrave of Hesse-Kassel agreed, in return for a subsidy, to supply 3,000 soldiers for three years. But without French money he could do little. He was soon forced to admit to his minister in Paris that 'the subsidies from the king [Louis XV] constitute my only income, for I draw nothing from my territories and Spain pays nothing [that is, of the money promised him in the Nymphenburg agreement of May 1741]'.[6] From this humiliating situation he was never to escape.

The position of Maria Theresa, by contrast, had strikingly improved. Austria had shown that it was still a substantial military power. In particular, contemporaries were impressed by the mobility and destructive power of the irregular forces raised in the eastern borderlands of the monarchy, the Croats, *pandours* and *tolpatches* (irregular infantry, from the Magyar *talpas*, a foot-soldier) who made up much of Barenklau's army.[7] Some of these, wearing white cloaks and red hoods and bristling with weapons of all kinds, had paraded before Maria Theresa in Pressburg during her dramatic visit to the city. They now led Charles VII (as Charles Albert had now become) to complain that 'Bavaria was overrun by vermin of this kind and the land devastated and ruined in a manner unheard of among Christians'.[8] Moreover, success helped to generate increased enthusiasm and fighting spirit among the Habsburg regular forces. When on 21 January 1742 Francis Stephen, who had just been given nominal command of those invading Bavaria, met Khevenhuller near Linz, he gave him a letter in which Maria Theresa thanked her general very warmly for his loyalty and achievements. When Khevenhuller read this out at a banquet it roused the officers there to the sort of emotion shown a few months earlier by the Hungarian nobles at Pressburg. Many of them kissed the hand of the grand duke, assuring him of their loyalty to his wife; and when a portrait of Maria Theresa and her son was unveiled they blew kisses towards it and brandished their swords.[9] The lethargy and pessimism which had marked the last days of Charles VI were being

6 P. C. Hartmann, *Karl Albrecht – Karl VII: glücklicher Kurfürst, unglücklicher Kaiser* (Regensburg, 1985), pp. 179–80, 190, 262, 268.

7 See below, pp. 221–2.

8 Hartmann, *Karl Albrecht*, p. 266.

9 Guglia, *Maria Theresia*, i, 136.

dispelled by the stimulus of conflict and the taste of success. Most important of all, the conquest of Bavaria gave the Habsburg cause an important asset in any future territorial bargaining. The electorate, so desirable in strategic terms, might well be retained as compensation for the loss of Silesia, or perhaps bartered for territory elsewhere, notably in Italy.

THE WAR BEGINS IN ITALY

Here the Spanish attack had been long in taking shape. For this France, and in particular Fleury, were responsible. The death of Charles VI became known in Madrid on 5 November; and at once Philip V and his wife began to press for French support for the establishment of Don Philip in an Italian principality of his own. In this they made great play with the fact that he had married in 1738 the favourite daughter of Louis XV. 'At this time there is a good opportunity to obtain something for the Infant, Don Philip', wrote Philip V to Louis, 'and at the same time I beg the King, my nephew, to think of his daughter on this occasion in order that their children may have something to live upon and may not remain Cadets.' Fleury remained for some time quite unresponsive.

> If the pretensions of the Elector of Bavaria had had any foundation [he told Philip on 24 November] we should have supported them and might have found in the dismemberment of the Emperor's inheritance some opportunity of profiting in favour of the Infant. But Your Majesties will have learned from what has passed at Vienna [a reference to the production there of the will of Ferdinand I; see p. 73 above] that it is clear that the House of Bavaria has no right to the Austrian Succession [a significant admission in the light of France's later policies]. We have, therefore, no resource but in the election of an Emperor by which the Empire may be divided and it may be possible to negotiate in favour of the Infant with the candidate elected.[10]

On 13 December, none the less, Fleury agreed, under the influence of the war party which was already gathering strength at Versailles, that the Italian territories of the Habsburgs were not covered by the Pragmatic Sanction, since they were not part of their hereditary possessions. By the end of January 1741 he was willing to allow Elizabeth Farnese to claim the duchies of Parma and Piacenza, and

---

10 S. Wilkinson, *The Defence of Piedmont, 1742–8: A Prelude to the Study of Napoleon* (Oxford, 1927), pp. 28–9.

perhaps also Mantua, as an apanage for Don Philip. But, to the intense irritation of Philip V and his wife, he insisted that the really important objective was not to act in Italy but to secure the election as emperor of Charles Albert who, once elected, would not oppose these Spanish claims. This point was forcibly made in the instructions given to the new French ambassador to Madrid, Vauréal, bishop of Rennes.[11] In May, by the treaty signed with Spain at his palace of Nymphenburg, just outside Munich, the elector did in fact recognise the Spanish claim to Maria Theresa's Italian territories.

Any military operations in Italy were certain to be decisively influenced by the attitude of the king of Sardinia, Charles Emmanuel III. As well as the backward and poverty-stricken island from which he took his royal title, he ruled the much more important mainland territories of Savoy and Piedmont. The strategic position of these, astride the Alps and controlling the routes from France to Italy, ensured them a certain importance. Combined with the abilities of a series of rulers, and the large and relatively efficient army they maintained, this had meant a steady increase in their international standing since the second half of the sixteenth century. Savoy-Piedmont had already shown its military potentialities in the very significant role it played in the Spanish Succession struggle. Charles Emmanuel was therefore a highly desirable ally. Though the Spanish government negotiated with him in early 1741 for an alliance and joint action against Maria Theresa, the king, showing the prudence and care for his own interests which was to mark him throughout his reign, refused to make any commitment until he was sure of the attitude of France.

For months on end, however, Fleury fobbed off Philip V and his domineering wife with vague hopes that if things went well in Germany Louis XV would then obtain something in Italy for Don Philip through negotiation with Maria Theresa. Moreover, Charles Emmanuel and his ministers were insistent that a balance of power must be maintained in the peninsula. Already a Spanish Bourbon, the second son of Philip V, had since 1735 been established in Naples and Sicily as King Charles III. If his younger brother were now set up in a large territory of his own in northern Italy, would this not mean Bourbon dominance of the whole peninsula with a

11 *Receuil des instructions données aux ambassadeurs et ministres de France depuis les traités de Westphalie jusqu'à la Révolution Française*, xxvii, ed. D. Ozanam (Paris, 1960), 12–13.

corresponding threat to the kingdom of Sardinia? If the Habsburgs were driven out of Italy completely, Francis Stephen would be unable to maintain his position as grand duke of Tuscany; what then would happen to this important state? What was to be the fate of Corsica, officially a Genoese possession but for over a decade chronically rebellious and ungovernable? If Charles Emmanuel and Don Philip were both to benefit from the break-up of Habsburg power, there must therefore be a very clear understanding as to what each was to gain. All these points were made by the marquis d'Ormea, the able Sardinian Foreign Minister, in complex negotiations which went on, first in Turin and then in Paris, throughout 1741. They also underlay two elaborate alternative schemes for a new territorial settlement in Italy which Charles Emmanuel sent to Paris in the first days of 1742.[12]

Some flexibility on the Spanish side might well have produced an agreement very threatening to Maria Theresa. But this was not forthcoming. In a long and difficult interview which Vauréal had with the king and queen in November 1741, in which as usual Elizabeth did almost all the talking, the queen told him that 'the king declares to you that his patience is at an end and that he would rather negotiate with the Grand Duchess [Maria Theresa] than with the King of Sardinia'. Later she was to refer to Charles Emmanuel on at least one occasion as 'that Italian brute'; while in March 1742 the Spanish ambassador in Paris suggested that by coming to some arrangement with France and Spain the Austrians might recover any territory they were forced temporarily to cede to Charles Emmanuel, and said that 'his master would prefer that the Queen [Maria Theresa] kept the Milanese rather than see it pass to the King of Sardinia'.[13] On his side Charles Emmanuel, if less forthright, was almost equally distrustful. In December 1741 he gave the British minister in Turin a memorandum which stressed the critical position of Maria Theresa: she must at once make peace with Frederick II and gain Russian support. He also undertook, however, to prolong negotiations with the Bourbon powers until he could come to an agreement with her: if in the meantime there were a Spanish invasion of Lombardy he would join her in resisting it.[14]

12 D. Carutti, *Storia della Diplomazia della Corte di Savoia* (4 vols, Turin, 1875–80), iv, 163–8.

13 Baudrillart, *Philippe V*, v, 72–4; Carutti, *Storia*, iv, 191; R. Butler, *Choiseul* i, *Father and Son, 1719–1754* (Oxford, 1980), p. 436.

14 Carutti, *Storia*, iv, 178.

On 31 January 1742 the Spanish force which had landed at Orbetello in November of the previous year was reinforced by another which got ashore at Spezia, in Genoese territory. Once more the British Mediterranean squadron under Admiral Haddock did nothing to prevent this: it was simply too weak to blockade effectively at the same time both Cadiz and Cartagena, the main Spanish Mediterranean naval bases. Clearly there was now, after months of futile diplomacy, to be fighting on a considerable scale. The Spaniards marched south into the papal state and were joined there by a Neapolitan force supplied by Charles III. There were great obstacles to any agreement between Maria Theresa and Charles Emmanuel. The king of Sardinia, as the one remaining descendant of Philip II of Spain, had inherited a claim to the duchy of Milan; and he expected to receive a large part of it in return for assisting her. He also demanded the marquisate of Finale, which Charles VI had sold in 1713 to the Genoese republic; this was strategically important, since it would greatly improve the access to the sea of almost landlocked Piedmont-Savoy. Maria Theresa was deeply unwilling to make such concessions. She had a sentimental attachment to her Italian possessions and dreamed of adding to them the kingdom of Naples which her father had had to surrender in 1735. She was encouraged in such hopes by assurances given her by secret emissaries that there was much support in the kingdom for a Habsburg restoration and that the appearance there of an Austrian army would set off a general rising against the Spanish regime.[15] But, faced by the threat of growing Bourbon power in Italy, the two rulers were able, on 1 February 1742, to reach one of the most peculiar of the numerous and short-lived agreements of these years. The Austrians would defend against the Spaniards Modena and Mirandola, which acted as the outer defences of the duchies of Parma and Milan: the Piedmontese would do the same for Piacenza and Pavia. While this alliance lasted Charles Emmanuel would not press his claim to Milan; but this was not in any way to prejudice his raising the issue in the future. He could do so at any time merely on condition of giving a month's notice of his intention, and could make any alliance he saw fit as a means of forwarding his claim. This provision brings out well the fragile and ephemeral nature of so many of the alliances of the period. As one historian has pointed out, the treaty 'reads more like a labour agreement than a political transaction'; and even contemporaries found it remark-

---

15 Arneth, *Geschichte*, ii, 174.

able. The French Foreign Minister called it 'the oddest treaty which has ever been concluded'.[16]

Nevertheless, the tide of military success ran in favour of the Austrians and Piedmontese in 1742. The strategically important duchy of Modena, whose ruler had taken the Bourbon side, was occupied by Charles Emmanuel in June. On 19 August a small British naval squadron (five ships of the line and four bomb-vessels) appeared before Naples, and its commander, Commodore Martin, threatened to bombard and destroy the city if the Neapolitan regiments were not at once withdrawn from the Spanish army in the papal state and a promise given that Naples would provide the Spaniards with no help in future. This ultimatum, delivered on the orders of the commander of the British Mediterranean squadron, Admiral Matthews, was completely successful. A letter signed by a Neapolitan minister, the marquis de Sales, gave these assurances the following day.[17]

These setbacks intensified the feeling in Madrid that France, by refusing to make any military commitment in Italy, had betrayed its ally. 'Ah monsieur', said Elizabeth Farnese to Vauréal in March, 'are you telling us that the King of France cannot give five or six thousand men to his son-in-law to use against a prince [Charles Emmanuel] who for the last year has been deceiving both crowns? We shall be able to convince no one of this and everyone will remain sure that this can be only through lack of friendship for us.' Six months later she still felt bitter that Louis XV could provide large armies to support Charles VII in Germany but would do nothing south of the Alps. She also complained, with more justification, that the Spanish government was kept in the dark by the French about their intentions. 'How will this finish?' she asked. 'By learning some day in the newspapers that a peace has been made about which we have been told no more than the republic of Lucca?'[18] This was in fact a fairly accurate forecast of what was to happen in the peacemaking of 1748.[19] By 1742, therefore, one fundamental characteristic of the struggle in Italy was well established. This was the deep division within each of the opposing power-groupings. On the one side, the ambitions of Charles

---

16 Sir R. Lodge, *Studies in Eighteenth-century Diplomacy, 1740–8* (London, 1930), pp. 46–7; Butler, *Choiseul*, p. 435.

17 Sir H. W. Richmond, *The Navy in the War of 1739–48* (3 vols, Cambridge, 1920), i, 212–15.

18 Baudrillart, *Philippe V*, v, 91, 108–9.

19 See below, p. 204.

Emmanuel could be gratified only at the expense of his ostensible ally, Maria Theresa. On the other, France and Spain were separated by deep differences of outlook and by a growing feeling in Paris that Spanish policy was far too much at the mercy of an obstinate and unreasonable woman. These disunities, and the resulting weakness of both alliances, were to mark the war in the peninsula from beginning to end.

FREDERICK II MAKES PEACE BUT REMAINS INSECURE

The collapse of the fragile Klein-Schnellendorff agreement left the king of Prussia in what he more and more felt to be a dangerously exposed position. When hostilities with the Austrians began once more at the end of 1741 he found cooperation with his French allies very difficult. He favoured an invasion of Moravia, through which Vienna itself could be threatened, whereas the Marshal de Broglie, who had now succeeded Belleisle as French commander in Bohemia, wished to move south to repel the Austrian invasion of Bavaria. Frederick did in fact advance on the Austrian capital in February and March 1742, when Prussian cavalry almost got within sight of the city; but lack of a siege-train, which the Saxons had promised to supply but did not, and the harassing of his communications by Hungarian irregular cavalry, forced him to retreat. He was now highly critical of the inaction and what he saw as the strategic mistakes of the French; and certainly Broglie, who was old, disliked his task, and was on bad terms with both Frederick and Belleisle, now subordinate to him, was a poor choice for the post he held. Also Frederick was now more and more hostile to Saxony, his ostensible ally. He was determined that Prussia should not fight to benefit this potentially dangerous neighbour. 'So long as I breathe', he told Belleisle on 8 January, 'I will never allow a métairie [that is, a small farm] of Bohemia to be detached in favour of the King of Saxony [*sic*: the Elector Augustus was also king of Poland].' A few days later he refused point-blank to evacuate any of his conquests in Moravia to ease the communication problems of the Saxon army: and at the end of the month he told Podewils that 'My great ambition is not to allow the Saxons to escape from my clutches.'[20] It is not surprising, therefore, that when Frederick, backed by his able younger brother Prince Henry, met Augustus and his chief

---

20 *Pol. Corr.*, ii, 7, 9, 25.

minister, count Brühl, in Dresden on 19 January the meeting merely confirmed the total lack of unity between the two rulers. Saxon ambitions now seemed to the king of Prussia more threatening than Austrian resentment; and he was well aware that bad luck or bad judgement could easily and quickly end the run of military success he had so far enjoyed. At the same time his appetite was whetted by the prospect of new territorial gains. The collapse of Bavaria and the increasingly difficult position of the French garrison in Prague, he felt, might strengthen his hand and allow him, when peace was made, to acquire part of Bohemia, the circle of Königgrätz. But he also feared that Britain and the Dutch might declare war on France and thus make it withdraw forces from Germany and leave Prussia to bear the brunt of the fighting there. At the very least they might, by providing garrisons for the barrier fortresses in the Austrian Netherlands, free more regiments for Maria Theresa to use against him in Germany. Yet on the other hand, if the struggle with her were pressed to the point of complete victory, would not this make France the arbiter of Europe, which he certainly did not want? This mixture of fears and hopes made the spring and early summer of 1742 a time of particular stress for him. 'The state of the King of Prussia', recorded the French ambassador later, 'was terrible, and as a result his appearance had become wild. All his remarks were harsh, his laugh forced and sardonic and his jokes full of bitterness. Everything worried him, everything aroused suspicion in that tormented soul.'[21] More and more he wished for peace if it could be had on acceptable terms.[22]

On the Habsburg side also there was a willingness to negotiate. Apart from anything else, Maria Theresa's financial position was still terribly weak. In May 1742 a British emissary sent on a trade mission to Vienna reported that the Austrian ministers admitted that without the British subsidy they would be unable to keep an army in existence.[23] The queen herself was still hostile and distrustful. Though she agreed to her husband making overtures to Frederick for peace, and perhaps even for some form of alliance against

21 *Mémoires des négociations du Marquis de Valori, ambassadeur de France à la cour de Berlin*, ed. Comte H. de Valori (Paris, 1820), i, 154.

22 The arguments for peace with Maria Theresa as he saw them are summed up in the undated memorandum drawn up by him in March or April 1742, in *Pol. Corr.*, ii, 99–100.

23 P. G. M. Dickson, *Finance and Government under Maria Theresia* (Oxford, 1987), ii, 160–1.

France, she believed and probably hoped that nothing would come of this. However, early in February Baron Pfütschner, the former tutor of Francis Stephen, had an interview with Frederick at Olmütz; and a month later Count Giannini, the bishop of Olmütz, saw the king in his headquarters at Znaim. Neither had any success. To Pfütschner, whose mission was largely exploratory, Frederick insisted that the position of Maria Theresa was still desperate. British money had given her merely 'a short respite in her misfortunes'. She could expect no help now from Russia. If she lost another battle she was doomed. He wanted the Habsburgs to remain a significant power; but the only way of achieving this was an immediate peace, based on concessions to Bavaria, Saxony and Prussia. Giannini was empowered to offer Frederick the county of Glatz in addition to what he had already seized; but in return Maria Theresa was to retain upper Silesia, while the king must support by arms her recovery of her other hereditary lands, in particular Bohemia and Moravia. Each ruler was to guarantee the territories of the other and to provide a force of 25,000 men if necessary to make good this guarantee. This went much further than Frederick was ready to contemplate: four days of negotiations therefore ended without result.[24]

However, the king was more and more anxious for peace. He too was now short of money. Though his financial position was much stronger than that of Maria Theresa, there remained of the ample resources with which he had begun the war in December 1740, according to his own much later account, only 150,000 crowns.[25] On 5 April he told Podewils that he regarded an end to hostilities as 'prudent and necessary for us'; if necessary therefore the demand for the Königgrätz circle must be given up.[26] Hyndford had already been approached to act as a go-between, though the Klein-Schnellendorff experience had somewhat blunted his appetite for the role; and Frederick now stressed his wish for better relations with the maritime powers (Great Britain and the Dutch Republic), and backed this by threats that if peace with Maria Theresa could not be achieved he would throw himself irrevocably into the arms of France. But the negotiations dragged on, to his growing unease. Maria Theresa still demanded that in return for what he claimed in Silesia he should guarantee the rest of her territories, or at least the

24 Arneth, *Geschichte*, ii, 470–2, 56–7.
25 *Histoire de mon temps*, ii, 128.
26 *Pol. Corr.*, ii, 107.

German ones, and join in driving the French from Germany; and this he was determined not to do. On 11 May he told Podewils that nothing could be hoped from Hyndford's negotiations and that he saw no way out of the impasse but by further fighting. Six days later he defeated the main Austrian army in Bohemia, now commanded by Prince Charles of Lorraine, the younger brother of Francis Stephen, at Chotusitz. This was far from a complete victory. The losses of the two sides were not very unequal, while Frederick made no effort to follow up his success. This was partly because his cavalry had suffered badly in the battle, but at least as much because his real objective was political, not military; to induce his opponent to make peace.

Even now there were forces in Vienna which wanted to go on fighting. Bartenstein still urged his mistress to continue the struggle. An agreement with Frederick now, he argued, would be fatal to the Habsburgs and to the peace and security of Europe. If she could hold out for another year she would win, for the Bavarian forces had been destroyed, the French and Saxon ones were in poor condition, and those of Prussia had been seriously weakened. The Austrians, on the other hand, had been strengthened by new Hungarian and Croat units; and if commanders in the field were chosen for ability rather than social rank (perhaps an indirect criticism of the slowness of movement and general indecisiveness of Prince Charles) victory could be expected.[27] But the need to recover Bohemia was now the dominant consideration in Vienna: the result was the agreement on 11 June at Breslau of preliminary peace terms. These were confirmed by a formal peace treaty signed at Berlin on 28 July. To the last moment Frederick hoped, in vain, to gain something in Bohemia; but he was now extremely anxious to have an agreement signed and ratified as soon as possible.[28] Maria Theresa ceded all Silesia, including Glatz, except for Teschen, Troppau and some minor territories. There was provision for the protection of the Catholic church and its privileges in the ceded areas, something to which she, as a devout Catholic, attached a good deal of significance. Frederick was to evacuate all other Austrian territory within sixteen days of the signature of the preliminaries; and Saxony was to be included in the peace if its forces also withdrew within sixteen days of the terms being communicated to the Elector Augustus. On 23 July Maria Theresa

27 Arneth, *Geschichte*, ii, 70.
28 *Pol. Corr.*, ii, 190.

made what was in effect a peace agreement with Saxony: peace was formally proclaimed in Dresden on 17 September. She had thus freed her hands, at least for the time being, for effective action against the French in Bohemia. But it was impossible to see this peace as anything but a defeat for the Habsburg cause. Bartenstein bitterly described it as 'the true tomus secundus of the peace of Belgrade [the disastrous peace with the Ottoman Empire made in 1739]'.[29]

Frederick knew very well that this second desertion of his allies was bound to reinforce the reputation for duplicity and unreliability which he had now acquired. As soon as peace terms had been agreed, therefore, he sent a stream of self-justifying letters to Fleury, Belleisle and Charles VII. The French and Saxons, he claimed, had totally mishandled the war in Bohemia: this meant that the whole weight of it had fallen on Prussia, which could not carry such a burden. 'I therefore look on this affair [the war with Austria]', he wrote to Belleisle on 18 June, 'as a voyage, undertaken by several people with the same purpose, but which, thrown off course by a shipwreck, puts each traveller in a position where he is entitled to look to his own safety, to save himself by swimming and getting to shore where he can.' To Fleury on the same day he had the effrontery to assert that 'the course of this war forms, so to speak, a tissue of marks of goodwill given by me to my allies'.[30] These protestations did little or nothing to lessen the anger which his conduct had aroused in France. Belleisle described him in a letter of 23 June as 'the faithless prince who has just betrayed his allies'. The French minister to the imperial diet spoke of the Breslau agreement as 'an unheard-of proceeding' and of the Prussian king as 'a faithless ally', while Valory in Berlin warned the king that this abandonment of France would one day rebound against him.[31]

But, the king reiterated, he had found himself bearing the whole weight of the war in Germany because of the poor performance of the French armies there, and could not allow himself to become its victim. He had not betrayed his allies: he had simply withdrawn from an enterprise which had become too big and too demanding for him. He did not regard his alliance with France as broken off: he might even become a mediator between it and Austria.[32] This

---

29 Arneth, *Geschichte*, ii, 482, fn. 42.

30 *Pol. Corr.*, ii, 206–9.

31 Butler, *Choiseul*, p. 323; Vicomte de Boislecomte, 'Le Maréchal de Belle-Isle pendant la Guerre de Succession d'Autriche', *Revue des Questions Historiques*, 65 (1899), 205; *Mémoires des négociations du Marquis de Valori*, i, 164–5.

32 *Mémoires des négociations du Marquis de Valori*, i, 284–9.

self-confident attitude, however, masked deep anxieties. Frederick was uneasily aware that hopes of revenge and the recovery of Silesia were still very much alive in Vienna. If Maria Theresa kept Bohemia, he told Podewils, he would have to fight her again in four or five years' time. He foresaw the possibility of a Franco-Austrian alliance against him of the kind which took shape in 1755–6, though he drew reassurance from the thought that in that case he would have Britain, the Dutch and Russia on his side.[33] His success had made Frederick the outstanding ruler of the day; but it had also induced in him fears which were never to leave him. This atttitude of suspicion and the consciousness of his own vulnerability which underlay it endured for the rest of his life.

How could he best protect himself against a Habsburg war of revenge? Something might be done by strengthening Charles VII, not merely by the restoration of his Bavarian electorate but perhaps by giving him also the small, detached Habsburg territories in south-west Germany, or land in Italy, secularised ecclesiastical principalities such as the archbishopric of Salzburg, or annexed imperial free cities such as Augsburg, Regensburg or Ulm. This would re-establish him as a significant force in south Germany and to some extent a counterweight to Maria Theresa. Frederick therefore tried in several ways to fortify the emperor's position: he supported the efforts of Charles to persuade the imperial diet to vote him money (the so-called Roman Months) and backed the choice of his brother as the new elector of Mainz.[34] Much more effective than any of this, however, would be a defensive alliance with some major power willing to help defend Prussia's Silesian conquest. France or Russia were his first choices for this purpose; but for different reasons neither was now available. The only remaining resource was Britain, supported by its traditional Dutch ally, and to the construction of an alliance with Britain Frederick devoted a considerable amount of effort in the second half of 1742. He now hoped for a general peace produced by the creation of a powerful German army made up of contingents from the different states and commanded by himself. This would safeguard the neutrality of the Holy Roman Empire and ensure the exclusion from it of all foreign armies; in this way he could appeal to the popular feeling of genuine German patriotism and resentment of foreign

33 *Pol. Corr.*, ii, 210, 213, 287.

34 A. Berney, *Friedrich der Grosse: Entwicklungsgeschichte eines Staatsmannes* (Tübingen, 1934), p. 172.

military incursions which undoubtedly existed in many parts of the empire. The idea came to nothing, in spite of serious efforts to persuade the German princes to accept it. Particularism was now too strong among them; and Charles VII himself deeply distrusted Prussia.[35] By the end of April 1743 Frederick had abandoned the scheme, at least for the time being. But he was willing to guarantee the integrity of Hanover and thus protect it against French attack, a major objective of British policy. This he felt was in Prussia's own interests; and he also hoped that Britain might support a number of relatively minor Prussian territorial claims, in Mecklenburg, East Friesland and the bishopric of Osnabrück.[36] The British government, for its part, had no real interest in the fate of Silesia and was quite unwilling to make any sacrifice merely to return it to Maria Theresa. The result was an Anglo-Prussian defensive alliance signed at Westminster on 29 November 1742. By this each state guaranteed the European possessions of the other and promised to back the guarantee with a force of 10,000 men if necessary.

BRITAIN BEGINS TO PLAY AN ACTIVE ROLE IN EUROPE

This agreement was one aspect of an important change in the international situation. Great Britain was now becoming an active participant in the struggle to preserve at least the non-German parts of the Habsburg inheritance. The early stages of the war saw little British comment, either in Parliament or the press, on the morality of Frederick's action in invading Silesia. Moreover, he could always call on still powerful religious sympathies, since he could easily be seen as a Protestant champion liberating fellow-Protestants from oppressive Catholic rule. A pamphlet of 1741, written to defend his alleged right to Silesia, spoke of him as 'this great Protestant Defender', and as freeing his new subjects from 'the petty Tyrannies of Cardinals, Priests and Jesuits' and from 'the unbearable Yoke of Austria'. Care was taken in the parliamentary debates and in the address of thanks for the king's speech from the throne in 1741 to avoid giving them any anti-Prussian colouring. On the other hand, there was complete agreement among politicians on the need to maintain a powerful Austria as an essential counterbalance to

35 Berney, *Friedrich*, pp. 177–8.
36 *Pol. Corr.*, ii, 278.

France; and the religious argument to some extent cut both ways. Catholic France, after all, could be seen as the greatest of all enemies of Protestantism. If Austria were the essential check to its power, then anything which weakened Maria Theresa must necessarily strengthen, at least indirectly, the anti-Protestant forces in Europe.[37] Walpole was deeply hostile to any British involvement in opposition to Prussia; from the beginning, his policy was to urge Maria Theresa to come to terms with her opponent. But domestic opposition to him was growing in 1741 and his ability to control British policy had been declining for some time, as the outbreak of war with Spain in 1739 had already shown. The convention of September 1741 which provided for the neutrality of Hanover[38] could easily be seen as a cowardly desertion of Maria Theresa. It aroused much opposition, even from members of the government who had hitherto been among Walpole's most loyal supporters. 'Have we, or do we, in the present circumstances, even treat the Queen of Hungary as a friend or an ally?' asked the duke of Newcastle rhetorically of the Lord Chancellor just before the convention was signed; and he went on to confess that 'I must admit freely to you, it goes to my heart, to think that France should have been able to overrun all Europe, to influence in such a degree all the measures taken by this Country, and that we should sit quiet and suffer them to do it, during the time of my being with my friends in the Administration.'[39]

The fall of Walpole in February 1742, to which this unpopular agreement contributed, opened the way for Britain to pursue more active policies. Carteret, as Secretary of State for the Northern Department, was for the next two and a half years to be the most prominent figure in their making. Unlike most of his fellow-ministers he was seriously interested in the affairs of continental Europe and well informed about them. This, and his ability to speak German, gave him the trust and support of George II. Moreover, he was self-confident to the point of arrogance, sure of his ability to play a leading role in these affairs and anxious to do so. He spoke of himself, with typical lack of false modesty, as 'knocking the heads of the kings of Europe together and jumbling

37 M. Schlenke, *England und das friderizianische Preussen, 1740–1763* (Munich, 1963), pp. 143, 120, 144.

38 See above, pp. 84–5.

39 P. C. Yorke, *The Life and Correspondence of Philip Yorke, Earl of Hardwicke, Lord Chancellor of Great Britain* (Cambridge, 1913), i, 269, 271.

something out of it that may be of service to this country'. Observers in London saw quickly that a new spirit was now at work in foreign policy. One of them told Robinson in Vienna in June 1742 that 'all has taken an amazing turn and the spirit of disquiet seems greatly to subside; Lord C. gains great esteem and ground by his unshaken resolution and *fermeté* and will carry matters, I doubt not, in such a channel that the people will be, as they daily are, more and more pleased'.[40] But Carteret was no more interested than Walpole in making any sacrifice to restore Silesia to Maria Theresa. To him as to every British statesman of the age France was the real enemy and the only real threat. His objective was the construction of a great anti-French alliance, of which he hoped both Frederick II and Maria Theresa would be members. 'His plan', wrote approvingly the Austrian minister in London in July, 'is no less than to drive the House of Bourbon from Italy, to return Lorraine to the House of Lorraine and to round off somewhat the territories of Her Majesty the Queen in Germany, to compensate her in this way for the sacrifice she has just made to the King of Prussia. I have every day new reason to admire the extent of his views, the solidity of his thinking and plans and his infinite application to the means of putting them into practice.'[41]

Such a policy meant during Carteret's first months in office continuing pressure on Maria Theresa to reconcile herself to the loss of Silesia. In return for this she was offered not merely money but the active assistance of British troops. In late April 1742 Parliament voted her a subsidy of £500,000; though the good effect of this in Vienna was largely nullified when a few weeks later Carteret made it clear that £200,000 of this would be diverted to Charles Emmanuel of Sardinia to support his struggle against the Bourbons in Italy. Since to Maria Theresa he seemed a rival in the peninsula almost if not quite as serious as Spain, this support for him was most unwelcome. More important was the decision to send British troops to fight on the continent. It had already been agreed in May 1741 to form an expeditionary force of 12,000 men under General Wade for use in the Netherlands or Hanover. Nothing came of this for a year: with the tide of military success running so strongly for France and Bavaria, and with no help to be looked for from Austria

---

40 Basil Williams, *Carteret and Newcastle, a Contrast in Contemporaries* (Cambridge, 1943), pp. 131, 135.

41 F. Wagner, *Kaiser Karl VII und die Grossen Mächte* (Stuttgart, 1938), p. 332 fn.

or Hanover, there seemed little that a small army of this kind could hope to achieve. The result was that throughout 1741 Britain's limited military strength continued to be squandered in ineffective efforts in the West Indies, the one area in which it seemed that it might make gains which could be used as bargaining-counters in any future peace-making. By the spring of 1742, however, the situation had changed significantly; and the new and much more interventionist regime in London now decided to send 16,000 men to the Netherlands. There they would join Austrian forces and hired Hanoverian and Hessian ones in Flanders to form a formidable composite army which could act directly against France.

In fact it achieved nothing of significance for the rest of the year. Divided counsels among its leaders meant delay and inaction. The British commanders, Lord Stair and General Ligonier, supported by the Austrian one, the duke d'Aremberg, favoured a bold stroke against either Rouen or Paris itself: Stair reacted angrily when the ministers in London turned this down as 'impractical and chimerical'. George II and Carteret, on the other hand, wanted this 'Pragmatic Army' to act in Germany and give more direct help to Maria Theresa. Disunity in its high command was to weaken the allied military effort in the Netherlands to the end of the war. An at least equally serious weakness was the unwillingness, indeed inability, of the Dutch Republic to give the anti-French allies in the southern Netherlands the help they had expected from it. It had indeed guaranteed the Pragmatic Sanction, and might conceivably have acted to make good its guarantee but for the discouraging effect of the convention of September 1741 for the neutralisation of Hanover, a disappointment which had a considerable impact on the Dutch government. But its army was no longer the force which had performed so well in the Spanish Succession struggle; most aspects of its economic life were in decline; and its policies were decided by the urban oligarchies of the province of Holland, which were deeply opposed to any involvement in the war or any large-scale military effort. Though the republic was soon to become a belligerent, it became and remained so merely as an auxiliary of Maria Theresa. Carteret himself went to Holland at the end of September 1742 in an effort to stir the Dutch government to greater activity, but with no success. This was the first of a series of British efforts of this kind during the years which followed. The ministers in The Hague remained understandably reluctant to declare war on France, and British and Austrian complaints of their weakness and lethargy steadily mounted. 'As for Holland', the marquis de Stainville, the representative in Paris of the grand duchy of Tuscany had written in November 1741, 'I regard her as a dead power who will be the victim of her drowsiness.'[42] Events were to show that this scathing judgement contained a formidable element of truth.

42 Butler, *Choiseul*, p. 339.

6 FROM BRESLAU TO DRESDEN; THE END OF THE WAR IN GERMANY, 1742-5

FRENCH DISAPPOINTMENTS AND FRUSTRATED AUSTRIAN HOPES

By the summer of 1742 the position of the French army in Bohemia was clearly very exposed and dangerous. When at the beginning of July Belleisle had an interview with the Austrian commander, Marshal Königsegg, he did so from a position of increasing weakness. Of the 40,000 men he had led across the Rhine a year earlier only 20,000 infantry and 4–5,000 cavalry remained; and the desertion of his French ally by Frederick II meant that this much reduced force was now in real danger of being forced to surrender and be made prisoner. It was also obvious that the Austrians were determined to press home the advantage they had now gained. Belleisle had hoped for an agreement by which, in return for a French evacuation of Bohemia, Maria Theresa's forces would leave Bavarian territory; but it became clear at once that there was no hope of this. In a second interview at the end of August Königsegg demanded that, in return for being allowed to leave Prague, the French army there should agree to evacuate the whole of Germany and not to serve again in the war for an agreed period of time; these conditions Belleisle indignantly rejected.[1] Maria Theresa was now bitterly hostile to the French: Robinson was struck by her 'inveterate hatred' of them. She dreamed of recovering Alsace and Lorraine for the Holy Roman Empire, or even Burgundy (which had been a part of the Empire in the Middle Ages) and was determined that the garrison of Prague should leave the city only as prisoners of war. Moreover, rivalry and bad feeling between Belleisle and Broglie was now more acute than ever; and each was supported by his own faction among the French officers in the Bohemian capital. At the

1 Duc de Broglie, *Frédéric II et Louis XV, 1742–1744* (2 vols, Paris, 1885), i, 3, 5–6, 15, 67–70.

end of July it was decided in Paris, after much argument among ministers which was ended only by the personal intervention of Louis XV, to send the army under Marshal Maillebois, which had for the last year been stationed in Westphalia to threaten Hanover and thus put pressure on George II, to the rescue of the endangered garrison. This was unsuccessful. Maillebois moved slowly; he had been ordered to be cautious since his army might have to be recalled at short notice if France were suddenly attacked by British and Austrian forces from the Netherlands. His advance allowed Charles VII temporarily to recover most of his electorate. But though he forced the Austrians in mid-September to raise the very loose siege of Prague they had been carrying on, he failed in the following month to link up with the garrison: difficult country, shortage of supplies and the hostility of the local population forced him to retreat into Bavaria.

The position of the French in the Bohemian capital was now acutely difficult. However, during the night of 16 December Belleisle, now in sole command there, left the city with all the men fit to face the rigours in store for them, about 14,000 in all. Nine days later, after a very difficult march in severe winter weather, he arrived at Eger (the present-day Cheb) about 100 miles west of Prague, where his army was at last in safety. This dramatic winter retreat was the most striking military episode of the entire Austrian Succession war and arguably its greatest military achievement.[2] But it was a very expensive one. The force left in Prague, made up mainly of sick and wounded men, was able to make good terms with the Austrian besiegers and return home: Chevert, the general left in command there, showed great ability in a hopeless situation and obtained an honourable capitulation by theatening to burn the city. None the less, of the French army which had entered Bohemia in the autumn of 1741 probably little more than a quarter left it. Such a setback was bound to provoke in France questions about the justification of the war and the wisdom of continuing the struggle.

When in January 1743 Fleury, whose end had been expected for months, died at last, Louis XV announced that he would have no more chief ministers. Henceforth he would rule in person and decide and control policy: French diplomats abroad were ordered to

2 There are detailed accounts of Belleisle's retreat in R. Butler, *Choiseul*, i, *Father and Son, 1719–1754* (Oxford, 1980), pp. 359–69; Comte P. V. C. de Pajol, *Les Guerres sous Louis XV*, ii (Paris, 1882), 244–51; and R. Browning, *The War of the Austrian Succession* (New York, 1993), pp. 123–7.

correspond directly with the king as had been done under Louis XIV. This soon proved to be an empty gesture. Louis was probably a more intelligent man than his great-grandfather; but he completely lacked the qualities needed for effective personal rule. Irresolute, pessimistic and lazy, he soon allowed effective authority to fall into the hands of a small number of ministers, each with his own views and policies, so that, as Frederick II later contemptuously remarked, 'France was governed by four subsidiary kings, independent of one another'.[3] This meant that French policy became, if anything, less consistent than it had been under Fleury. There was strong feeling in Paris that the country should now cut its losses in Germany and adopt a much less ambitious and essentially defensive political and military strategy; and this is easy to understand in view of the sacrifices the war was now demanding. Critics calculated that in 1742 the French army had lost 60,000 men in Germany without fighting a single significant battle.[4] Yet the scale of France's military effort was growing. In 1743 the total strength of its army rose to 330,000 men; and in January of that year it was decided to raise additional militia levies from which new regiments for the regular army could be formed. Paris, which had hitherto been exempt from the very unpopular militia system, was now for the first time to make a contribution; while even the sons of respectable artisans and small merchants were to be called on to serve – something, it was indignantly claimed, which had not been seen even under Louis XIV. In fact only 2,200 men were raised in this way in the capital; and in the following year the government replaced this dangerously unpopular expedient by a money payment made by the Parisian *corps de métiers*. But the demands of the war were clearly being felt: the drawing of lots for militia service in 1743 produced riots in at least two substantial provincial towns, Tours and Sens.[5] Total government expenditure had reached about 330 million livres in 1742: from 1744 it was running an annual rate of 350 million,[6] while it was estimated in 1743 that the fighting in Germany and Bohemia had so far cost France 300 million. But so great an expenditure of men and money had produced little or no result

3 *Histoire de mon temps*, ii, 3.

4 Barbier, *Chronique de la Régence et du Règne de Louis XV (1718–1763), ou Journal de Barbier* (4 vols, Paris, 1885), iii, 434.

5 Barbier, *Chronique*, iii, 400; J. Delmas, ed., *Histoire militaire de la France*, ii, *De 1715 à 1871* (Paris, 1992), p. 19.

6 P. G. M. Dickson, *Finance and Government under Maria Theresia* (Oxford, 1987), ii, 167.

apart from the election of an emperor who, for most of his reign, had been a poverty-stricken fugitive from his own hereditary lands. The feeling of disillusionment in French ruling circles was marked and was well expressed in a letter from Jean-Jacques Amelot, the Foreign Minister, to Belleisle in January 1743.

You know better than anyone [he wrote] that in the first place the war was undertaken in the belief that it would not last long, and that in the second place the alliance with the king of Prussia was an essential part of the scheme. Events have turned out quite differently; the king of Prussia, whom we trusted too much, has let us down at the most critical moment; the war has been prolonged without our being able to see a way out of it; the king is bearing alone all the weight of it; we are today much less further on than at the beginning, and we shall be very lucky if the allies on whom we have counted do not declare themselves against us.[7]

This foreboding was quite justified, for by the end of 1742 Charles VII was putting out feelers in both Vienna and London in search of an acceptable peace. He was now on bad terms with his French backers and ready in his turn to feel that he had been left in the lurch by them. Early in June 1743 he wrote to his minister in Paris from the imperial free city of Augsburg, to which he had been forced to flee, 'So I am now compelled to seek refuge here and my hereditary lands are completely surrendered to my enemies. . . . This is the bitter fruit of French help.'[8] His demands, considering his position as a *Vagabundkaiser* (his own term) were still pitched remarkably high: recognition of his imperial title, which Maria Theresa continued to refuse; the return of his Bavarian territories, with gains in the Tyrol or Bohemia, or on the upper Rhine; and a hereditary royal title for future rulers of Bavaria. There was no question of the queen of Hungary accepting such conditions. At most she was prepared to allow Charles to remain emperor for his lifetime, on condition that her husband should succeed him; but she was now determined to hold on to her Bavarian conquests if possible as compensation for what she had lost in Silesia. As soon as the terms agreed at Breslau had made it clear that, for the time being at least, the loss of Silesia could not be undone, she had begun to think in terms of securing an 'equivalent'; and Bavaria was by far

7 Broglie, *Frédéric II et Louis XV*, i, 390.

8 P. C. Hartmann, *Karl Albrecht – Karl VII: glücklicher Kurfürst, unglücklicher Kaiser* (Regensburg, 1985), p. 281.

the most attractive one available. If Alsace could be recovered from the French, or Naples and Sicily from Charles III, one of these might be used to compensate Charles VII for his lost electorate. But Bavaria she very much wished to have. Without it, she felt, the house of Habsburg would be under permanent threat; and from the late summer of 1743 she began to demand that the Bavarian nobility do homage to her, and to set up her own administrative system in the electorate under a kind of Austrian viceroy, count von Goess. If Charles wanted to recover Bavaria he must at least join her in reconquering from France the lost German territories of Alsace and Lorraine.[9] Clearly the emperor was quite prepared to desert his ally if it served his interests to do so; while the French government felt that, for the time being at least, it could do little more for him. Belleisle, whose influence was now rapidly declining, was ordered to tell him as much before returning to Paris, and did so in an acrimonious interview in January 1743. When in March the Marshal de Noailles, old and strongly conservative, became a member of the royal council, this marked the final abandonment of the hopes of a quick and easy victory which had run so strongly in 1741 and which Belleisle personified.

If there was disillusionment in Paris, however, there was corresponding optimism in Vienna. Maria Theresa was disappointed by the escape of most of the French garrison from Prague; and her financial position was as difficult as ever. But she had now better prospects than ever before of effective military help from Britain, while she was strengthened by the anti-French feeling which was running strongly in much of Germany. In April 1743 she won an important political success when count von Ostein, her former minister in London, became the new elector of Mainz. This meant that the electorate, and its vote in any future imperial election, was now under Austrian and not French influence.

The campaigning of 1743 was, however, in general disappointing to the anti-French allies. In the early summer Maria Theresa's forces reconquered most of Bavaria, where Munich surrendered to them once more on 9 June. Elsewhere less was achieved. The Austrian government, supported by George II, wanted to use in Germany most of the British regiments which had been

9 E. Wagner, *Kaiser Karl VII and die grossen Mächte* (Stuttgart, 1938), pp. 329–42; Broglie, *Frédéric II et Louis XV*, i, 244–50; E. Guglia, *Maria Theresia: Ihre leben und ihre Regierung* (2 vols, Munich–Berlin, 1917), i, 190; Hartmann, *Karl Albrecht – Karl VII*, p. 284.

sent to the southern Netherlands in the previous year, largely in the hope that this would help to strengthen anti-French feeling among the smaller German states. By May the British had reached the river Main, and together with substantial Hanoverian and Austrian contingents made up a powerful force. In June this 'Pragmatic Army', with George II in at least formal command (the last appearance of any British monarch on a battlefield), won a rather fortuitous victory over the French, commanded by the Marshal de Noailles, at Dettingen. Both the Austrian and the French immediate reactions to this battle were disproportionate to its real significance. In Vienna the news was greeted with 'a genuine storm of rejoicing'. Maria Theresa, who was in Linz when she heard of the victory, made a triumphal entry into her capital: at the Hofburg she was greeted by her son, the two-year-old Archduke Joseph, who waved a little flag from a window. In Paris the defeat deepened the atmosphere of despondency, particularly as it had been preceded by the retreat of Broglie, with the second French army in Germany, from the parts of Bavaria which were still under French control.[10] Noailles gloomily told Louis XV that that the allied infantry were 'so superior to ours that they cannot be compared', and a week or two later urged him to make peace as soon as possible on the best terms that could be obtained.[11]

But both the rejoicing and the despondency were excessive. The battle had been fought when the Pragmatic Army, seriously short of supplies, was in retreat; and it had been won only because of serious errors by Noailles's second-in-command, the duc de Grammont. The allied wounded had to be abandoned on the battlefield to the mercies of the French. More important, no effort was made to follow up the victory. Though the Pragmatic Army was joined by an Austrian one under Prince Charles of Lorraine which had just driven Broglie from Bavaria, the allies did nothing to exploit their success. Their leaders were deeply divided on strategy: there were disagreements between George II [who had prevented any pursuit of the French after the battle] and the Austrian generals, Neipperg and d'Aremberg, who were themselves divided. According to one British soldier, 'whatever Lord Stair [the British commander] proposed was strenuously opposed by the Duke of Aremberg and the Marshal

---

10 A. von Arneth, *Geschichte Maria Theresias* (10 vols, Vienna, 1863–79), ii, 262; Wagner, *Kaiser Karl VII*, p. 447.

11 *Correspondance de Louis XV et du Maréchal de Noailles*, ed. C. Rousset (Paris, 1865), i, 123, 167.

[Neipperg]'. To Prince Charles, when he arrived on the scene, the allied headquarters seemed 'a republic, for everybody talks and appears to have a different opinion'.[12] From the British standpoint, an invasion of eastern France, which for a moment seemed quite possible, might be dangerous. It could produce a French declaration of war against Britain (the French, it will be remembered, were still formally fighting only as the auxiliaries of Charles VII, the British as those of Maria Theresa); and this it was very desirable to avoid until Britain had some guarantee of active Dutch support in such a war, of which there was as yet no sign. The result was that nothing effective was done. In October the Pragmatic Army returned to winter quarters in the Netherlands and that under Prince Charles to the small detached Habsburg territories in south-west Germany. France had escaped virtually unscathed from a potentially dangerous situation; and Noailles was quite justified in telling Louis XV in October that 'we are heavily indebted to the irresolutions of George the Second'.[13] In the Netherlands also the year 1743 saw the same allied disunity and ineffectiveness. Any chance of taking one of the French fortified frontier cities – Lille, Condé, Maubeuge or Valenciennes – was lost because of the lack of a siege train and Dutch insistence that the British pay the cost of any siege, while the Austrians refused to pay for the horses needed to bring up the heavy siege-guns from Antwerp.[14] Any effective action was made impossible by the squabbling which was to mark the allied effort in the Netherlands to the end of the war.

THE WAR IN ITALY AND THE HANAU NEGOTIATIONS

In Italy also the fighting of 1743 was indecisive. At the end of the previous year the Spaniards had occupied Savoy after a campaign in which the army of Charles Emmanuel suffered serious losses. The count de Gages, who had now succeeded the duke de Montemar as Spanish commander in the peninsula, was spurred on to greater activity by Elizabeth Farnese but found his way barred by Marshal Traun, the best Austrian commander of the entire war. At Camposanto, on the river Panaro in the papal state early in

---

12 Arneth, *Geschichte*, ii, 518, fn. 15.
13 *Correspondance de Louis XV et du Maréchal de Noailles*, ii, 39.
14 R. Whitworth, *Field-Marshal Lord Ligonier: A Story of the British Army, 1702–1770* (Oxford, 1958), pp. 86–7.

February, was fought an indecisive battle which was followed by a Spanish retreat. Traun, however, did not follow this up effectively; and the following months saw little activity of much importance. Both in Madrid and Vienna there was dissatisfaction with the lack of military success. Elizabeth Farnese pressed more than once for an attack on Piedmont through the Alps by a second Spanish army which was now based in south-eastern France; but by then it was too late in the year for this to have any prospect of success. Maria Theresa for her part still had hopes of conquering Naples. In July she ordered Traun to march south and attack Charles III there; but he argued that without reinforcements and more money this was impossible and asked to be relieved of his command. This was done in mid-September, when Field-Marshal Prince Christian Lobkowitz was appointed governor of Milan and Habsburg commander-in-chief in Italy, also with orders to move against Naples. This was not a change for the better. Traun had been cautious and slow-moving in the way which had now become traditional among Austrian generals: it was this which had irritated Maria Theresa. But he was a competent professional soldier who was soon to win the admiration of Frederick II himself.[15] Lobkowitz, whose very lax blockade of Prague in the later months of 1742 had made possible the escape of Belleisle and most of the French garrison, was to show himself much inferior to his predecessor. Early in October he began a march south to Bologna and Rimini (yet another violation of the neutrality of the defenceless papal state); but the year ended with little achieved by either side.

In 1743, as in 1742, the struggle in Italy was one of diplomats at least as much as of soldiers; and in this Britain, in the person of the autocratic and self-confident Carteret, was now to play a larger role than ever before. His first objective was the construction of a powerful alliance of German princes directed against France. If this could be achieved, it would mean that most of the energies of Britain's great enemy would be absorbed east of the Rhine and thus not available for attacks, much more dangerous from the British point of view, on the Netherlands or perhaps even on Britain itself. Events from 1744 onwards were to add much weight to this reasoning. It could even be argued that France would be more seriously damaged by setbacks in Germany than by direct attacks on its own territory. But for the building of such an alliance it was essential to persuade Charles VII, now in a very weak position and

15 See below, p. 135.

on bad terms with his French backers, to change sides. The duke of Newcastle put this attitude well at the end of May. 'I dread France and Spain singly on our hands,' he wrote to Carteret. 'The Emperor is the weak point of their question; he is more than half conquered already; there we must press France, and there we shall get the better of them.'[16] The result was a complex and fruitless negotiation in the German city of Hanau during the summer of 1743 between Carteret and the representatives of Charles VII, with Prince William of Hesse acting as a partly self-appointed intermediary.[17] The central difficulty was the continued insistence of Maria Theresa on retaining all or most of Bavaria as compensation for what she had lost in Silesia, and the refusal of Carteret to accept this. In Vienna there was still a willingness to compensate Charles VII in Naples if it could be taken from the Bourbons, or in Alsace if it could be reconquered from France, or perhaps even in the Austrian Netherlands. But Bavaria was by far the most desirable quid pro quo for Silesia. Ruled from Vienna it would consolidate the position of the Habsburgs as unmistakably the greatest of the German dynasties and strengthen them as no territorial gain detached from the main body of their central European lands ever could.

But Carteret was quite unwilling to contemplate anything of this kind. For the Holy Roman Emperor, even one for the time being forcibly driven into exile, to be permanently denied any significant territorial foothold at all in the German world would be fatally damaging to his prestige and to that of his office. It would offend German national feeling which, though still largely embryonic, was none the less already a factor of political importance. The addition of Bavaria to the existing Habsburg lands would tilt the religious balance in Germany markedly towards the Catholic side, a consideration which still carried real weight, not least with British public opinion. Most important of all, such a strengthening of Maria Theresa's position was certain to be bitterly opposed by Frederick II, who regarded Charles VII as an emperor of his own creation; and without at least his neutrality there was no hope of building up an effective anti-French alliance among the German states. He had already shown that he would not oppose a peace

---

16 Sir R. Lodge, *Studies in Eighteenth-century Diplomacy, 1740–8* (London, 1930), p. 22.

17 The most detailed discussions are those in Wagner, *Kaiser Karl VII*, pp. 429–46, and Lodge, *Studies*, chap. I. There is a briefer one, written from the British standpoint, in J. B. Owen, *The Rise of the Pelhams* (London, 1957), pp. 162–5.

between the emperor and the queen of Hungary; but this must not be based on a crushing victory for Maria Theresa. A way out might be found by allowing Charles VII to strengthen himself by secularising a number of bishoprics, independent abbeys and imperial cities; and in January 1743 Frederick almost casually invited the emperor to indicate which of these it would suit him to take – a good indication of his attitude to any legal right not backed by military power. Perhaps Maria Theresa might cede to Charles the small detached Habsburg territories in Swabia and take in exchange only the secularised bishopric of Passau. But the king of Prussia became immediately suspicious when faced by any suggestion that she might be given really substantial compensation for what she had ceded in the Breslau settlement. In mid-July, therefore, when it seemed that Carteret's negotiations might be close to bearing fruit, Frederick despatched one of his most trusted diplomats, Count von Finckenstein, to Hanau with instructions to force his way into the proceedings at all costs so that he could safeguard the interests of his master.[18]

The fundamental difference of attitude between the British and Austrian governments meant that the so-called treaty of Hanau (really no more than two documents drawn up by Carteret and dated 15 July) never came into effect or, in all probability, ever had any chance of doing so. In these documents Charles VII agreed to cut his links with France and dismiss his French auxiliary forces. He would give up his claims to Maria Theresa's territories and use his influence as emperor to persuade the German states to cooperate with Britain and the Dutch in forcing France to agree to an acceptable peace settlement. In return he would recover his lost hereditary dominions with some gains which would increase his revenues; and the rulers of Bavaria would acquire a royal title. Finally, when these terms had been carried out, he would receive a British subsidy. Nothing came of all this. Carteret's fellow-ministers in London increasingly resented his high-handed attitude, his 'reserved and contemptuous' treatment of them, his failure to keep them informed of what he was doing, and his influence over George II and wish to gain 'the power and reputation of a Prime Minister and Favourite'.[19] This helped to ensure their rejection of the Hanau

18 *Politische Correspondenz Friedrichs des Grossen*, ed. J. G. Droysen *et al.* (46 vols, Berlin, 1879–1939), ii, 313, 329, 339–42; Lodge, *Studies*, pp. 19–20.

19 P. C. Yorke, *Life and Correspondence of Philip Yorke, Earl of Hardwicke, Lord Chancellor of Great Britain* (Cambridge, 1913), i, 320–1.

terms; and this in turn ended any prospect of the British subsidy for Charles VII which was an essential element in them. In Vienna too they would in all probability have been rejected. But they were never presented at all to Maria Theresa and her ministers in their final form: they flew too openly in the face of their desire to retain Bavaria. However, while he was negotiating in Hanau, through Prince William of Hesse, with Charles VII, Carteret was simultaneously trying to construct an alliance between Maria Theresa and Charles Emmanuel of Sardinia; and to this he attached far greater importance than to a settlement with the emperor.

THE TREATY OF WORMS AND ITS RESULTS

Charles Emmanuel was indeed a more valuable ally than the poverty-stricken and rather pathetic Charles VII. (When Noailles met the emperor in Frankfurt some days after the battle of Dettingen he had to make him a personal loan of 40,000 crowns, so desperate was his financial position.)[20] Yet no agreement between the king of Sardinia and Maria Theresa of the kind Carteret was determined to achieve could be reached without substantial concessions on her part in Italy. To combine a demand for these with an almost simultaneous one for what could be regarded as a surrender to Charles VII in Germany was impossible. The negotiation with the emperor at Hanau therefore was not followed up, in order to make possible a more successful, though still difficult, one with Charles Emmanuel. The king of Sardinia held strong cards, for he was now being courted by both sides; and he showed both ability and lack of scruple in playing each off against the other. There was, in fact, a marked symmetry about the position in this respect. On the one hand, the French government, well aware of the strategic and military advantages of an alliance with Charles Emmanuel, was pressing the very reluctant Philip V and Elizabeth Farnese to swallow the need to make substantial concessions to him. On the other, Great Britain was urging an equally reluctant Maria Theresa to even greater sacrifices for the same purpose. By August 1743 Charles Emmanuel had accepted in principle a treaty which the marquis de Saint-Necterre, the French minister in Turin, had been authorised to sign. This would have given him the whole of the duchy of Milan and some other territories on the left bank of the river Po, with the title of king of Lombardy. Don Philip for his part

20 *Correspondance de Louis XV et du Maréchal de Noailles*, i, 141.

was to have most of the duchy of Mantua, parts of those of Parma and Piacenza, and the island of Sardinia, also with a royal title.[21] Philip and Elizabeth did not like this arrangement, which they thought, with typical lack of moderation and common sense, did not go far enough in meeting the claims of their son: they also objected particularly to the fact that Charles Emmanuel was to have overall command of the allied armies in Italy against the Austrians. Nevertheless they accepted it. Simultaneously, however, Charles Emmanuel was negotiating actively at Worms, through Carteret, with the Austrians; and he was no more willing to see Austrian power in Italy destroyed than he was to see that of the Bourbons disappear. The discussions at Worms were difficult, indeed bitter. Maria Theresa and her ministers deeply resented the concessions which the king, backed by Carteret, demanded from them; and only a Sardinian ultimatum brought matters to a head. On 2 September the marquis d'Ormea, the Foreign Minister of Charles Emmanuel, told Villettes, the British minister in Turin, that unless Maria Theresa accepted his master's terms within the time needed for a messenger to go to Worms and return the king would be forced to accept a French alliance. Eleven days later Carteret, Ignaz Johann von Wasner representing Maria Theresa and the cavaliere Giuseppe Osorio-Alarcon on behalf of Charles Emmanuel, signed the Treaty of Worms.[22]

By this Charles Emmanuel and Maria Theresa guaranteed to each other the territories they currently possessed, or ought to possess in virtue of a number of earlier treaties which were specifically enumerated. Charles Emmanuel abandoned his claims to the duchy of Milan and guaranteed the succession to the Habsburg lands laid down by the Pragmatic Sanction. In return, Maria Theresa ceded to him a number of Italian territories – Vigevano, part of the Pavese, Piacenza and parts of the Piacentino, Anghiera and her rights over the marquisate of Finale. She agreed to maintain in Italy an army of 30,000 men; Charles Emmanuel was to supply one of 40,000 infantry and 5,000 cavalry. Britain, for its part, undertook to maintain a fleet in the Mediterranean and to pay Charles Emmanuel an annual subsidy of £200,000. There were three secret articles, of which the second was the most significant. By this

21 A. Baudrillart, *Philippe V et la Cour de France* (5 vols, Paris, 1890–1902), v, 155–6, 158–9.

22 The Worms negotiations are discussed in Wagner, *Kaiser Karl VII*, pp. 446–64; Lodge, *Studies*, chap. II; and Browning, *War of the Austrian Succession*, pp. 142–8.

it was agreed that if the Bourbons were defeated in northern Italy the allies would attempt to drive Charles III from Naples and Sicily: if they were successful in this Maria Theresa was to have Naples and Charles Emmanuel Sicily. These terms represented a clear victory for the king of Sardinia over the queen of Hungary. It was one made possible only by continuous British pressure on the Austrian government and its representative at Worms. Almost to the end Maria Theresa struggled to hold Bavaria. On 27 August Wasner was given new instructions which demanded that in return for what was being asked of her in Italy – notably, the abandonment of Piacenza, which was a particularly bitter pill to swallow – she must be given a written British guarantee of compensation for what she had lost or was about to lose. If Bavaria were annexed to the Habsburg monarchy Charles VII could be compensated in Tuscany or perhaps the Austrian Netherlands. At the same time Robinson reported from Vienna that count Corfiz Ulfeld, the holder since the previous year of the new office of Hof-und-Staatskanzler, had told him that if the British persisted in their demands, 'we shall not be able to work together for long'. But all Carteret was willing to agree to was a promise by George II to obtain for Maria Theresa 'without however entering into any specific engagement, the best compensation possible given the circumstances and the success of the war'. Wasner at first refused to accept this very half-hearted concession and asked for time to obtain new instructions; but he then gave way in face of the Sardinian threat to accept the competing French proposals. He justified in Vienna his signature of the treaty by saying, with much justice, that a knife had been put to his throat.[23] The Worms agreement, inevitably, was badly received in the Austrian capital. Apart from the territorial concessions which had been extracted from her, Maria Theresa objected strongly to the British subsidy promised to Charles Emmanuel. This was to be deducted from the £500,000 a year already voted her by Parliament; moreover, its payment was guaranteed for the duration of the war or as long as the need for it lasted, while the remaining £300,000 which she would receive was not protected in this way. (Carteret had agreed by a supplementary convention attached to the treaty that her subsidy also should continue 'as long as the war and the need shall last'; and this convention also incorporated the vague promise of

23 A. F. P. Pribham, ed., *Österreichische Staatsverträge: England*, i (Innsbruck, 1907), 606–11.

compensation which he had already suggested. His cabinet colleagues, however, refused to accept these additional undertakings.)

British support therefore had allowed Charles Emmanuel to emerge from these negotiations with a very favourable settlement, one which seemed to some contemporaries to pave the way to even greater success in the future. Cardinal Tencin, a member of Louis XV's council, prophesied soon after the treaty had been signed that 'one day the King of Sardinia would be master of all Italy'.[24] The provision regarding Finale was a particularly telling illustration of British partiality for Charles Emmanuel. This little coastal territory had been sold by the Emperor Charles VI to the Genoese Republic in 1713. The right of redemption of the marquisate which Maria Theresa ceded at Worms was worthless, in fact non-existent, as she explicitly admitted. As early as February she had told Wasner that any promise of Finale to the king of Sardinia would be 'a wrongful forcible act'.[25] Yet the treaty clearly envisaged its acquisition by him. He understandably wanted a better outlet to the sea for his territories; and from the British standpoint this was an ambition to be supported. If in addition to Finale he gained Sicily his kingdom might well become a respectable Mediterranean naval power, and one of considerable potential use to Britain as an ally against France. Here as elsewhere British and Sardinian interests seemed compatible in a way in which British and Austrian ones were not.

The Treaty of Worms was in many ways an example of eighteenth-century international relations at their least inspiring. It was none the less important, perhaps the most important of all the shifting and unstable agreements of this exceptionally complex period. It is quite conceivable, as several historians have pointed out, that the war could have ended in 1743. By then two fundamental decisions had been taken and were not to be overturned by the events of the following years. Most of Silesia was now Prussian and was to remain so. The rest of the Habsburg territories in central Europe had successfully resisted conquest and partition and would continue to do so. Moreover, Franco-Habsburg antagonism, for more than two centuries the central pivot of international relations in Europe, was now showing some signs of weakening. In France, disillusionment and pessimism meant that escape on acceptable terms from a war which had been expensive

24 Butler, *Choiseul*, p. 446.
25 Guglia, *Maria Theresia*, i, 196.

and unsuccessful and from which it had now little to gain seemed the only reasonable objective. From early in 1743 there were tentative and exploratory contacts in Berne between French and Austrian agents, while in Vienna even Bartenstein was willing to envisage better relations with the traditional enemy. So indeed was Maria Theresa herself, though she was reluctant to weaken what, in spite of many disappointments, she still saw as the fundamental Austrian alliance with the maritime powers. In July and August Cardinal Tencin sounded the Tuscan envoy in Paris, the marquis de Stainville, about possible peace, perhaps even alliance, with Austria.[26] Louis XV himself had no doubt that France should now make peace as soon as possible. The country was still supporting Charles VII, not because it hoped for any real advantage in Germany but merely because if it abandoned him this might produce a stampede of the smaller German rulers to the anti-French side. This would allow Britain to recruit from their territories all the soldiers she needed. It would also send a very discouraging signal to Spain, which might in its turn abandon its French ally.[27] It was not unreasonable in the summer of 1743, therefore, to hope for an early end to fighting in Europe.

The Treaty of Worms radically changed this situation. It produced in Paris a strong feeling that Charles Emmanuel had betrayed France after he had seemed on the point of allying himself with it. Louis XV, when he learned of the signature of the treaty, told his nephew in Madrid, 'I have resolved to unite my forces with those of Your Majesty to take vengeance for such black perfidy.'[28] On 25 October, therefore, the Treaty of Fontainebleau, the second Family Compact, was signed by the two Bourbon powers. This was a very unequal agreement. Louis XV undertook to declare war on Charles Emmanuel before the next campaign began; as his share of what came to be known as the 'Gallispan' effort in Italy he agreed to provide thirty battalions of regular troops and five of militia, thirty squadrons of cavalry and an appropriate amount of artillery, all of these to be under the command of Don Philip. He was also to enter the war against Britain and Austria as a principal, obtain Milan, Parma and Piacenza for Don Philip, and help recover Minorca and Gibraltar for Spain. He guaranteed Charles III's possession of Naples and Sicily but agreed that he should remain

---

26 Guglia, *Maria Theresia*, i, 197–8; Butler, *Choiseul*, pp. 450–1. 454–5.
27 *Correspondance de Louis XV et du Maréchal de Noailles*, i, 149–50, 167, 192.
28 Baudrillart, *Philippe V*, v, 161.

neutral in the struggle. In return for these far-reaching concessions, France was merely to recover from Charles Emmanuel the relatively minor fortresses of Exilles and Fenestrelle, lost in the Utrecht settlement of 1713. There have been few more one-sided treaties than this in the history of European international relations. It was the outcome of pique and hasty misjudgement in Paris, and it is not surprising that Louis and his ministers soon ceased to regard it as binding on them.

FREDERICK II RE-ENTERS THE STRUGGLE BUT WITH LITTLE SUCCESS

The most important result of the Worms agreement, however, was its effect on the king of Prussia. The end of active military conflict had done nothing to assuage the bad feeling between Prussia and Austria. In Vienna resentment of the loss of Silesia was as strong as ever. The idea that Charles VII should be strengthened by being allowed to annex a number of secularised bishoprics and abbeys, which was supported by Frederick II, had been opposed by Maria Theresa, partly because she naturally disliked any strengthening of the emperor's position and partly because of her sincere Catholic faith. She had also angered Frederick by insisting that the election of Charles as emperor had been illegal, since she as legitimate ruler of Bohemia had not been able to vote in it, and that all imperial acts since it took place were therefore invalid.[29] The king of Prussia for his part had opposed both the entry of the Pragmatic Army into Germany and any suggestion that Charles VII should lose Bavaria and be compensated with either Naples or Tuscany. He had also done his best to block suggestions that Francis Stephen should be elected as King of the Romans, in other words as the recognised successor of Charles VII. Throughout 1743 and the first half of 1744 he remained watchful and became increasingly uneasy.

The most obvious response to a potentially dangerous situation was to strengthen his army; and in 1743–4 he added to it nine new field and seven garrison battalions, as well as twenty squadrons of light cavalry, so that by the summer of 1744 he had available for combat over 94,000 infantry and 29,000 cavalry – a sharp increase from the already disproportionately large force of 83,000 he had inherited. But more than purely military measures were called for.

29 Broglie, *Frédéric II et Louis XV*, i, 132–5.

He was, as always, very anxious to remain on good terms with Russia, repeatedly urging Mardefeld in St Petersburg to do everything he could, including the use of bribery, to check British and Austrian influence there and if possible bring about the fall of Bestuzhev.[30] He went so far as to hope for at least token Russian support in any renewed military action he might have to take against Maria Theresa: even a small force of Cossacks would have the psychological effect he wanted. But on the other hand the possibility that another palace coup might unseat the Empress Elizabeth was a continual source of worry to him.[31] He was uneasy about the attitude of Saxony: he knew that the Elector Augustus was a potentially serious rival and that his favourite and chief minister, count Brühl, was his confirmed opponent. The possibility of a Saxon alliance with either Austria or Russia alarmed him, while he was well aware of the continuing bitter dislike felt for him by George II.[32] Any idea that Maria Theresa should be compensated for the loss of Silesia, and any suggestion that a final peace might be made in Germany without his own participation, he found even more threatening: a settlement in which Prussia had no share might well involve some effort to make him disgorge the conquered province, or part of it.[33] By the end of September 1743 he was once more hoping for the creation of a large composite army which would drive foreign – in other words, British and Austrian – forces out of Germany. This would be made up of contingents supplied by most of the German states and backed by French subsidies. In it Prussian regiments would bulk large, and Frederick, as its commander, might receive for himself and his successors the title of lieutenant-general of the forces of the Holy Roman Empire. If all went well, he hoped, he might by July 1744 be at the head of a force of this kind big enough to compel Britain and Austria to make peace with France.[34]

The Treaty of Worms (whose terms became known when in February 1744 it was published in a number of Dutch newspapers) intensified this sense of insecurity and gave Frederick a partly plausible grievance. It guaranteed a number of past treaties, some of which, such as those signed in Vienna in 1731 and 1738, were

30 *Pol. Corr.*, ii, 369–70, 406–7, 411–12, 459; iii, 118.
31 *Pol. Corr.*, ii, 411–12, 427–8; iii, 8–10, 47.
32 *Pol. Corr.*, ii, 292, 393–4, 416–17, 468.
33 *Pol. Corr.*, ii, 339–42, 380–1, 424–5, 435.
34 *Pol. Corr.*, ii, 425, 431–2, 483–4.

difficult to reconcile with the terms of the Breslau settlement. In the Worms agreement Charles Emmanuel had guaranteed the Pragmatic Sanction; but this guarantee contained no reference to the cession of Silesia. More serious in Frederick's eyes was the fact that by another article the king of Sardinia agreed that if the French and Spaniards were driven out of Italy he would become responsible for the defence of Lombardy. This would allow Maria Theresa to move substantial forces from Italy to Germany and thus increase her chances of waging there a successful war of revenge against Prussia. Frederick later claimed and probably believed that the treaty contained 'the germ of an offensive alliance prepared against the King of Prussia'.[35] He failed to grasp how much Maria Theresa was now concerned, at least in the short term, to hold Bavaria rather than to recover Silesia.

The attitude of Saxony in particular worried him more and more. The agreement which the Elector Augustus had signed with Maria Theresa in December 1743 was purely defensive; but another in May of the following year looked to the defeat of Prussia and the recovery by the Habsburgs of Silesia. Disagreement over the territories which Augustus should receive for his help in achieving this meant that it had no immediate effect; but his hostility to Frederick was clear. Like George II in Hanover, he exemplified the envious dislike which any German ruler was all too ready to feel for an obviously successful neighbour; and an important element in Frederick's desire for good relations with Russia, with which Saxony had traditionally close relations, was a belief that it would be a restraining influence on the elector. By February 1744, however, the Prussian king was thinking not merely in defensive terms but in those of conquering Bohemia with the help of France and of a defensive, and if possible also offensive, treaty with Russia. He felt that he must act soon, for the longer he delayed the stronger Maria Theresa would become; and he consoled himself with the reflection that such a war would be an essentially preventive one. By the beginning of April he was hoping to be ready for a new struggle by the end of July.[36]

For a successful new trial of strength with Maria Theresa Frederick needed, most of all, effective French support. In Paris, however, there was understandable reluctance to be drawn again

---

35 *Histoire de mon temps*, ii, 32ff.
36 *Pol. Corr.*, iii, 82.

into large commitments in Germany. Amelot, the Foreign Minister, and even more Maurepas, the Minister of Marine, were hostile to any large-scale action east of the Rhine. But Cardinal Tencin, and still more the Marshal de Noailles, favoured a more active and interventionist policy; and this was strongly supported by the chevalier de Chavigny, the energetic new French representative at the imperial diet in Frankfurt.[37] These conflicts culminated in the dismissal of Amelot at the end of April and a declaration (which very quickly proved completely hollow) by Louis XV that henceforth he would act as his own foreign minister. The interventionist forces in Paris were now firmly in the saddle. On 22 May the Union of Frankfurt was created, ostensibly for the defence of the emperor and the Reich. This was hardly the wide-ranging combination of German states contributing to a joint army under his own command which Frederick had hoped for. It was simply an alliance of the emperor, the Elector Palatine (the most pro-French of all the significant German rulers), the landgrave of Hesse-Kassel and Frederick himself, based on the historical precedent of the French-inspired Rheinbund of 1658, which was later joined by France in a secret agreement. One German historian has dismissed it as 'a conspiracy of princes in the pay of foreigners';[38] and indeed the keeping secret of the French accession to it was a concession to German national feeling. Nevertheless, it was a further step towards the new struggle with Austria which Frederick had long been contemplating. In a separate article of the treaty which created the union he undertook to conquer Bohemia and reserved for himself the parts of it which bordered on Silesia. A few days before the union was formed, moreover, he had drawn up two memoranda in which he discussed in some detail the possible course of the campaign on which he was about to embark. The war of 1744 was therefore much more the product of deliberation and long-term planning than the original attack on Silesia in December 1740.

On 6 June the essential diplomatic step was taken, when Cardinal Tencin and count von Rothenburg (a Prussian major-general who had been sent to Paris earlier in the year, when the need for military cooperation with France became pressing), signed a Franco-Prussian alliance. From the French point of view there were plausible arguments for such a treaty. France's

---

37 Broglie, *Frédéric II et Louis XV*, ii, 165, 187.

38 A. Berney, *Friedrich der Grosse: Entwicklungsgeschichte eines Staatsmannes* (Tübingen, 1934), p. 183.

involvement in the war had now become deeper and more formal than before; and between July 1743 and April 1744 there had been issued a stream of ordinances aiming at the strengthening and improvement of its army in all its branches – uniforms, arms, supply and administration. In particular, the disappointments of 1743 and the anti-French schemes of Carteret had produced in Paris a desire to hit back at Britain, which some of the French ministers, notably Noailles, now regarded as a much more serious enemy than Maria Theresa. From the beginning of the war Jacobite exiles had been pressing for a French landing in the British Isles, which they confidently and quite wrongly claimed would be supported by a widespread popular rising in favour of the exiled dynasty. By the end of 1743 it had been decided to make such an attempt.

On 10 December, Louis XV wrote to Philip V in his own hand announcing a projected invasion of England and received an enthusiastic reply from his nephew.[39] In late 1743 and early 1744 a variety of plans were put forward for a landing in Essex or even an attack directly up the Thames on London itself; and a considerable fleet of transports was assembled at Dunkirk. But bad weather and indecision caused delays, news of the scheme leaked out in London, and early in March two severe storms destroyed a number of the transports and blew out of the Channel the French squadron which had been intended to cover the invasion. On 13 March the expedition, about which some French ministers, notably Noailles, had always been lukewarm, was abandoned.[40] During the same month, however, war was declared on Great Britain and Hanover. In May came a similar declaration against Maria Theresa. The Treaty of Fontainebleau had already committed France to a direct share in the struggle in Italy. All this meant that the possibility of an early end to the war, which had seemed quite large in the summer of 1743, had now disappeared. What had begun as an apparently rather undemanding military intervention in Germany had now become a long and exhausting struggle in which fighting in the Netherlands, to a lesser extent in Italy and perhaps even in Great Britain, would be increasingly important.

A large French army, commanded by the Marshal de Saxe, the illegitimate son of the Elector Augustus II of Saxony who had

---

39 F. J. McLynn, *France and the Jacobite Rising of 1745* (Edinburgh, 1981), pp. 16–17.

40 *Correspondance de Louis XV et du Maréchal de Noailles*, ii, 73–4; on this abortive French invasion scheme in general see J-P. Bois, *Maurice de Saxe* (Paris, 1992), pp. 311–14.

already a distinguished record in French service and had just become a marshal of France, crossed the frontier into the Austrian Netherlands in May 1744. It met little resistance. The allied forces facing it, British, Dutch, Austrian and Hanoverian, were as disunited as ever, and correspondingly ineffective: the difficulties in the way of effective concerted action by them were almost insuperable. Feeling between the Hanoverian contingent and the British was particularly bad; and George II, who would have liked to take personal command as he had done in the previous year, found his ministers determined to prevent this. There were disagreements between Marshal Wade, the recently promoted British commander, and the duke d'Aremberg, the Austrian one, which led to much indecision; so that later in the year Wade complained that 'partial and private considerations seem to influence our actions here, and if we don't alter our measures, our treasure will be exhausted to little purpose'.[41] The Austrian contingent was pitifully small (only 3,000 men by the end of May). The Dutch, who were still not at war with France and were involved only as the allies of Maria Theresa, were patently reluctant to fight. Wassenaer, the envoy of the States-General, met Louis XV in the French camp near Lille at the opening of the campaign in an abortive effort to persuade him to abandon it; and the garrisons of the Dutch-held barrier fortresses, which were in any case under strength, showed little will to resist attack. The result was inevitable: Courtrai, Menin, Ypres, Furnes, fell to the French within a matter of weeks.

But these successes were completely overshadowed by the threat to France from the east which took shape in the summer of 1744. A powerful Austrian army under Prince Charles of Lorraine (who had recently married the younger sister of Maria Theresa and thus become doubly her brother-in-law) began to cross the Rhine on the last day of June and soon was in control of most of Alsace. From there an advance on Lorraine, even on Paris itself, seemed quite possible. Stanislaus Leszczynski, the former king of Poland who had been established as ruler of Lorraine in 1735, fled from his palace in Lunéville, while his wife, carrying all her jewels with her, took refuge in Versailles. Prince Charles had already told his wife in mid-June that once he had crossed the Rhine he would soon be writing to her from Paris;[42] and it seemed for a moment that his

41 Arneth, *Geschichte*, ii, 387–8, 546; Yorke, *Life and Correspondence of Philip Yorke*, i, 360.
42 Guglia, *Maria Theresia*, i, 214.

optimism might be justified. 'What a change', wrote an exulting British observer, 'from this time two years – the Queen of Hungary, with an army of 100.000, penetrating into France!'[43] This critical situation meant a large diversion of French strength from the Netherlands. Early in August Noailles and Louis XV himself arrived in Metz with an army of 25,000 men. But almost immediately any further French activity was paralysed by the sudden and serious illness of the king, who for several days seemed on the point of death. Should he die and the queen become regent for her young son, this would probably mean the fall from power of all those closely associated with the existing regime, not least Noailles himself, a consideration which for the time being inhibited any decisive action. If, on the other hand, Louis recovered, an interventionist policy in Germany would almost certainly be continued. If Prince Charles had been more ready to take advantage of this situation, with all its uncertainties, the French army in Alsace and Lorraine might very well have been in serious difficulties.

The whole situation was transformed when, on 15 August, Frederick II launched the invasion of Bohemia which had been so carefully prepared. The march of his army through Saxony, still neutral territory, was justified by a published declaration which attacked Maria Theresa's efforts to undermine the position of Charles VII, the lawfully elected emperor: she had, it claimed seized his hereditary lands 'to the last patch (*flecken*)' and driven his forces from imperial territory.[44] The attack came as a considerable surprise in Vienna. There news of the anti-Habsburg union formed at Frankfurt had been received with scepticism; and as late as 30 July Bartenstein was still assuring Francis Stephen that as the invasion of France was going so well Frederick would not dare to make a move.[45] It was a sign of the increasing bitterness of the struggle in Germany that the invasion, unlike that of Silesia in 1740, aroused genuine popular hostility in the Habsburg lands and especially in Vienna, where the house of Count von Dohna, the Prussian ambassador, had to be protected against possible mob attack.[46] But Frederick's action was very threatening. Maria Theresa and her husband went at once to Pressburg and tried, with very limited

43 *Annals and Correspondence of the Viscount and the First and Second Earls of Stair*, ed. J. M. Graham (Edinburgh–London, 1875), ii, 315.
44 Guglia, *Maria Theresia*, i, 223.
45 Arneth, *Geschichte*, ii, 555, fn. 51.
46 Arneth, *Geschichte*, ii, 413.

success, to rouse support in Hungary as had been done in 1741. Although Francis Stephen told his brother on 22 August that he hoped for aid on twice the scale of three years earlier, many of the Hungarian counties provided fewer men than they promised and others none at all. Money, as always, was also very scarce. There was only one thing to be done: on 23 August Prince Charles was ordered to abandon the campaign in France and march back at once to Bohemia to protect the territorial core of the monarchy. Before the end of the month his army had recrossed the Rhine with little loss or interference from the French: this considerable achievement owed much to Marshal Traun, now the prince's chief adviser. It can be argued that Noailles here threw away one of the few great military opportunities of the war and that more enterprise on his part might well have inflicted a crushing defeat on the retreating Austrians.

At first the Prussian offensive in Bohemia went well. Prague was taken on 16 September; and Frederick then advanced up the Moldau valley hoping to catch Prince Charles between his own army and the French and Bavarian forces which he assumed to be in hot pursuit of the Austrians. In fact this was not the case. Noailles did send some French regiments into Bavaria to support the forces there, commanded by Marshal Seckendorff, which still remained to Charles VII. The Austrians quickly evacuated the electorate and the emperor was able to re-enter Munich on 23 October. But the bulk of the French army settled down to a long siege of Freiburg-im-Breisgau, the chief city of the scattered Habsburg territories in south-west Germany. From Frederick's standpoint this was quite useless; he knew well that the Austrians would not detach a single man from the decisive field of operations in Bohemia merely to protect these isolated and vulnerable small possessions. He now found himself in a dangerously exposed position, particularly when in the first days of October Saxony joined Maria Theresa against him. During the last weeks of 1744, sometimes outmanoeuvred by Traun, now in command of the forces opposed to him, he was forced into a demoralising and expensive retreat. When he crossed the Elbe on 9–10 November he hoped to find respite behind it; but he was forced to continue the withdrawal into Silesia. By the end of the year his army had lost about a quarter of its original strength and doubts about his abilities as a commander were being expressed. Of the 36,000 Prussian soldiers who finally reached Silesia it was estimated that half then died of dysentery.[47] Frederick

47 C. Duffy, *Frederick the Great: A Military Life* (London, 1985), p. 56.

was generous in the tribute he later paid to his adversary. Traun's handling of the campaign, he said, had been 'a model of perfection',[48] though it seems likely that the Austrians might have won a really decisive victory if they in their turn had shown a little more activity and aggression.

By the last months of 1744, then, the hopes of Frederick's opponents were high. One plan, probably the work of Brühl, his bitter enemy, envisaged a devastating partition of his territories, with Silesia reverting to Maria Theresa, Magdeburg to Saxony, East Prussia to Poland in return for concessions to Russia on its eastern borders, and Halberstadt to Hanover. There was even discussion of declaring him an enemy of the empire, deposing him and replacing him with his younger brother, Augustus William.[49] So difficult was his position that he wrote to Elizabeth of Russia in the hope that she might mediate a peace between him and his enemies, an idea which Mardefeld had already put forward on his own initiative. But although the empress was flattered by the idea of playing such a role, and made overtures in London as to the site of a possible peace conference, nothing came of the suggestion.[50]

The most important casualty of the campaigning of 1744, however, was Franco-Prussian relations. Frederick had from the beginning been very much alive to the risk of being left by his ally to face alone the full might of the Habsburgs, and therefore insistent that France must act effectively in Germany. He expected France to protect the detached western provinces of Brandenburg-Prussia, Cleves and Mark, against the Austrians and their allies, to hold Hanover in check and prevent it attacking him (something to which he attached considerable importance), and to continue to subsidise Charles VII even after he had recovered his electorate. As his position became more difficult he repeatedly demanded the sending of a French army to Westphalia, while at the same time he hoped that Belleisle, and the forward policy which he personified, might regain their former influence in Paris.[51] On the French side there was a well-founded suspicion that Frederick would never hesitate to throw over any ally when it suited him to do so. 'Past experience',

48 *Histoire de mon temps*, ii, 76–7.

49 U. Dann, *Hanover and Great Britain, 1740–1760* (Leicester–London, 1991), p. 59.

50 W. Mediger, *Moskaus Weg nach Europa: Der Aufstieg Russlands zum europäischen Machstaat im Zeitalter Friedrichs des Grossen* (Braunschweig, 1952) p. 275.

51 *Pol. Corr.*, iii, 171–2, 207–8, 209–10, 228–30, 297–9, 302–5.

wrote a prominent member of Louis XV's court, 'has made us judge with reason that one ought not to count on the words, even the treaties, of the King of Prussia.'[52]

By the end of the year Frederick, side by side with his overtures in St Petersburg, was trying hard to influence George II and British public opinion in his favour.[53] Here the fall from power of Carteret in November, brought down by his own arrogance and secretiveness (Newcastle complained of his 'obstinate and offensive silence') and the hostility of his fellow-ministers in spite of the continuing favour of the king, was one gleam of light in an otherwise dark picture. Henry Pelham, Newcastle's younger brother, who now became, as First Lord of the Treasury, the most important member of the cabinet, knew little about the politics of the continental states. He was more and more preoccupied by the growing cost of the war and its impact on Britain's finances. There seemed, therefore, some reason to hope, though Newcastle remained as bellicose as ever and there was no fundamental change in the British attitude, that the ambitious interventionist policies of Carteret might now be diluted or even abandoned. Certainly Carteret's fall gave much pleasure to Frederick;[54] and this is understandable, for in September Carteret had put forward to the Dutch and Austrian governments a plan for a great anti-Prussian alliance which involved, among other things, Russia putting 50,000 men in the field. The proposal, like so many others of the period, had no result; but not until the dark days of the Seven Years War was the king of Prussia to experience setbacks worse than those of the last months of 1744.

THE WAR IN ITALY AND FRANCO-SPANISH DIVISIONS

In Germany, then, Maria Theresa had achieved a good deal in 1744. She had lost control, at least for the time being, of most of Bavaria. But she had successfully warded off the Prussian attack in Bohemia, inflicted on Frederick II the first serious military setback of his reign, and gained the alliance of Saxony. In Italy the picture was less satisfactory. The conquest of the kingdom of Naples was her major ambition in the peninsula; and her hopes were nourished by the knowledge that the Neapolitan army was badly and irregularly paid

52 Duc de Luynes, *Mémoires sur la cour de Louis XV (1735–58)* (Paris, 1859–64), v, 160.
53 *Pol. Corr.*, iii, 336, 360–1, 362–6.
54 *Pol. Corr.*, iii, 368–70.

and by the belief that there would be widespread support there for the restoration of Habsburg rule. Plans for such a restoration were not wanting. Traun had sent one to Vienna at the end of 1742; and in the spring of 1744 his successor Lobkowitz sent to a number of sympathetic Neapolitan nobles a proclamation intended to pave the way for a Habsburg conquest of the kingdom. There were also expectations elsewhere in Italy that there would indeed be a revolt against Bourbon rule in the kingdom if this were likely to be supported by an Austrian army.[55] Such plans and ambitions underlay the unsuccessful effort which began in March 1744 to push southwards from Rimini, where Lobkowitz had spent the winter, and invade Naples. In spite of a victory in August at Velletri over a combined Spanish and Neapolitan force, this accomplished little, largely because of the indecisiveness of the Austrian commander and the slowness of his movements. By the beginning of November Lobkowitz and his army were retreating northwards through the papal state.

This retreat had been forced on the Austrians largely by the need to support Charles Emmanuel in northern Italy. There the French and Spaniards had in April captured Villefranche, the Piedmontese port which had hitherto been a useful base for the British Mediterranean squadron. They followed this up with some considerable successes in Piedmont and defeated Charles Emmanuel at the end of September at Madonna dell'Olmo. But they were then halted by the minor fortress of Coni (Cuneo), which they besieged unsuccessfully and at high cost in casualties, and forced to retreat before Lobkowitz and his army could come into play at all.

The real lesson of 1744 in Italy, however, was one which was to be repeated with monotonous regularity in different contexts throughout the war: the extreme difficulty of inducing the armed forces of different states, and their commanders, to cooperate effectively. This was particularly marked where France and Spain were concerned. There was much argument in the spring, for example, over whether the Gallispan armies should move against Charles Emmanuel through Dauphiné as the French wanted and as eventually happened, or by the much more difficult coastal route along the Genoese riviera, as Elizabeth Farnese insisted. There was more disagreement over the siege of Coni and the retreat after its

55 Arneth, *Geschichte*, ii, 337, 364, 370. See, e.g., the comments of Sir Horace Mann, the British minister in Florence, in *The Yale Edition of Horace Walpole's Correspondence*, xviii (London–New Haven, Conn., 1955), 446.

failure. In spite of the dynastic connection since 1700 there was no tradition of friendship between the two powers; and in an age still deeply sensitive on points of etiquette and precedence irritating disputes on issues of this kind were almost unavoidable. Since the French commander, the prince de Conti, belonged to a junior line of the royal family, there were opportunities for much argument between him and the at least equally royal Don Philip. The fact that Louis XV had decided that the Spanish prince should be regarded as a *fils de France* provoked protests from other members of the French dynasty, who felt that this might threaten their places in the line of succession to the throne. There was argument, again, over whether French or Spanish forces, when both were on the march together, should have the place of honour on the right; it was finally agreed that it should be taken by the Spaniards, as the French were fighting technically as auxiliaries of Spain.[56]

The tensions were therefore only too plentiful. They had already been raised to a dangerous level early in the year by events at sea. On 22 February an indecisive naval battle was fought off Toulon between French and Spanish squadrons and a British fleet under Admiral Mathews. On both sides it was a botched and unsatisfactory affair which produced bitter recriminations. The French and Spanish ships retreated to Spanish ports; but Mathews, who had shown little capacity for leadership and had been poorly supported by his second-in-command, Admiral Lestock, did not press the pursuit. Henceforth the Bourbon powers were never able to send any substantial military force to Italy by sea, as the Spaniards had done in November 1741. In this sense the outcome was a strategic success for Britain, though there was deep dissatisfaction there with the failure to win a more decisive victory, and the battle was followed by acute disagreements and a series of courts-martial. On the Gallispan side most of the fighting had been done and most of the losses suffered by the Spaniards, who claimed that the French had failed shamefully to support them. At the ports of Málaga and Cadiz placards were displayed urging that Frenchmen be killed as traitors. Philip V told the French ambassador that Spanish naval officers would ask to retire rather than cooperate again with French ones, and ostentatiously rewarded the Spanish commander, Admiral Navarro, with a title (marques de la Victoria) which underlined the belief of many Spaniards that the

---

56 Baudrillart, *Philippe V*, v, 178–9.

battle had been a success negated by the cowardice of their allies. On their side, the French criticised the Spanish officers and claimed that Navarro had himself shown cowardice during the battle.[57] This bad feeling was carried over into the war on land and intensified by the haughty and intractable attitude of the new Spanish commander in Italy, the marquis de la Mina. In July Conti complained that he distributed among his officers copies of the French movement orders, which meant that they could not be kept secret, and that it was 'impossible to carry on war with an ally whose incapacity, ill will and bad faith upset every arrangement'.[58]

Underlying personal antagonisms and operational disputes, however, were real policy differences. Louis XV sincerely wished to help his son-in-law; and this meant that the Spaniards were given more latitude than they really deserved in the conduct of the war. The French war minister told Conti in July, quite correctly, that 'the King's sole object and interest in the war in Italy is to help obtain the Duchies which the Queen of Spain wants for Don Philip'. This meant, he went on, that even though their military plans were bad ones 'we are bound to meet the wishes of the Spaniards'.[59] But this was a shaky foundation on which to build a joint military effort. Elizabeth Farnese's dominance of Spanish policy was much disliked in Paris, and Vauréal, as ambassador in Madrid, commented scathingly in his despatches on her irrational suspicions and lack of both knowledge and intelligence.[60] In particular, the French government did not share her deep hostility to Charles Emmanuel. In Paris there were still not unreasonable hopes that he could be induced to change sides; and this difference of attitude was soon to lead to really serious disagreement. Between Austrians and Sardinians there were also very real sources of disunity and potential conflict. Charles Emmanuel was as unwilling as ever to see the Bourbons driven from Italy and Habsburg power dominant there. His ambitions in Lombardy, whatever ostensible limits might have been put to them by the Treaty of Worms, were still very much alive and impossible to realise except at the expense of Maria Theresa. Austrian and Sardinian commanders in the field were almost as likely to quarrel as French and Spanish ones. In 1744,

57 Baudrillart, *Philippe V*, v, 186–8, 191.
58 S. Wilkinson, *The Defence of Piedmont, 1742–8: A Prelude to the Study of Napoleon* (Oxford, 1927), p. 140.
59 Wilkinson, *Defence*, p. 141.
60 Baudrillart, *Philippe V*, v, 210, 232–3.

however, it was the divisions of the Gallispans which were the more obvious and important.

FREDERICK II'S DIFFICULTIES AND EVENTUAL TRIUMPH

The early months of 1745 were a period of severe strain for the king of Prussia. At the beginning of the year he was uneasy about signs of Russian military preparations in Livonia, anxious for a final settlement with Maria Theresa if one could be obtained on acceptable terms, and hopeful that British mediation might help to bring this about. On 20 January, however, the now almost phantom emperor Charles VII died in Munich, when an Austrian army was once more threatening his capital. This was a blow to both France and Prussia. The imperial title which they had snatched from the Habsburg grasp after three centuries now seemed very likely to revert to its traditional holders: the Grand Duke Francis Stephen, although not himself a Habsburg, was much the strongest, indeed the only plausible, candidate for it. 'Certainly the emperor could not have died more inopportunely for our interests', Frederick told Louis XV, 'and this event unsettles all our plans.'[61] Charles's successor as elector of Bavaria, his young son Max Joseph, was very ready to come to terms with Maria Theresa. Though he took the title of archduke of Austria it was significant that he did not assume that of king of Bohemia, which his father had taken after his coronation in Prague in 1741. (Frederick in fact approved of this, since any assertion of Bavarian claims to Bohemia would tend to push Saxony more firmly into the arms of Austria.) A last military effort by the new elector was a failure. The Habsburg generals Batthyany and Browne quickly reconquered most of his electorate: by the middle of April 1745 the last Bavarian forces in the field had been routed. On 22 April, in spite of the efforts of Chavigny to keep him in the French camp, Max Joseph made peace with Maria Theresa by the Treaty of Füssen. In exchange for the return of his electoral lands he promised to vote in the forthcoming imperial election for Francis Stephen and to influence the Elector Klemens Frederick of Cologne, his uncle, in the same direction. Maria Theresa did not insist that Bavaria join her in her continuing struggle with France and Prussia; but Max Joseph undertook to provide forces to support the work of general pacification in Germany and was promised a subsidy of 400,000 gulden to help him maintain these. This treaty was a serious setback for the opponents of Maria Theresa. The election as emperor of Francis Stephen would be a still more serious one; and yet it was one clearly very difficult to prevent. In France the new foreign minister, the marquis d'Argenson, was deeply opposed to acceptance of the grand duke as emperor. In January he told Stainville, Francis Stephen's representative in Paris, that to prevent this France would continue the war for forty years if necessary.[62] But other French ministers, notably Tencin and Noailles, did not share this determination and were prepared to accept that there was now little chance of preventing a Habsburg recovery of the imperial dignity. By mid-February it had been agreed with Frederick II that the marquis de Valory, the French envoy to Berlin, should go to Dresden and try to persuade the Elector Augustus to become a candidate in the forthcoming election; but this effort to put forward a credible rival to Francis Stephen was a failure. Neither Brühl nor Father Guarini, the elector's influential confessor, was willing to press Augustus to support it. Both, with good reason, feared Frederick, while Brühl suspected that if the elector achieved the imperial title his own influence over him would be undermined. Even the fact that Valory was empowered, if all else failed, to offer Augustus a substantial subsidy with which to maintain a much bigger army could not tilt the balance.[63] At the end of April the duke of Campo-Florido, the Spanish ambassador in Paris, proposed that the Bourbon powers make a virtue of necessity and help Francis Stephen become emperor: Maurepas and Tencin, and a few days later Noailles, accepted the idea, though d'Argenson disdainfully rejected it.[64] For months the foreign minister clung desperately to the hope that Augustus could still be persuaded to become a French-backed candidate; but he now felt that France had lost all military superiority in Germany and that this could be replaced only 'by negotiation, that is, by money'.[65]

62 Butler, *Choiseul*, p. 574.

63 *Mémoires des négociations du Marquis de Valori, ambassadeur de France à la cour de Berlin*, ed. Comte de Valori (Paris, 1820), i, 211–15.

64 Baudrillart, *Philippe V*, v, 276.

65 E. Zevort, *Le Marquis d'Argenson et le Ministère des Affaires Etrangères du 18 Novembre 1744 au 10 Janvier 1747* (Paris, 1880), pp. 122–3.

Frederick II was now more and more alarmed by the direction of events. On 8 January there had been signed at Warsaw a quadruple alliance of Austria, Great Britain, Saxony and the Dutch Republic, which was clearly aimed at Prussia. Saxony was to receive substantial subsidies – £100,000 from Britain, 550,000 florins from the Dutch – and also territorial gains after 'the common enemy' had been defeated. (These were defined in a separate agreement with Maria Theresa which was not signed until May.) In return, the Elector Augustus renewed his guarantee of the Pragmatic Sanction and promised an army of 30,000 men to help defend Bohemia against any new Prussian onslaught. When it was out of danger he would provide, for use elsewhere in the Holy Roman Empire or the Netherlands, 10,000 men in return for a proportionately reduced subsidy (£60,000 from Britain; 330,000 florins from the Dutch). The Polish Republic and, far more menacing, Russia, were to be invited to accede to the treaty. Frederick felt clearly the threat to Prussia. It now seemed all too likely that France might make easy gains in the southern Netherlands and Spain realise the ambitions of Elizabeth Farnese in Italy, while he had to bear the main weight of the war against a formidable hostile coalition. From this uncomfortable position he for some time hoped to escape by making advances to Britain. On 27 January, only a day after he heard of the death of Charles VII, he ordered his minister in London, Andrié, to sound the earl of Harrington, Carteret's successor as Secretary of State for the Northern Department, on the British attitude to the new development. Three weeks later he was even hoping for an Anglo-Prussian agreement which would lay down the terms of a settlement with Maria Theresa to which she would be forced to agree, and in which Bavaria, the Palatinate and Hesse-Kassel would be included.[66] The attitude of Saxony, which was demanding compensation for the damage done when the Prussian army marched through its territory *en route* to Bohemia in August of the previous year, was another worry, especially as Frederick feared that its claims might be backed by Russia. By the end of March he had begun to see Russian mediation as his best hope of ending a war he was now very anxious to escape from, and was ready to offer handsome bribes to Bestuzhev, and to count M. L. Vorontsov, the Vice-Chancellor, if they would help him achieve this.[67]

---

66 *Pol. Corr.*, iv, 26–7, 55–7.
67 *Pol. Corr.*, iv, 89.

Any hopes he placed in a Saxon candidacy for the imperial title, or in Britain or Russia, were doomed to disappointment. By the beginning of April Frederick had realised that France would not be able to bring a majority of the imperial electors to support Augustus as the next Holy Roman Emperor. By the second half of the same month he had given up hope of British mediation. On the 23rd of April count P.G. Chernyshev, the Russian envoy to Berlin, presented a note in which the Empress Elizabeth explicitly refused to mediate between him and Maria Theresa. Frederick was now in desperation contemplating a move of the Prussian government from Berlin to Magdeburg, where it would be more secure from attack; and his tone in his correspondence with his diplomats and ministers became increasingly apocalyptic. 'I have passed the Rubicon', he told Podewils at the end of April, 'and either I shall maintain my power or all will be lost and the name of Prussia will be buried with me.'[68] He now drew comfort from the example of his great opponent: Maria Theresa, he pointed out, had not despaired even when her enemies were at the gates of Vienna. A month later he had begun to feel that 'in this critical and uncertain situation only a diversion by the Great Turk (*Grosstürken*) can deal the Queen of Hungary a deadly blow and support effectively the views of the King of France and his allies.'[69]

While the king of Prussia was racked by anxieties, the French in the Netherlands were making impressive headway. This was not surprising. Here for the next three years almost everything was in their favour. They had the enormous advantage of unity of command, a striking contrast to the quarrels and indecisions which continually afflicted the allies. They had a highly competent commander in Saxe, soon to become a marshal of France. They had a superiority in numbers which at times threatened to become crushing. Before the opening of the campaign Saxe told his half-brother, the Elector Augustus, that 'if one compares our resources to those of the Austrian alliance in effect only a miracle can tilt the balance in its favour. . . . However much the negotiators on the Austrian side try they will have difficulty in finding the means of giving even an appearance of equality to their forces.'[70] The first real battle of the war in that area, therefore, at Fontenoy on 11 May, was a French victory, though a hard-fought

---

68 *Pol. Corr.*, iv, 102–3, 126, 133, 134.
69 *Pol. Corr.*, iv, 167.
70 Pajol, *Les Guerres sous Louis XV*, ii, 368,

one. It was soon followed by the fall of Tournai and Ghent; and once more the disunity of the allies was exposed. There was bitter British criticism of the behaviour of the Dutch regiments in the battle: the government in the official account of it published in London toned down some of the comments on them made by the British commander, the duke of Cumberland, the younger son of George II (he spoke in a private letter of their 'inexpressible cowardice') so as not to 'create any uneasiness in so ticklish and necessary an ally'. The duke's secretary for his part thought the fall of Ghent showed the 'indolent timidity' of the Dutch.[71] Also at the end of July Prince Charles Edward Stuart landed with a tiny handful of followers in Argyllshire. Though the seriousness of the rebellion he was to set off was as yet not anticipated in London, the news that he had raised the Jacobite standard meant that Cumberland was at once ordered to send home ten battalions of infantry. This was the beginning of a process which was soon greatly to reduce the strength of the British army facing Saxe; and a convention of 8 June by which an Austrian corps of 8,000 men was taken into British pay for use in the Low Countries did little to reverse this.[72] The Dutch government was further discouraged by the withdrawal of British forces: in August Harrington found it 'extremely alarm'd at the thought of such a weakening of the combined army in Flanders at this most critical juncture and ready to give up the game in despair if it should take place'.[73] The Bourbon powers for their part tried to encourage a revolt which pre-empted so much of Britain's military strength at little cost to them; in August Charles Edward received from Campo-Florido in Paris promises of support in money, arms and troops, though France did little and Spain nothing to make these good in practice. The French government therefore had good reason to concentrate its military effort in the Netherlands, where the situation was so favourable to it, rather than in Germany, the scene of so many disappointments.

71 F. H. Skrine, *Fontenoy and Britain's Share in the War of the Austrian Succession* (Edinburgh–London, 1906), pp. 207, 231; Hon. E. Charteris, *William Augustus, Duke of Cumberland, His Early Life and Times (1721–1748)* (London, 1913), p. 199. The most recent detailed account of the battle of Fontenoy is in Browning, *War of the Austrian Succession*, pp. 206–13.

72 The text of this convention, in *Österreichische Staatsverträge: England*, i, 714–17, in its detailed provisions regarding the payment and maintenance of these troops is a good illustration of the overriding importance of money in eighteenth-century warfare.

73 Skrine, *Fontenoy*, p. 259.

In Italy also 1745 was a good year for France and its Spanish ally. Marshal Maillebois, the new French commander there in succession to Conti, was a competent professional soldier with an excellent staff; by comparison Schulenburg, his new Austrian counterpart, was a mediocrity. In spite of the inevitable disagreements between French and Spaniards, Tortona, Piacenza, Parma and Pavia were captured. At the end of September Charles Emmanuel was defeated at Bassignana. In mid-December Don Philip occupied Milan, though against the opposition of Maillebois, who thought this a strategic mistake.

When campaigning began once more on the Silesian border (perhaps significantly, it was the Austrians under Prince Charles who made the first move), Frederick stressed that he was resolved to conquer or die. He was determined, he said, to present to misfortune 'a brow of bronze'.[74] In fact he quickly won, on 4 June at Hohenfriedberg, a victory which he claimed was the most complete since Blenheim. But neither on the political nor the military level did it have the results he hoped for. The Austrians still showed no sign of giving him the only thing he wanted; an end to the war which left him in possession of Silesia. Though he advanced into Bohemia he got no further than the line of the Elbe; his supply position was difficult, the population was hostile and once more he got no effective help from France. Repeated pressure for French subsidies produced only an offer which he rejected in almost brutal terms at the beginning of September as totally inadequate.[75] A fortnight later he began a slow retreat into Silesia; and though on the 29th he won another victory at Soor, which owed much to his personal abilities as a commander, this did little to improve his position. A month earlier he had managed to make with George II an agreement which seemed for a moment to offer an escape from his difficulties. On 26 August the convention of Hanover was signed, by which the two rulers guaranteed each other's territories. This gave George some degree of protection for his electorate, on which he once again feared a French attack. To Frederick it gave valuable support for his continued possession of Silesia, which the convention specifically mentioned as a Prussian territory. He also undertook not to cast his electoral vote against Francis Stephen. Maria Theresa was to be given six weeks in which to accede to the

74 Berney, *Friedrich*, p. 202.

75 *Pol. Corr.*, iv, 271–2. For Frederick's own account of his difficult position in Bohemia, see *Histoire de mon temps*, ii, 142–3.

agreement and end the war with Prussia; but there was never any chance of her doing so. When at the beginning of August Robinson had an interview with her at Schönbrunn and urged her to make peace, arguing that even if Prince Charles won a battle this would not be enough to recover Silesia, while if he were defeated this would ruin her, she replied, 'If I had to make peace with King Frederick tomorrow I would still strike him a blow this evening.' Moreover, a new Austro-Saxon alliance signed on 29 August (the result in part of bribery of Brühl to bring it about) did something to justify her defiance: in spite of military setbacks there was still confidence in Vienna in the possibility of victory.[76]

Between Great Britain and Austria the divergence of outlook now seemed wider than ever. Maria Theresa complained of the 'despotic demands' of Robinson, and argued forcibly that so long as Frederick remained as strong as he was her territories could never be really safe.[77] In London, on the other hand, what was seen as the foolish obstinacy of Austria aroused growing irritation. As early as the first days of April the duke of Newcastle had been insisting that Maria Theresa's best policy was to face facts, cut her losses and secure the imperial title for her husband by making peace with Frederick II.[78] The dogged determination with which she clung to hopes of recovering Silesia underlined once more the fundamental differences of objective which separated the two powers. 'The King of Prussia is still ready to make up with the Queen of Hungary, notwithstanding his last victory,' wrote Newcastle in October. 'I really think if the Queen of Hungary does not comply, there will be no more question here about her.'[79] The diplomat who complained that 'so much pride and stubbornness was never seen as that court [Austria] has shown even to their benefactors and supporters [Great Britain]' spoke for the whole of British official opinion.[80]

Maria Theresa's 'pride and stubbornness' were understandable, however. Against the military defeat at Soor could be placed an important political victory. On 13 September in Frankfurt her husband was proclaimed Holy Roman Emperor: on 4 October, his name-day, he was crowned. This meant that she had achieved one

---

76 Guglia, *Maria Theresia*, i, 261, 263.

77 Guglia, *Maria Theresia*, i, 270–1; Arneth, *Geschichte*, iii, 436.

78 *Private Correspondence of Chesterfield and Newcastle, 1744–46*, ed. Sir R. Lodge (London, 1930), p. 39.

79 British Library, Additional MSS.32705, fols. 249–50.

80 *The Private Correspondence of Sir Benjamin Keene, KB*, ed. Sir R. Lodge (Cambridge, 1933), p. 73.

of her most important objectives. The election of Francis Stephen (now the Emperor Francis I) was a defeat for France and Prussia. But it was one which neither was willing or able to do much about. D'Argenson made it clear that he was unwilling to use the French army under the prince de Conti, which was still stationed in west Germany, to influence the election directly; and this attitude was supported by many French ministers and commanders, notably by Saxe, who wanted to concentrate France's military effort on the Netherlands and continue his advance there. Frederick II also accepted the *fait accompli*. His representative at Frankfurt refused to vote for Francis Stephen and left the city the day before the election. But he rejected French suggestions that he should protest formally against the choice which had been made: he saw well enough how useless such a gesture would be. What had happened in Frankfurt, he told Podewils, was regrettable; but there was nothing to be done about it.[81]

In spite of his victories, therefore, his position in the last months of 1745 was by no means easy. The strains and uncertainties of the long struggle were having their effect on him. He was full of renewed complaints about the failure of France to support him. It had not provided the large army in west Germany which was needed to divert Austrian resources away from the struggle in Bohemia, for French successes in the Netherlands were quite useless in this respect.[82] The subsidies France offered him were only half of what he had asked for and were to be paid in twelve monthly instalments and not in the two six-monthly ones which he wanted. This, he told Valory contemptuously, 'might be suitable for a Landgrave of Darmstadt'; but he would try to find resources of his own to take the place of what he was offered by 'ungrateful friends'.[83] Yet he was very conscious of his need for money. In April he had decided to demand from France an annual payment of 4 million crowns, without which, he claimed, he could not carry on the war. After French failure to supply what he asked, he tentatively broached the possibility of raising a loan in London.[84] His desire for good relations with Britain and for its help in achieving peace with Maria Theresa was as strong as ever: once such a peace had been

81 *Pol. Corr.*, iv, 303, 305.

82 *Pol. Corr.*, iv, 289, 303–4, 305; *Histoire de mon temps*, ii, 109.

83 Duc de Broglie, *Marie-Thérèse impératrice* (Paris, 1888), ii, 150–3, 156; *Pol. Corr.*, iv, 271–2.

84 *Pol. Corr.*, iv, 335–6.

made, he emphasised, he would be willing to send Prussian troops to help suppress the increasingly threatening revolt in Scotland.[85] Most of all he was uneasy about the attitude of Russia, and with reason. Bestuzhev was as hostile as ever; and Augustus of Saxony had been asking for Russian help ever since the first move of the Prussian army through his territory in August 1744. After Hohenfriedberg these pleas became more insistent, and the Empress Elizabeth, still reluctant to commit herself to decisive action, was becoming more and more hostile to 'the Prussian Nadir Shah', as she called Frederick. At the end of September she told the state council in St Petersburg that she had decided to support Saxony if Prussia once more attacked it.[86]

From this accumulation of anxieties Frederick was finally delivered by military victory. The Austro-Saxon plan of campaign, which in November might have cut him off in Silesia from the core of his dominions, the electorate of Brandenburg, was carried out too slowly. In any case, it had already become known in Berlin through the Swedish minister in Dresden, who had passed it on to his opposite number in the Prussian capital.[87] On 15 December the Saxons were completely defeated by Prince Leopold of Anhalt-Dessau at Kesselsdorf, a few miles north of Dresden. This was decisive. The Saxon capital surrendered the following day; and the Elector Augustus was forced into humiliating flight. On 25 December the Austrian plenipotentiary, count Friedrich Harrach, signed the Treaty of Dresden which once more confirmed Silesia and Glatz as Prussian territory. Frederick for his part recognised the Emperor Francis I and guaranteed the Pragmatic Sanction. Augustus of Saxony recovered all his territories in a separate treaty signed on the same day but had to pay an indemnity of a million crowns, while the Electress Maria Josepha, a Habsburg archduchess before her marriage, renounced any claim she might have to Silesia.

Frederick had thus abandoned his French ally for the third time. The difficulties of his position, and in particular the danger of a disastrous Russian intervention against him if the war had lasted much longer, go far to justify his action in this case. At the beginning of January 1746 (that is, before news of the Dresden settlement had reached St Petersburg), orders were given there for

85 *Pol. Corr.*, iv, 314, 318, 321.
86 Mediger, *Moskaus Weg*, pp. 270, 284, 287. Nadir Shah was the despotic and aggressive ruler of Persia, a military adventurer, who was assassinated in 1747.
87 *Histoire de mon temps*, ii, 148.

the formation of an army of thirty regiments in Courland, Esthonia and Livonia, and for the preparation of Cossack and Kalmuck units of the kind Frederick feared most of all. Bestuzhev told the Saxon minister in the Russian capital that Elizabeth was now determined to deprive Prussia of its conquests and to ensure that satisfaction was given for the losses Saxony had suffered; and Hohenholz, the Austrian representative in St Petersburg, also believed that the empress was at last ready to act. The danger to Frederick from the east was therefore a real one.[88] He defended himself strenuously against any charge of having betrayed his ally. The essence of his apologia was not new: his arguments were those he had used to justify the Breslau settlement more than three years earlier. France, he claimed, had only itself to blame for his making peace, since it had given him no effective help in either men or money and had let down all its allies in 1744–5 – Charles VII, the Elector Palatine and William of Hesse as well as himself. He had been 'entirely abandoned' by the government in Paris.[89] Since he had left Berlin on 14 November, he told one of his confidants on 4 December, he had lived through 'a political storm greater than any I have yet experienced',[90] and his desire for a quick peace was intense and entirely understandable. None the less, the Dresden settlement, following the surreptitious truce made at Klein-Schnellendorff and the short-lived peace agreed at Breslau, confirmed his reputation as a dangerously unreliable ally.

A REALIGNMENT OF FRENCH POLICY?

French policy in Germany in 1745 was confused and uncertain, the product of conflicting personalities and ideas. The attitude of the Foreign Minister was clear. D'Argenson was a convinced and largely uncritical partisan of Frederick II. He was also an idealist, the only idealist in a position of authority in any European state in a cynical and materialist age. France in his eyes was as powerful as it needed or could hope to be. Further expansion on its part would merely arouse the fears and jealousies of its neighbours. 'The French crown is today too great', he wrote, 'too territorially complete (*arrondie*)

88 Mediger, *Moskaus Weg*, pp. 291–2; Guglia, *Maria Theresia*, ii, 275.
89 *Pol. Corr.*, iv, 390–2; *Mémoires des négociations du Marquis de Valori*, ii, 297–8.
90 *Briefwechsel Friedrichs des Grossen mit Grumbkow und Maupertuis (1731–1759)*, ed. R. Koser (Leipzig, 1898), pp. 197, 198.

and too well placed for trade, still to prefer territorial gain to a high reputation. It should no longer think of anything but moral leadership in Europe, which gives it peace and dignity. It is clear that in this way France would reach a degree of greatness and prosperity of which there are few examples in the world.'[91] As Foreign Minister he showed clearly that his idealism was genuine. Immediately after the victory at Fontenoy he wrote to the French chargé d'affaires in the Dutch Republic and ordered him to propose to the States-General that a peace congress be held in some Dutch town; and this initiative he repeated in September. He was reluctant to use French troops to support the Jacobite rebellion in Scotland, partly at least because he had genuine scruples about the forcible imposition on any nation of a regime to which it was opposed.[92] But if d'Argenson sought no territorial gains for France, he none the less wished to carry on its traditional policy of weakening the Habsburgs. 'As soon as France ceases to work for her own grandeur', he wrote in June 1742, before becoming Foreign Minister, 'and strives only for the breaking-up of Austrian power, the individual interests of the states will be served.'[93] For such a policy Frederick seemed the ideal instrument; and d'Argenson had a sincere regard for the abilities of the king of Prussia.

Among the French ministers, however, he was isolated. Orry, the able Controller-General of Finance, was very unwilling to provide more subsidies for Prussia. Tencin argued that French resources should be used to support the Jacobites by landing a substantial invasion force in Britain; and Noailles tended to take the same line. Louis XV himself was torn between resentment of the new emperor (he regarded Francis Stephen, originally a mere duke of Lorraine, as an inferior) and irritation generated by the unflattering remarks which Frederick II made, with indiscreet and undiplomatic frankness, at his expense.[94] There was therefore now in Paris a greater willingness than at any time in the last four years or more to consider serious negotiations and a lasting settlement with Maria Theresa. Early in September count Brühl surprised the comte de Vaulgrenant, the French minister in Dresden, by suggesting that the empress might be prepared to receive proposals for a peace

91 *Journal et mémoires du Marquis d'Argenson*, ed. E. J. B. Rathery (Paris, 1859–67), iv, 135.

92 Broglie, *Marie-Thérèse impératrice*, i, 441–2, ii, 123–5.

93 *Journal et mémoires*, iv, 16.

94 Broglie, *Marie-Thérèse impératrice*, ii, 337–9.

agreement with France. Almost simultaneously count Chotek, the Austrian representative in Munich, made similar suggestions to the Saxon minister there, who passed them on to Chavigny in Frankfurt. A few days later Maria Theresa, on her way to Frankfurt for the imperial election, had a meeting in Passau with Chotek and the Saxon minister. This resulted merely in a note given to Chavigny confirming that she was ready to listen to any proposals the French government might make; but in conversation with Chotek, in her coach on the journey between Passau and Regensburg, she made it clear that she was now prepared for serious peace negotiations with France.

The majority of the ministers in Paris, supported at least tacitly by the king, was in favour of exploring this possibility. D'Argenson could not refuse; but he held firm to his prussophile attitude. 'Whatever reason for discontent the King may have with the King of Prussia', he wrote to Vaulgrenant on 22 September, 'H.M. is completely unwilling to discuss stipulations tending to deprive him of Silesia or to prejudice him elsewhere.'[95] A fortnight later he told Chavigny that, 'as for the negotiation proposed by the Queen of Hungary [the French government still refused to recognise Francis Stephen as emperor and therefore to give Maria Theresa the title of empress] enter into it but support it as little as you can'.[96] The negotiations were thus carried on in the main through Vaulgrenant in Dresden and von Saul, the Saxon minister in Vienna. The difficulties were considerable. On both sides a long history of enmity had to be overcome; and there were difficult specific issues to resolve. The desire of Louis XV to obtain a substantial territory for Don Philip in Italy was an obvious example; this the Austrians were willing to concede, but only on condition that the creation of such a principality should not involve territorial loss for Charles Emmanuel. There were demands for substantial gains for France in the Netherlands – Ypres, Tournai, Furnes and Nieuwport. Most important of all, there was in Paris no readiness to see Frederick II, however unsatisfactory he might have proved as an ally, deprived of Silesia; while in Vienna the recovery of the lost province was the ultimate objective of any improvement in relations with France. When, at the end of November, count Harrach was sent to Dresden with full powers to agree peace terms with France, he was

95 D. B. Horn, 'Saxony in the War of the Austrian Succession', *English Historical Review*, xliv (1929), 35 fn.

96 Broglie, *Marie-Thérèse impératrice*, ii, 232.

disappointed to find that Vaulgrenant not merely demanded more territory for Don Philip in Italy than the Austrians were willing to concede but also insisted that Silesia must remain Prussian. It was this political setback more than the defeat of the Saxons at Kesselsdorf which inclined Maria Theresa towards ending the war in Germany.[97] On 3 December Harrach was given full powers to negotiate terms with Prussia 'in the extreme case' (that is, if Saxony were forced to make a separate peace). He still clung to the hope that Frederick II could be defeated. On 18 December he suggested to Ulfeld a combined attack on Prussia by Austrian, Saxon and Hanoverian forces supported by Russian ones; but the inability of the Saxons to go on fighting made such ideas quite visionary. On the following day he was given explicit instructions to make peace; and the arrival in Vienna two days later of news of the fall of Milan to the Spaniards further strengthened the case for this. When Harrach arrived in Dresden on the evening of the battle of Kesselsdorf, with the Prussian army on the point of entering the city, he had discussions with Vaulgrenant on a possible Austro-French alliance which went on throughout the night; but without result. He refused to agree to Don Philip having Alessandria and Tortona, which were hereditary possessions of the king of Sardinia; and though he seemed rather more accommodating on the Netherlands, even there he refused to give way over Tournai and Nieuwport, which he insisted must remain in Austrian hands. The peace with Frederick II which was signed ten days later thus became inevitable.

DECISION IN GERMANY: BUT THE WAR CONTINUES

The most important result of this long and complex series of struggles had now been achieved. Silesia was Prussian. The standing in the affairs of Europe of Prussia and its ruler had risen very sharply.[98] Frederick's success had not been easily won; and he knew well how deeply the loss of Silesia was resented in Vienna. He was now anxious for a period of peace. 'The future is beyond human reach,' he said when he was warned that Maria Theresa would never abandon the lost province. 'I have won territory; let others keep it. I fear nothing from Saxony or Austria for the ten or twelve years of life that remain to me: in future I shall not attack a cat

97 Guglia, *Maria Theresia*, i, 278.
98 See below, pp. 211–12.

except to defend myself, and I would see Prince Charles at the gates of Paris without stirring.'[99] His position was still far from entirely comfortable. The fear and dislike he inspired in some of the German states and their rulers were genuine and deep. He alienated Saxony still more, and strengthened the position there of Brühl, by failing to keep his promise to return Saxon prisoners of war when peace was made and using many of them as forced recruits for his own army. The envy and hostility of George II were unabated. More distant but potentially much more threatening, the forces hostile to him in St Petersburg had lost none of their strength. None the less, he had transformed the political and military balance in Germany; and for a decade to come there was to be no overt challenge to what he had achieved. Maria Theresa, for her part, had saved the core of the Habsburg monarchy and placed her husband on the imperial throne, and in doing so had shown a courage and determination which made her admired throughout Europe. 'Whatever sacrifice she makes', wrote a well-informed French commentator in September 1745, 'it must be agreed that this war will always be in history infinitely glorious for this princess.'[100] The fact that, as a woman, her ability effectively to control her commanders in the field was limited, and also that during these years of trial and danger she was frequently pregnant (she gave birth to her eighth child in February 1746) throw her achievement into still sharper relief.

By the end of 1745 the war, in so far as it was about the Austrian Succession, had been decided. Its most dramatic episodes – the Austrian recovery at the end of 1741, the French retreat from Prague a year later, the rapid Prussian success in December 1745 – were in the past. But the secondary struggles to which the central one in Germany had helped to give birth were still unresolved. Spanish ambitions in Italy, the efforts of the anti-French allies to defend the Netherlands, even the naval and colonial ambitions of Great Britain, were to ensure that a general peace was still almost three years in the future.

99 Broglie, *Marie-Thérèse impératrice*, ii, 374–5; *Mémoires des négociations du Marquis de Valori*, i, 255–6, 293–4.
100 Barbier, *Chronique*, ii, 86.

7 ITALY AND THE NETHERLANDS, 1745-8

FREDERICK II's CONTINUING FEARS

After the treaty of Dresden the struggle for power in Germany, hitherto the central theme of the war, ceased to be an active one. It had by no means ended, for Austro-Prussian rivalry was still intense; and in Vienna the desire for revenge was as strong as ever. But neither power was willing to renew the conflict. Frederick II was well aware that he would have to live, in all probability for the rest of his life, with the deep antagonism he had aroused in his great neighbour. The anxious watchfulness which was never henceforth to leave him was still very much in evidence. The signature at the beginning of June 1746, after months of negotiation, of an essentially defensive alliance between Maria Theresa and the Empress Elizabeth seriously alarmed him. He feared that a peace between Austria and France, which might not be far distant, would be followed by an attack on him by Austria and Russia, one in which Saxony, Hanover and perhaps Denmark might well join. Such an onslaught, he told Podewils only a few days after the treaty was signed, would be especially dangerous at that moment because of the economic difficulties of Prussia and the food shortage which made it impossible to assemble a large army. He must therefore rely on diplomacy for protection and 'clothe myself in a fox's skin after having worn that of a lion'.[1] Even after he had realised that his fears were exaggerated he still, in the last weeks of 1746, hoped that Turkish hostility, perhaps even a declaration of war by the Porte, might seriously weaken Maria Theresa in Germany.[2]

Nor were his fears, however exaggerated, totally unfounded. A secret article of the Austro-Russian treaty provided that if Frederick

1 *Politische Correspondenz Friedrichs des Grossen*, ed. J. G. Droysen *et al.* (46 vols, Berlin, 1879–1939), v, 62–3, 64–5, 66–7, 114.
2 *Pol. Corr.*, v, 241, 246, 248, 264, 267.

should attack either of the signatories, or the Polish republic, this would at once restore to Maria Theresa all her former rights in Silesia and Glatz; moreover, each of the two powers undertook to hold in readiness on its frontiers a force of 30,000 men to act if needed against Prussia, and to raise this number if necessary to 60,000. If Maria Theresa should recover her lost territories with Russian help, she would within a year pay her ally 2 million Rhenish florins in recompense for the assistance she had received.[3] Clearly, both powers saw war with Prussia as a real possibility. Also Bavaria had now gone over to the anti-French, and hence still by implication to some extent anti-Prussian, side. In July 1746 Max Joseph made an agreement with Austria, later supplemented by one with the maritime powers, by which he agreed, in return for a subsidy, to supply 7,000 soldiers for the war against France. From 1746 onwards, therefore, Frederick pinned his hopes of strengthening his international position largely on the achievement of better relations, perhaps even an alliance, with Britain. He now realised that Britain was better placed than any other power to withstand a long and costly war. Through its financial strength, he told Podewils in February 1747, it could treat all Europe as 'a great republic created to serve her'. A year later, when negotiations for the peace which would at last end the war were well under way, he was still sure that an understanding with the maritime powers was the best foundation for his inevitably anti-Austrian policies.[4] Moreover, in spite of his now very bad reputation as an ally, and what one British statesman called his 'abandoned perfidy and falseness',[5] there was a growing tendency in London, as irritation with Maria Theresa and her ministers grew, to look to the king of Prussia as a potentially useful ally. However faithless Frederick might be, after all, there was no gainsaying the quality of his army; Prussia's military power now meant that alliance with her could never be altogether unattractive.

---

3 The German text of the article can be found in *Receuil des traités et conventions conclus par la Russie avec les puissances étrangères*, ed. F. de Martens, i, *Autriche, 1648–1762* (St Petersburg, 1874), pp. 169–73.

4 *Pol. Corr.*, v, 314; vi, 48.

5 P. C. Yorke, *Life and Correspondence of Philip Yorke, Earl of Hardwicke, Lord Chancellor of Great Britain* (Cambridge, 1913), i, 650.

THE NETHERLANDS, 1746: FRENCH SUCCESSES

But the war was now being fought not in Germany but in the Netherlands and Italy; and this meant that it became more and more predominantly an Anglo-French one. These powers alone had the resources to sustain a long and large-scale struggle and to subsidise less powerful allies. On the British side the Dutch Republic (still not formally a belligerent), Sardinia and even Austria, on the French one Spain, thus found themselves increasingly relegated to a position of inferiority. More and more they were forced to accept decisions which they might greatly dislike but which they could not undo or even modify. For a moment it appeared, in the last days of 1745 and the first ones of 1746, that the Jacobite rebellion, backed by a French invasion, might overthrow the Hanoverian regime in Britain and end the war at a stroke. The victory of Charles Edward's Highland army at Prestonpans in September 1745 made it seem in Paris that the rebellion was worth supporting and ended the scepticism which until then some ministers had felt about its chances of success. At the end of November the French government asked, unsuccessfully, for the sending of 2,000 Spanish troops to support the rising;[6] and Sir James Stuart, sent by Charles Edward to France to urge an attack across the Channel, had several audiences with Louis XV in December, in all of which the king promised full support for the prince. By the end of the year preparations were under way for a French invasion to be launched from Calais and Boulogne. The duc de Richelieu, who was to command it, was equipped with 3,000 copies of a manifesto drawn up by Voltaire himself, to be distributed when the invasion force got ashore.

But the project was as complete a failure as that of the previous year. The slowness of the preparations, bad weather and technical problems, all conspired against it. Richelieu, who lacked energy and drive, became steadily more pessimistic about its chances of success. More significantly, there was once more disunity in the French government. The War Minister, the comte d'Argenson (brother of the Foreign Minister) and Noailles wished to concentrate France's energies on the war in continental Europe; and in this they were supported by Saxe. Maurepas, as Navy Minister, wanted to devote resources rather to the maritime and colonial struggle with Britain. It could be argued also that by overthrowing a Protestant dynasty in

---

6 A. Baudrillart, *Philippe V et la Cour de France* (5 vols, Paris, 1890–1902), v, 328.

the British Isles France risked alienating the Protestant rulers of Germany, on whom it had frequently relied during the last two centuries for support against the Habsburgs: this was a consideration which carried weight with Louis XV himself.[7] By mid-February 1746, therefore, the invasion plan had been in effect abandoned; and early in March the king admitted to Maurepas that there was no hope of carrying it out. The direct French help given to the Jacobites was small: a later estimate by one of them was that it amounted merely to 1,200 men, with £15,000 in cash and a small quantitiy of artillery and war material.[8] A small Swedish force recruited during the winter of 1745–6 by the French government for use in Scotland never left Gothenburg.

In spite of the crushing of the Jacobite rising, however, 1746 was a gloomy year for Britain on the battlefield. The French advance in the Netherlands went on. Brussels fell to Saxe in February, a success which earned him the supreme ceremonial honour of the *grandes entrées* of the king's chamber and the use during his lifetime of the splendid royal château of Chambord. Mons was taken in July and Namur in September; and on 11 October Saxe once more defeated the allies, commanded by Prince Charles of Lorraine, at Rocoux. The French army was substantially bigger than the one it faced: at Rocoux it numbered about 120,000 against 80,000 British, Dutch and Austrians. (These figures bring out the growing scale of the conflict: not until the age of Napoleon were such forces again to confront one another on the battlefield.) But quite apart from this material advantage the French still benefited greatly from a unity of command which their opponents conspicuously lacked. Disputes and rivalries between the allied commanders were as frequent and divisive as in the past. Sir John Ligonier, as commander-in-chief of the British forces, had great difficulties with a number of Dutch and Austrian generals to whom he was technically junior and who as a result claimed precedence over him in councils of war. He therefore finally refused to attend such meetings and instead fell back upon private ones with the Prince of Waldeck, who commanded the Dutch forces, and the Austrian Marshal Batthyany.[9] The universal feeling among British

7 F. J. McLynn, *France and the Jacobite Rising of 1745* (Edinburgh, 1981), pp. 160–3.

8 F. J. McLynn, *France and the Jacobite Rising of 1745*, pp. 195, 234–5.

9 R. Whitworth, *Field-Marshal Lord Ligonier: A Story of the British Army, 1702–1770* (Oxford, 1958), p. 122.

ministers that the Austrians were not pulling their weight in the Netherlands, and that Britain was not being given full value in military terms for its subsidies, meant that the government in London now began to attach to such payments strict and detailed provisions about the numbers, location and state of readiness of the Austrian forces it was maintaining. The subsidy treaty signed at The Hague at the end of August 1746 by representatives of George II, Maria Theresa and the States-General, which provided for the sending of an additional 20,000 Austrian soldiers to the Netherlands, is a good case in point. It carefully specified the regiments which were to make up this force, while British officers were to have the right to inspect it to ensure that the full complement of men had in fact been provided, and any deficiency in this respect was to mean a proportionate reduction in what Britain paid.[10] A document such as this, essentially no more than a contract of employment, brings out well the lack of trust and absence of any sense of engagement in a true joint enterprise which now more than ever marked relations between the anti-French allies.

ITALY, 1746: D'ARGENSON'S PLANS AND THEIR RESULTS

In Italy the Austrians, in spite of their underlying rivalry with and distrust of Charles Emmanuel, did well in 1746. This was in large part the unintended work of the marquis d'Argenson. His idealism, in some ways far-sighted but in the short run completely impractical, had in Italy freer play and took a more radical form than anywhere else. He hoped for the formation of a federation of Italian states, a new Italy freed from all foreign influences. In it the Grand Duke Francis Stephen, since he was now Holy Roman Emperor, must hand over Tuscany to his brother Charles, while Austria's Italian possessions would be divided between Sardinia, which would acquire most of the Milanese, Don Philip, who would gain part of the Milanese with Parma and Piacenza, and Venice, which would take Mantua. The duke of Modena would recover his lost duchy, while Genoa acquired the whole Ligurian coast up to the French frontier. D'Argenson's policy, as he put it, was to 'concentrate the Italian powers within themselves (*concentrer les*

---

10 Text in A. F. P. Pribham, ed., *Österreichische Staatsverträge, England*, i, (Innsbruck, 1907), 727–9.

puissances italiques en elles-mêmes)'; and he insisted that the peninsula should develop its political life freely and not be under any outside tutelage. Foreign princes might reign over Italian states; but if they did they must become completely Italian in outlook. If they inherited thrones outside Italy they must abandon their Italian territories to some other ruler. This principle to him was fundamental.[11] More than any other French minister, moreover, he wanted good relations with Sardinia and its ruler. This expansionist state in northern Italy, he pointed out with some acuteness, had somewhat the same relationship to the Habsburgs in the peninsula as Prussia in Germany. It therefore deserved French support. Sardinia's territorial growth was not a threat to France, for 'we must have neighbours, and what can one do better than to strengthen the small ones at the expense of the greater ones?'[12] His ideas had no realistic chance of success: the Venetian representative in Paris thought they 'verged on the chimerical'.[13] They were little understood in Italy; and of the Italian states only Sardinia and Naples were strong enough to give any help in realising them. In Turin it was suspected that his federalist scheme might merely be camouflage for a French protectorate; and when the British minister there heard of it at the end of 1745 he feared that Louis XV might assume the title of emperor in Italy, thus making himself the equal in ceremonial terms of the Holy Roman Emperor.[14]

Most important of all, d'Argenson's ideas were quite impossible to reconcile with the ambitions of Elizabeth Farnese and Philip V; and he was deeply hostile both to these ambitions and to the queen herself. Spain, he complained, was 'restless, distrustful and jealous' where France was concerned. Elizabeth wanted to 'eat up Italy' and was irrationally hostile to any territorial gain whatever by Sardinia. The war in the peninsula 'costs us more than it does the Court of Vienna', while Spain gave France no help at all in the Netherlands and Germany, the areas which really mattered to it.[15] Such attitudes could only worsen the already very strained relations between the two Bourbon powers.

11 *Journal et mémoires du Marquis d'Argenson*, ed. E. J. B. Rathery, (Paris, 1859–67), iv, 269.

12 *Journal et mémoires*, iv, 278.

13 C. Baudi di Vesme, *La Pace di Aquisgrana* (1748) (Turin, 1969), p. 130.

14 C. Baudi di Vesme, *La Pace*, p. 126; Sir R. Lodge, *Studies in Eighteenth-century Diplomacy, 1740–8* (London, 1930), pp. 101–2.

15 Baudrillart, *Philippe V*, v, 303; *Journal et mémoires*, iv, 272–3; E. Zevort, *Le Marquis d'Argenson et le Ministère des Affaires Etrangères du 18 Novembre 1744 au 10 Janvier 1747* (Paris, 1880), p. 33.

In October 1745 secret talks began between Champeaux, the French resident in Geneva, and count Mongardino, the intendant of the extensive French estates of the Princes of Carignano, a junior branch of the Sardinian ruling house. In these Champeaux put forward d'Argenson's proposals for an Italian federation. It was also suggested that all the Italian rulers should agree to a declaration asserting their complete independence of all control by the Holy Roman Empire; that there should be some kind of Italian diet or parliament made up of representatives of the different states (the Holy Roman Empire, the Dutch Republic and the Swiss confederation were in d'Argenson's mind as examples here); and that there might be an embryonic Italian national army, to be commanded in wartime by the king of Sardinia.[16] It was clear from the outset that anything as far-reaching as this would not be acceptable in Turin, where it was argued that the open throwing off of all imperial authority in Italy, an authority which after all did not limit or threaten Sardinia in any way, would arouse unnecessary hostility in Germany. Moreover, the proposed strengthening of Genoa would make it more difficult for Savoy and Piedmont to have any secure outlet to the sea, one of the major ambitions of Charles Emmanuel in the war. A proposed free port at Villefranche was not seen as an adequate answer to this objection. Most important of all, if Habsburg influence were excluded from Italy this would open the way to a dangerous Bourbon predominance there.[17]

Nevertheless, the negotiations went on. On 26 December Champeaux and the marquis di Gorzegno, who had succeeded Ormea as Sardinian chief minister in June, signed a joint memorandum which somewhat modified the details of the proposed territorial settlement. Champeaux also agreed, without having any authority to do so, that in a continuing struggle with Maria Theresa France and Spain would give Charles Emmanuel subsidies equivalent to those he was receiving from Britain. In Paris it was decided to turn the memorandum into a formal treaty; but d'Argenson refused to agree to an armistice with Sardinia until a preliminary peace agreement had been signed. An armistice, however, was the essential immediate objective of Charles Emmanuel and his government. The fortress of Alessandria, which had been under siege by the French for some time, was almost certain to fall soon. The Sardinian

16 These proposals are discussed in detail in D. Carutti, *Storia della Diplomazia della Corte di Savoia* (4 vols, Turin, 1875–80), iv, 251–4.
17 Carutti, *Storia*, iv, 256–8.

ministers, Gorzegno, count Bogino, the War Minister, and the marquis di Breglio, agreed that news of an armistice must reach Turin by 20 February if Alessandria were to be saved; and Bogino persuaded the king to agree to military action against the French if this did not happen or if the negotiations were unduly prolonged. The attitude of the Sardinian government had now changed considerably. When the memorandum of 26 December was signed there had still seemed some prospect of the Jacobite rebellion succeeding, and Maria Theresa was apparently still deeply involved in her struggle with Frederick II. A few weeks later it was clear that the Jacobites would almost certainly be crushed and, much more important, that the empress was now able, after making peace with Prussia, to pour troops into Italy and greatly improve her military prospects there. Agreement with France had become correspondingly less necessary and less attractive.

On 17 February d'Argenson, after some hesitation, signed the armistice agreement (which included a provision for the immediate lifting of the blockade of Alessandria). But its publication was delayed until the comte de Maillebois, d'Argenson's son-in-law and the son of the Marshal de Maillebois, now the French commander in Italy, could be sent to Turin as a special emissary and agree with his father on the date when it could best be made public. The Foreign Minister had in fact already sent to the marshal a month earlier a letter urging him to remain inactive and do nothing against the Sardinian forces until peace had been made. What was needed, d'Argenson said, was 'a simple defensive attitude and tranquillity until a treaty has been signed'.[18] This, however well-intentioned, was a serious mistake. It gave Charles Emmanuel all the benefits of an armistice without any corresponding advantage to France. The comte de Maillebois, when he reached Sardinian territory in late February, made it clear that the publication of the armistice, for which the government in Turin was very anxious, could take place only on conditions. The blockade of Alessandria would now be lifted only to the extent of allowing a week's supply of food to reach the garrison at any one time; the duration of the armistice must be unlimited and not, as had at first been agreed, restricted to two months; and it must be made clear that it was a result of the agreement of 26 December, which would thus be given a more formal and public character. The discussion of these points, which

18 Zevort, *Le Marquis d'Argenson*, p. 291.

went on for several days, was not in itself very important.[19] The real significance of the protracted negotiations was that the Marshal de Maillebois, and the French army generally, now assumed that peace was imminent. Charles Emmanuel declared formally that if an armistice had not been concluded by 1 March he would consider himself free to act as he wished; but d'Argenson failed to pass on this very important information to the French commander. The Sardinians, who had always thought largely in terms merely of saving Alessandria, were still far from agreement on the content of an eventual peace treaty. They also saw clearly that it would be very difficult to persuade the Spanish government to agree to any peace terms acceptable in Turin, an important point to which d'Argenson had given little thought. They therefore took advantage of the situation to make a sudden attack on the French-held city of Asti. The garrison, nine battalions in all, was taken completely by surprise and surrendered almost without resistance during the night of 7–8 March. This meant the immediate abandonment of the siege of Alessandria; and on the night of 18–19 March the Spanish army evacuated Milan.

ITALY, 1746: FRANCO-SPANISH DISUNITY

The military setback was serious and humiliating. But more important was the effect of this complicated fiasco on Franco-Spanish relations. When news of the negotiations with Charles Emmanuel reached Don Philip and his advisers in Milan their immediate reaction was to assume that they had been betrayed and an agreement made behind their backs. The surrender at Asti seemed to them a deliberate act of treachery, one arranged by Marshal de Maillebois with the Sardinian government. There was even talk in the Spanish army of arresting him and disarming the French regiments in Italy.[20] Villettes, the British minister in Turin, reported on 19 March, with obvious pleasure, that 'as for our enemies, the jealousy, rancour, and animosity between them cannot be greater. The Spaniards at Milan, from the general down to the

---

19 A good deal has been written on these negotiations; detailed accounts can be found in Carutti, *Storia*, iv, 255ff.; Duc de Broglie, *Maurice de Saxe et le Marquis d'Argenson* (Paris, 1891), i, 118ff.; Zevort, *Le Marquis d'Argenson*, pp. 286–300; and S. Wilkinson, *The Defence of Piedmont, 1742–8: A Prelude to the Study of Napoleon* (Oxford, 1927), pp. 229–37.

20 Baudrillart, *Philippe V*, v, 384.

last private man, openly call the French traitors, and both their letters and their discourse make no scruple of saying they have bargained to sacrifice them to the Piedmontese and the Germans.'[21] In Madrid, also, feeling was very bitter, and with justification. In the original negotiations with Mongardino Champeaux had been authorised to make it clear that if Spain refused to agree to the terms of a Franco-Sardinian peace the French army would be recalled from Italy and Don Philip left to his own devices; d'Argenson repeated this threat in a despatch of 16 January to Vauréal. At the end of February he told the ambassador once more that it was time to restore peace to Europe and that 'they should not flatter themselves at Madrid that the King is willing to subordinate these great objectives to the unbridled ambition of the Queen of Spain'.[22] News of the attempt to make peace with Charles Emmanuel was greeted with fury in the Spanish capital.[23] Philip V was particularly angered by the way in which France had embarked on secret negotiations with a ruler he considered Spain's worst enemy and was now confronting him with a *fait accompli*. He also complained that France had broken the promises made in 1743 in the Treaty of Fontainebleau. The defeats Maria Theresa had suffered in both Germany and the Netherlands, he argued, coupled with the Jacobite rebellion, meant that the Bourbon powers were now in a stronger position than when that treaty had been signed; it was therefore quite wrong to claim, as d'Argenson was doing, that the objectives agreed to in 1743 were impossible to achieve.

Louis XV, after some momentary hesitation, insisted that the alliance with Spain must be preserved. He told d'Argenson that 'Spain must not be abandoned in Italy for anything in the world' and assured Don Philip, in a personal letter of 5 April, that 'Marshal Maillebois will act in all things in concert with you and by your orders . . . accordingly you can and must again place your confidence in him as you did before'. He followed this up by ordering the marshal to join the Spanish army with all the forces under his command, without being concerned primarily, as Maillebois wished, for the safety of his communications with France.[24] The king was now willing, in effect, to endanger his army in Italy in order to regain the confidence of Philip V and his

21 Lodge, *Studies*, pp. 118–19.
22 Baudrillart, *Philippe V*, v, 366.
23 Baudrillart, *Philippe V*, v, 349–53.
24 Wilkinson, *Defence*, pp. 248, 251.

formidable wife. On both sides there were diplomatic initiatives meant to heal, or at least paper over, the breach between the French and Spanish courts. As soon as he heard of the negotiations with Charles Emmanuel Philip V decided to send a special ambassador, the duke of Huescar, to Paris to make his resentment clear. On the French side the Marshal de Noailles, now more hostile than ever to the Foreign Minister (in conversation with Campo-Florido he spoke of 'that animal d'Argenson'), urged successfully that he be sent on a similar mission to Madrid to mend fences and rebuild trust there. Such was his anxiety for the task that he offered to forgo any salary and be content merely with the payment of his expenses (which were in the event considerable – about 100,000 francs).[25]

Noailles had some success in smoothing ruffled feelings in Madrid; indeed, even before his arrival it had been realised there that there were powerful forces in Paris hostile to d'Argenson and his ideas. But deep-rooted suspicions remained. The Franco-Dutch contacts in the spring of 1746[26] aroused fears that Noailles's mission might be intended to conceal a new French diplomatic initiative which would damage Spanish interests; and when he returned to Paris in June he came as the bearer of a secret memorandum which showed that the ambitions of Philip and his wife were still as great as ever. Parma and Piacenza must go to Elizabeth Farnese for her lifetime; this demand, said Philip, he would never withdraw. Don Philip might give up his claim to Milan and Mantua, even though these had been promised him in the Treaty of Fontainebleau. But he must none the less have a substantial Italian principality, not merely because of the justice of his claims but for reasons of dynastic pride, to 'maintain the greatness of his birth' and ensure that he could never be looked down upon as a negligible minor ruler. He should be given a subsidy, paid in equal shares by France and Spain, to help him fortify the territories he was given; and they should also supply him with troops to garrison these fortresses. Finally, the French government should promise that if in the future Spain failed to fulfill its share of these arrangements France would itself, if necessary, assume the entire burden of them. This remarkable proposal was clearly meant to guard against the now imminent death of Philip V: it was known that his successor,

---

25 *Receuil des Instructions, données aux Ambassadeurs et Ministres de France des Traités de Westphalie jusqu'à la Révolution Française*, xxvii (Paris, 1960), 30; Zevort, *Le Marquis d'Argenson*, p. 16.

26 See below, p. 194.

the Infant Don Ferdinand, his son by his first wife, was unlikely to give strong support to the claims of his half-brother Don Philip. These very one-sided arrangements, it was claimed, would be as advantageous to France as to Spain, since they would make Louis XV 'the arbiter of all Italy'.[27] Quite clearly, Spanish pride and intractability remained a major obstacle to any general peace. Franco-Spanish relations were strained yet again during the summer of 1746 when Louis XV refused to agree to the remarriage of the dauphin with the Infanta Antonia, the sister of his recently dead wife. His conscientious scruples about allowing his son to enter into a union which was at least technically incestuous were genuine; though a papal dispensation to permit the marriage could certainly have been obtained without difficulty. Nevertheless, Philip V, who had strongly urged the marriage, had some justification for feeling that Louis's attitude weakened the Bourbon alliance. D'Argenson, true to his anti-Spanish attitude, hoped, though in vain, for the marriage of the dauphin to Princess Marie-Thérèse of Savoy; this, he thought, might pave the way to a peace settlement on moderate terms with Charles Emmanuel. In the event the dauphin married the daughter of Augustus of Saxony; but yet again a damaging divergence between French and Spanish attitudes had been displayed.

D'Argenson's ill-judged efforts at a settlement with Charles Emmanuel were not, however, totally fruitless. If they envenomed Franco-Spanish relations they also strained still further the already very difficult ones between Maria Theresa and the king of Sardinia. Charles Emmanuel had, after all, been privy to negotiations which envisaged the complete destruction of Habsburg power in Italy. This inevitably deepened Maria Theresa's distrust and sense of grievance where he was concerned. She had bitterly resented the concessions to him made at Worms; and she now felt strongly that his conduct in negotiating secretly with her enemy deprived him of any right to benefit in the way promised in that treaty. The loss of Silesia was a heavy enough blow in itself; but that in addition so treacherous an ostensible ally should take yet more territory from her in Italy seemed to her outrageous. In this attitude she was supported particularly by Bartenstein, pugnacious as ever in defending the interests of his mistress. The efforts of Robinson to persuade the empress to satisfy Don Philip in Italy and at the same time observe all the terms of the Treaty of Worms, he felt, showed that Britain

27 *Receuil des Instructions*, xxvii, 36–40.

aimed at 'the complete humiliation (*gänzliche Erniedrigung*)' of the house of Habsburg.[28] This deep-seated resentment and sense of injury was to underly the whole Austrian attitude in the final peacemaking.[29]

ITALY, 1746–8: THE INVASION OF PROVENCE, THE REVOLT OF GENOA, FINAL STALEMATE

In spite of these deep differences the course of the war in Italy ran strongly for the Austro-Sardinian alliance in 1746. The Gallispans were badly beaten on 16 June at Piacenza. This was the first time during the war that an Austrian army had defeated a French one in a pitched battle, and the victory was correspondingly gratifying to Maria Theresa. The officer bearing the official despatch with news of the battle made his entry into Vienna in a carriage drawn by twelve horses, amid the acclamations of the crowd. The defeat might well have had serious results for the French and Spaniards, who were extricated from a difficult position largely by the professional skill of Maillebois. Moreover, the death of Philip V a week or two later, on 9 July, temporarily immobilised the Spanish forces. Don Philip and his officers were unwilling to make any significant move until they had fresh instructions from the new king, Ferdinand VI; and it was soon clear that there was now, as indeed everyone had expected, a new attitude in Madrid. Ferdinand, in his first letter as king to Don Philip, suggested negotiations with Charles Emmanuel, something Philip V and his wife had always sought to avoid; but the king of Sardinia was unwilling to talk of peace at a moment when he and his ally were so successful.

However, that success was limited once more by the disunity which marked the Austro-Sardinian war effort almost, if not quite, as much as the Franco-Spanish one. The victory at Piacenza was not exploited as it might have been because of disagreements between Charles Emmanuel and the new Austrian commander, the marquis Botta d'Adorno (Maria Theresa's minister in Berlin at the time of the invasion of Silesia). The king wanted to force the Gallispans to withdraw to the north or east, if necessary into the duchy of Milan, and thus spare his own territory the exactions which would be levied by the retreating enemy. For the same reason Botta wished to

28 A. von Arneth, *Geschichte Maria Theresias* (10 vols, Vienna, 1863–79), iii, 190.
29 See below, pp. 204–5.

drive them west, into Piedmont, and thus spare his mistress's lands this burden. Also, an important point, to drive the Gallispans into the north-west corner of Italy would leave open the road south to Naples, the conquest of which was still a main objective of the empress. In fact, the French and Spaniards retreated westwards, through Tortona to Nice. Once more their operations were hindered by disagreements between rival generals. Maillebois found it impossible to work with the new Spanish commander, La Mina, who was stubborn and difficult to deal with even by the standards of Spanish generals, and asked to be relieved of his command. Yet again, however, the position of the Bourbon forces was made easier by the divisions of their opponents, in this case over the port of Savona, of which both the Austrians and the Sardinians hoped to take possession.

The Franco-Spanish retreat opened the prospect of a successful invasion of Provence; for the only time during the entire war apart from the summer of 1744 France's own territory was now under serious threat. Also it was a threat which it might have to meet with little assistance from its Spanish ally. At the end of the year La Mina refused to help the Marshal de Belleisle, who had now replaced Maillebois, resist the impending invasion: this drew bitter complaints to Paris from the French commander. In the first days of 1747, with the county of Nice lost, the line of the river Var forced, and Antibes under siege, there was real fear in Provence of what the enemy might achieve. The still numerous Protestants of the province seized the opportunity to complain of the religious discrimination from which they continued to suffer, while there were rumours of British agents inciting them to rebel.[30] More immediately, the Austrians won a very important success when they captured the great port of Genoa early in September 1746. The Genoese Republic had signed an alliance with France and Naples at Aranjuez on 1 May 1745 and agreed to support them with an auxiliary force of 10,000 men. As a point of entry for Spanish forces coming to Italy by sea, Genoa had always great potential importance; but fighting spirit there after the French and Spanish retreat was notable by its absence. Though the city was well fortified and had a garrison of 10,000 men (2,000 of them, according to the French consul, deserters from the Austrian army), it surrendered to Botta without resistance.

---

30 Broglie, *Maurice de Saxe et le Marquis d'Argenson*, ii, 124–5.

But lack of moderation and common sense meant that this great achievement was quickly thrown away. Botta was himself Genoese, but the son of a nobleman who had been condemned to death and gone into exile in 1689 for an act of tyranny committed against one of the republic's dependent territories. This, coupled with his own autocratic temperament, meant that very severe terms were imposed on the city when it surrendered. They were also drawn up without consultation with either the Sardinians or the British, which provoked protests from Charles Emmanuel both to Botta himself and to Vienna. Once more the crippling lack of real cooperation between the different anti-Bourbon forces was exposed. The gates of the city and all strong points in its surrounding territory were to be handed over to the Austrians; a very large indemnity was to be paid to them; and the doge and six senators were to go from Genoa to Vienna within two months to seek ratification of these terms and to remain there as hostages for the full performance of any others Maria Theresa might prescribe. A first instalment of the indemnity of 9 million livres within five days was demanded and paid; and by the end of November almost another 9 million had been handed over. This did not prevent the Austrians making new and heavy financial demands in an ultimatum of 30 November; and a few days later, on 5 December, a spontaneous popular revolt against the occupiers broke out. It was provoked by the attempt of the Austrians to collect and remove from the city artillery needed for the siege of Antibes, and after a few days of confusion was successful, helped by the fact that the Genoese garrison had not been disarmed and had been left in control of much of the fortifications. By 10 December Botta had been driven from the city.[31]

This was one of the decisive events of the Austrian Succession war. An invasion of Provence had always been a favourite strategy of the British government. As in 1707 during the war of the Spanish Succession, it was hoped that the capture of Toulon might cut off at its roots French naval power in the Mediterranean. But neither Maria Theresa nor Charles Emmanuel shared this enthusiasm.

31 For an account of the rising see G-E. Broche, *La République de Gênes et la France pendant la Guerre de la Succession d'Autriche, 1740–1748* (Paris, 1935), iii, 9ff.; E. Pandiani, *La cacciata degli Austriaci da Genova nell'anno 1746* (Turin, 1923); and F. Venturi, 'Genova a metà del Settecento', *Rivista Storica Italiana*, 79 (1967), 732–5. The last of these brings out well the acute social tensions within the city and the hostility to the ruling patrician group which played an important role in the revolt.

Though in January 1747 they agreed, in return for British subsidies and the provision of a substantial British naval squadron, to supply large forces (60,000 men from Austria, half as many from Sardinia) for use in France, this had not the results which were hoped for in London. Neither stood to gain much even if the invasion were a success. The empress still saw Naples as the most alluring of the territorial gains for which she might hope, while Charles Emmanuel disliked the possible weakening of the defences of his own territories if he provided a large army to invade southern France. The loss of Genoa, and the resulting threat to the communications of the Austrian and Sardinian armies with their bases in Italy, destroyed any hope of success in Provence. The Austrians were now committed to a long and ultimately unsuccessful siege of the city, which played an important role in much of the fighting of 1747 in Italy. The successful defence was made possible largely by French and Spanish help: 3,000 French soldiers arrived in March 1747 to reinforce the garrison, and others followed in spite of the generally unsuccessful efforts of the British navy to intercept them. The Austrians on their side obtained, by an agreement of 3 March, a promise of substantial Sardinian help in the siege – twelve regular battalions, 1,500 militia and a train of artillery – but none the less made little progress.[32] The besieging forces were unenterprising and inefficient. As the siege dragged on, the British minister in Florence complained in June of the 'tedious and neglectful' conduct of the Austrians; of 500 carriages for their artillery sent from Milan only eighty had been found usable. Nor did Austria's relations with its allies in Italy improve. To Maria Theresa the regaining of Naples, in which the British had little interest and which Charles Emmanuel was likely to oppose, remained as always the ultimate objective. The same diplomat reported a month later that 'The Austrians abuse us vastly for having prevented them making that conquest instead of going to ruin their army in Provence, which, and all their misfortunes after, they attribute to us.'[33]

In Paris there was a good deal of hesitation as to the wisdom of making sacrifices to help the Genoese. D'Argenson, until his fall from office in January 1747, remained very pessimistic about the whole Italian situation; and his successor as foreign minister, the marquis de Puysieulx, was little more enthusiastic. There was a

---

32 For an account of the siege, see Broche, *La République de Gênes et la France*, iii, chap. I.

33 *The Yale Edition of Horace Walpole's Correspondence*, xix (Oxford–New Haven, Conn., 1955), 406, 423.

feeling, largely justified, that the Genoese patriciate, the rulers of the republic, were unreliable allies. Many French soldiers wished to concentrate the country's military energies on the Netherlands, where France was beginning to enjoy a tradition of success, rather than on Italy, the scene of so many disappointments.[34] In Madrid on the other hand, though interest in Italian affairs in general was rapidly declining, it was argued that national honour demanded an effort to relieve Genoa; and this helped to produce still more friction between the Bourbon armies in the peninsula. In the campaigning of 1747 Belleisle wished to raise the siege by an invasion of Piedmont which would pose a clear threat to Turin and force Charles Emmanuel to concentrate his forces on the defence of his capital. La Mina, on the other hand, insisted on a direct advance on Genoa along the Ligurian coast; and heavy political pressure through the duke of Huescar, who had now replaced Campo-Florido as Spanish ambassador in Paris, forced the French to give way.

They did so with a bad grace. The comte d'Argenson, still War Minister after the fall of his brother, complained bitterly of the obstinacy of the Spaniards 'of which I can understand neither the motives nor the objective', and said that in his discussions with Huescar 'the patience of angels would have given way'.[35] When, in July, the French did attempt an advance into Piedmont through difficult mountainous country, they were very badly defeated on the ridge of the Assietta. A frontal attack on an almost impregnable Piemontese position was beaten back with heavy losses; and the French commander, the chevalier de Belleisle, the younger brother of the marshal, was killed. This was one of the most complete military victories of the war; but its strategic and political results were slight. In Vienna Bartenstein, still full of fighting spirit, suggested a renewed attack on Genoa; and the new Austrian commander, General Browne, was authorised to try once more to retake the city. But any plan of this kind was made impractical by the continuing absence of any effective cooperation with the Sardinians. The British government for its part, as the tide of French success in the Netherlands continued to flow,[36] pressed for another invasion of Provence which might force diversion of French strength away from Flanders and Brabant. Maria Theresa, though she would have preferred to retake Genoa and then invade the kingdom of Naples,

34 Baudi di Vesme, *La Pace*, pp. 159–60.
35 Wilkinson, *Defence*, p. 267.
36 See below, pp. 172–4.

agreed to such a move; but growing exhaustion and war-weariness in her territories were now making it difficult for her to play a decisive role of any kind. By January 1748 the pay of Austrian officers serving in Italy was seven months in arrears, and some of them were selling their clothes to live.[37]

Dissensions between Austrians and Sardinians remained as acute as ever as the war slowly ground to a close. In the last weeks of 1747 and the first ones of 1748 more than two months of haggling in London and The Hague over the details of the respective allied contributions to the war was complicated by long arguments as to whether Charles Emmanuel should have the supreme command in Italy, as he claimed, even though his military effort there was only about half that made by Maria Theresa. It was finally agreed that he should be supreme commander in operations where he was present in person; but as the end of the war approached disputes of this kind were ceasing to have much practical significance. A last French victory at Voltri in February 1748 meant the final abandonment of any idea of recapturing Genoa (the fruitless siege had ended in effect in June of the previous year), and the end of the war in Italy, after so much effort on both sides, in stalemate.

THE NETHERLANDS, 1747–8: FRENCH SUCCESS AND DUTCH COLLAPSE

Italian frustrations and setbacks were more than counterbalanced, from the French standpoint, by success in the Netherlands. At the beginning of 1747 Saxe was given the rank of *maréchal-général des camps et armées*, one which had in the past been held only by Turenne, the greatest French commander of the seventeenth century, and in the last months of his life by Marshal Villars. Resistance to the powerful French army he commanded continued to the end of the war to be hampered, as it had been from the beginning, by disagreements between the allies and most of all by the growing weakness and lack of fighting spirit of the Dutch Republic. A convention of 12 January 1747, signed at The Hague, specified in detail the forces to be provided by the British, Austrians and Dutch for the defence of the Netherlands;[38] but it was symptomatic of the situation that the States-General pressed for the agreement to take,

---

37 C. Duffy, *The Wild Goose and the Eagle: A Life of Marshal von Browne, 1705–1757* (London, 1964), p. 175.
38 Text in *Österreichische Staatsverträge; England*, i, 736–51.

so far as they were concerned, as informal a shape as possible. It was hoped that the allies could now assemble forces of unprecedented strength, 180,000 men or more; yet the summer's campaigning was even more disastrous than that of the previous two years. Saxe had now been given permission to act directly against the Dutch by invading their territory. This was something he had wanted to do a year earlier, after his victory at Rocoux; but d'Argenson's moderation and hopes of an early peace[39] had stood in the way. Even now, the permission was given in rather half-hearted and ambiguous terms.[40] But its effects were swift and dramatic.

The opening weeks of the campaign of 1747 saw much of Dutch Flanders overrun by the French: the republic seemed in greater danger than at any time since the crisis year of 1672, when the armies of Louis XIV had threatened its complete conquest. The reaction was similar to that three-quarters of a century earlier. Imminent danger, coupled with the humiliating ineffectiveness of the Dutch defences, produced a violent popular reaction against the republican regime which, pacific and cautious, dominated by the merchant interests of the province of Holland and particularly of Amsterdam, had ruled for a generation or more. Popular Orangist feeling, centred on the landward provinces and relatively pro-British, was now in the ascendant; and demands for the restoration of the stadtholderate were becoming irresistible. The States-General, faced by the growing menace of an Orangist seizure of power, even in desperation thought for a moment of offering the office of stadtholder to Frederick II; but he inevitably and wisely refused to have anything to do with the idea which, he pointed out, meant embroiling himself with both Britain and France.[41] As the French threat loomed nearer, a popular rising broke out, first in the port of Veere and spreading thence through Zeeland and then to Rotterdam and the province of Holland itself. By the end of the first week in May, with Orangist flags flying from state buildings in The Hague, William IV of Orange had been made stadtholder of most of the provinces and voted captain-general and admiral of the Dutch · forces. He entered The Hague in triumph on 15 May. For the moment at least the victory of Orangist and monarchist influences was complete.

39 See above, p. 150.
40 Broglie, *Maurice de Saxe et le Marquis d'Argenson*, ii, 177–9.
41 *Pol. Corr.*, v, 395.

It was a victory for British influences in the Dutch Republic and a defeat for the neutralist or pro-French ones which the great commercial interests of Amsterdam represented. It also owed a good deal to British encouragement: the prompt sending of a British squadron to the Scheldt to protect the revolt in Zeeland played a significant role in the Orangist success. The duke of Newcastle based high hopes on the restoration of the stadtholderate. He told the duke of Bedford, the First Lord of the Admiralty, at the beginning of May that 'by it, in all probability, the republic of Holland will recover its ancient weight and strength, and England will have a useful friend and ally instead of a jealous, timid, and burthensome neighbour'.[42] So strong was anti-French feeling now in the Dutch provinces that Chiquet, the unofficial French agent in The Hague, was for a time afraid to leave his house and feared it might be attacked at any moment.[43] The military effects of the revolution, however, were negligible: the hopes it had inspired in London very soon proved quite unfounded. In July Saxe once again defeated the allied army, now once more commanded by the duke of Cumberland, at Laufeldt. It was by no means an overwhelming victory; and the French losses may well have been greater than those of the allies.[44] Saxe did not follow it up energetically, which aroused suspicions in Paris (as had already happened after his success at Rocoux) that he wished to prolong a war which had so much strengthened his own prestige and influence. Also, Cumberland was able after the battle to prevent any attack on the great fortress of Maastricht, which had been Saxe's original objective.

None the less, the initiative remained completely with the French. On 16 September they took by storm Bergen-op-Zoom, the key fortress of Dutch Brabant, amidst the worst scenes of pillage and destruction of the entire war in the Netherlands. Its fortifications were strong: the pathetically weak defence offered by its garrison therefore reinforced the very low estimate of Dutch fighting spirit long held by the British and Austrians. Already at the end of July Cumberland had told Lord Chesterfield, the Secretary of State for the Northern Department, that 'I am convinced every day of the melancholy consideration that we must actually reckon on the

42 *The Correspondence of John, Fourth Duke of Bedford* (London, 1842–6), i, 210.

43 Broglie, *Maurice de Saxe et le Marquis d'Argenson*, ii, 195.

44 Hon. E. Charteris, *William Augustus, Duke of Cumberland, His Early Life and Times (1721–1748)* (London, 1913), p. 318; cf. J-P. Bois, *Maurice de Saxe* (Paris, 1992), pp. 402–5.

Dutch troops as *nothing*'; and his secretary dismissed the Dutch commander at Bergen-op-Zoom as 'that wretched doating animal who was trusted with the defence of this most important fortress'.[45] (The officer in question, General Cronstrom, had the excuse that he was then eighty-six years old.) The atrocities which accompanied the capture of Bergen, a scene of which one French officer said 'far from depicting it, I want to forget it for ever'[46] did indeed stimulate a new burst of furious anti-French feeling in the Dutch provinces; and William IV issued a proclamation promising that he would lead his army in person. But all this again had no military value. By the autumn of 1747, when active campaigning ended for the year, the situation of the allies seemed very serious. French military superiority was more threatening then ever. Maria Theresa was near the end of her resources and increasingly dependent on British subsidies. Worst of all, the Dutch were close to collapse: and if Saxe overran the Dutch maritime provinces Britain itself would be in danger. 'Holland seems gone', wrote Horace Walpole in October, 'how long England will remain after it, Providence and the French must determine.'[47]

From this situation there appeared, if the struggle were to be continued, to be only one escape. Russia, the greatest reservoir of military manpower in Europe, might be brought into play. A large Russian force, obtained by spending yet more British money, might still turn the tide. The idea of some agreement of this kind had already been put forward more than once by Bestuzhev: if it could be made it would provide the Russian government with the money it was in continual need of, and at the same time gratify his and Elizabeth's deep, and in the case of the empress growing, hostility to Frederick II.[48] Already in November 1746 Lord Hyndford, now British ambassador in St Petersburg, had been ordered to open negotiations for 30,000 Russian auxiliaries for use in western Europe: Bestuzhev was to be offered a 'loan' of £10,000 as an

---

45 Charteris, *William Augustus, Duke of Cumberland*, pp. 332, 333fn. For similar comments from a British officer in the field, see 'Military Memoirs of Lieut.-General the Hon. Charles Colville', ed. J. O. Robson, *Journal of the Society for Army Historical Research*, xxviii (1950), 6–7.

46 R. Butler, *Choiseul, i, Father and Son, 1719–1754* (Oxford, 1980), p. 707.

47 *The Yale Edition of Horace Walpole's Correspondence*, xix, 442.

48 W. Mediger, *Moskaus Weg nach Europa: Der Aufstieg Russlands zum europäischen Machtstaat im Zeitalter Friedrichs des Grossen* (Braunschweig, 1952), p. 299.

inducement to press for such an arrangement.[49] By January of the following year, however, there had been a change of plan in London. Instead of using this force in the Netherlands, where it could not arrive until the campaign was at least half over, it had now been decided to ask for 'a sufficient body' of Russian troops, paid for by Britain, to be held in readiness in Livonia and Courland. There they could frighten Frederick II into remaining neutral and prevent his launching any further attack on Bohemia or Hanover. A convention to this effect was signed in the Russian capital on 23 June 1747. In return for a payment of £100,000 Russia agreed to keep 30,000 men in readiness in Livonia and to provide forty or fifty galleys for use in the Baltic if necessary.

Six weeks later, as the situation in the Netherlands worsened, Hyndford was instructed to go a step further. A second force of 30,000 was now asked for; and this was to be used either in the Netherlands or on the Rhine, a scheme which had the active support of William IV.[50] These new negotiations dragged on for longer than had been hoped in London. The Russian College of Foreign Affairs irritated Hyndford by the slowness with which it handled business; and the Dutch, who were to share the cost, were dilatory in sending Swartz, their minister in St Petersburg, full powers to sign such an agreement. A second convention was, however, signed on 30 November 1747. Russia was to provide a second force of 30,000 men for two years in return for an annual subsidy of £300,000 paid at four-monthly intervals in advance.[51] But too much time had been lost. Hyndford pressed for the Russians to begin their march to the west at once; but he had to admit that even if this happened the French army would be in the field for three months in 1748 before these auxiliaries could be brought into play. There was also protracted argument about payment for their subsistence while they were on the march, so that an exasperated Chesterfield told Hyndford in January 1748 that dealing with the Russian ministers 'cannot any longer be called negociating with your court, but treating in effect with usurers and extortioners'.[52]

---

49 *Sbornik Imperatorskogo Russkogo Istoricheskogo Obshchestva*, ciii (St Petersburg, 1897), 120.

50 *Sbornik*, ciii, 346–8; *Archives ou Correspondance inédite de la Maison d'Orange-Nassau*, 4th ser., i, ed. Th. Bussemaker (Leyden, 1908), 40–1.

51 The texts of the Anglo-Russian agreements of 1747 can be found in Martens, *Receuil*, ix, 147–65.

52 *Sbornik*, ciii, 509.

The advance of the Russians across Poland *en route* to the Netherlands was painfully slow (3 miles a day in flat country and 2 in hilly, with a rest every third day, according to General Mordaunt, the British military commissary who accompanied them).[53] Their appearance as a new factor in the war nevertheless aroused considerable uneasiness in more than one quarter. In Poland a number of anti-Russian nobles drew up a protest against their infringement of the republic's territory and neutrality, though in the event few dared to sign it. The French government tried to slow their movements still further by making it difficult for them to obtain supplies of food in the areas through which they marched. In Germany there was discussion of the possible creation of a league of neutrality to oppose their passage; but this foundered on the refusal of Frederick II to play any part in the scheme.[54] The convention signed at The Hague on 26 January 1748 by representatives of George II, Maria Theresa, Charles Emmanuel and William IV[55] envisaged the Russians as forming part of a huge allied force of 192,000 men in the Netherlands; but long before they could be brought into play there events had forced the hand of the British government and serious peace negotiations were under way.

It was the exhaustion and demoralisation of the Dutch which made it almost impossible for Britain to continue the war. Charles Bentinck, when he was sent to England as representative of William IV at the end of February, was given instructions which showed clearly how difficult it would be to go on fighting. He was to stress very heavily the extreme danger in which the Dutch provinces now stood. It was unlikely that the coming campaign would be favourable to the allies. The season would be well advanced before the arrival of the Russians could give them a numerical superiority. Their preparations were tardy and inadequate: in particular, the magazines of supplies around Maastricht for the British contingent were not ready. Most serious of all, the financial position of the Dutch was now so bad that they must have a British loan of £1,100,000–1,300,000 if they were to go on fighting at all.[56] Henry Pelham, the First Lord of the Treasury and effective head of the government, who had for long been complaining loudly of the prodigal expenditure to little effect of British money on the continent,

53 Charteris, *William Augustus, Duke of Cumberland*, p. 341fn.
54 *Pol. Corr.*, vi, 5, 9.
55 Text in *Österreichische Staatsverträge; England*, i, 759–68.
56 *Archives ... de la Maison d'Orange-Nassau*, 4th ser., i, 152–5.

had no doubt that this was impossible. Quite apart from any other consideration, Parliament would never sanction such a loan. No other minister, not even Newcastle who had for months been the most determined to continue the struggle, seriously disagreed with this reading of the situation. By the early months of 1748 it was clearly impossible to put any reliance on the Dutch. Henry Legge, on his way to Berlin as British minister in an effort to mend fences with Frederick II, reported in scathing terms that they had no idea how many troops they had available, 'not that their numbers exceed all Arithmetick, but because they really don't know where they are, or whether they have any at all'.[57] Yet, if the Dutch were driven out of the war, it was impossible for Britain to fight effectively, or indeed at all, in Europe. Peace must be made. The tentative and complex negotiations which had been intermittently in progress for many months were now at last to bear fruit.

---

57 Quoted in N. A. M. Rodger, *The Insatiable Earl: A Life of John Montague, Fourth Earl of Sandwich, 1718–1792* (London, 1993), p. 49.

8 THE NAVAL AND COLONIAL STRUGGLE

THE NAVIES AND THEIR WORK

The war between Britain and Spain at sea and in America which broke out at the end of 1739, and in which from the beginning France seemed destined to play a leading role, found none of these three powers adequately prepared for it. All, most of all Britain, had powerful navies. In Spain José Patiño, during his long period as Intendant-General of Marine (1717–36), had presided over a remarkable rebirth of naval strength, the revival of a fleet which had virtually ceased to exist during the first years of the century. Organisation had been reformed, often on French models; many out-of-date practices had been swept away; a new naval base had been created at Ferrol. By 1737 the Spanish fleet was a respectable force of twenty-nine ships of the line (in effect those mounting fifty guns or more), eleven frigates and a number of smaller vessels; and by 1746, when there were thirty-two of the line, it had even grown somewhat in spite of wartime losses.[1] In France, where also the early eighteenth century had seen a marked though less catastrophic decline in naval strength, there had been a comparable revival: in 1739 it had about fifty ships of the line. Britain, with 124 such vessels, had on paper a comfortable margin of superiority over the Bourbon powers even if they were able to combine effectively against it; but of this imposing total forty-four were unfit for service and only thirty-five ready for immediate use.[2]

Navies, in the eyes of most contemporaries, did not exist primarily to fight battles at sea. They were needed instead partly to protect the movement of armies across stretches of water where they

---

1 C. Fernandez Duro, *Armada Española desde la unión de Castilla y Aragon* (Madrid, 1895–1903), vi, 210–25, 382.

2 Sir H. W. Richmond, *The Navy in the War of 1739–48* (3 vols, Cambridge, 1920), i, 14.

were exposed to enemy attack, as with the Spanish landings in Italy in 1741–2 or the projected French invasion of England in 1744 and 1746.[3] Most clearly of all, however, to the majority of observers, their function was to defend in time of war the seaborne trade of the states which maintained them. This feeling was strong in all the major maritime powers. In Britain it was seriously proposed in 1742 to earmark a number of ships exclusively for the protection of trade in the seas between England and Cape Finisterre, the area in which French and Spanish privateers were most active. These would be available for other duties only in case of 'great necessity' and even then not beyond Cape Finisterre; and a special commissioner was to superintend everything that concerned them. Such a scheme, which looked back to precedents in 1695 and 1708 during earlier struggles with France, would have created a kind of secondary and independent navy devoted entirely to commerce protection. It had no result; but throughout the war the pressure of merchant interests for every possible protection to be given to British trade was a factor which no government could ignore. Colonial governors also, both in the West Indies and North America, constantly pressed for the allocation of more ships to trade protection in their own areas. Sometimes they had considerable success. In 1745, when the Jamaica and Leeward Islands squadron was briefly outnumbered by the combined strength of the French at Martinique and the Spaniards at Havana, both the Mediterranean and Channel squadrons were weakened in order to reinforce it. In France such preoccupations were at least equally strong. During the war of 1744–8 with Britain the French government limited its naval effort in the West Indies, the most commercially valuable of all the areas of European imperial expansion, almost completely to the defence of trade: except for two small forces in 1745 it sent no naval expedition of any significance to the Caribbean. It even adopted a systematic policy of hiring warships to French merchants trading with the West Indies for the protection of the convoys which went there, receiving in payment a percentage of the value of the cargoes these ships escorted safely back to France.[4]

---

3 See above, pp. 77, 99, 131 and 156–7.
4 Richmond, *The Navy*, ii, 193.

THE WEST INDIES AND NORTH AMERICA

After the disastrous initial British efforts of 1740–2,[5] the West Indies saw relatively little large-scale fighting. The high proportion of the country's naval strength concentrated in the Caribbean by 1741 was never again approached during the war. Frederick II's attack on Silesia and all the ambitions and complications it unleashed forced both Britain and Spain to focus their attention and resources much nearer home; as a leading British minister remarked in August 1741, 'now America must be fought for in Europe', and the Caribbean became a secondary and peripheral theatre of conflict. British attacks on La Guayra and Puerto Cabello, on the coast of what is now Venezuela, in February–March 1743 were a complete failure; and the years which followed saw only a few small-scale and indecisive naval actions. An attack on Santiago in Cuba in March 1748 was also fruitless, while a little battle off Havana on 1 October of the same year, in which a British squadron had some success against a Spanish one, took place only after peace had been made though before news of it had crossed the Atlantic. In the Anglo-French war of 1744–8 neither belligerent, particularly perhaps the British, really wanted to gain new possessions in the Caribbean. On both sides there was a fear that to do so would lower the price of sugar and thus the profits of vocal and influential sugar-planters; and in Paris the prospect of newly acquired territories attracting settlers and resources away from France's existing colonies was an unwelcome one.[6]

Britain faced considerable difficulties in the West Indies. In particular, as almost always in the eighteenth century, it found it very hard to keep up to strength its ships' crews and its regiments there, because of the ravages of disease and the extreme unpopularity of service in the area. Soldiers or sailors sent to the islands 'were often more prepared to risk punishment for desertion, than to wait for death from yellow fever'; and losses by death and desertion could be truly crippling. In 1741 in one small ship 94 per cent of its rated complement (98 out of 110) deserted. This was a quite exceptional case; but in the same year at least eighteen others lost 30 per cent or more of their crews by death and disease.[7]

---

5 See above, pp. 18–19.

6 On these issues, see R. Pares, *War and Trade in the West Indies, 1739–1763* (Oxford, 1936), chap. v.

7 D. Crewe, *Yellow Jack and the Worm: British Naval Administration in the West Indies, 1739–1748* (Liverpool, 1993), pp. 63, 75.

Sometimes quite extreme measures had to be used. In July 1746, 250 Jacobite prisoners captured after the crushing of the 1745 rebellion were shipped to Antigua to strengthen a regiment there, while 100 others were sent in the same way to Jamaica.[8]

Yet if the government in London had pursued a more consistently aggressive policy in the area Britain might well have made significant territorial gains. The French islands, especially small ones such as Guadeloupe and Grenada with economies geared entirely to the production of sugar for export, were very vulnerable to blockade and often critically short of food. Sometimes they had only a few weeks' supply in hand; and during the last months of the war, when there was serious scarcity in France itself because of a bad harvest, their position was often desperate. Slaves, essential to their economy, were also in very short supply: during the last three years of hostilities only 149 reached Saint Domingue (the present-day Haiti), the largest and richest French possession in the Caribbean, and the French slave trade was completely destroyed by the war.[9] Colonial governors sometimes feared revolt in the French islands because of shortages there and discontent over the government's failure adequately to protect their trade. A number of devices were used to keep them supplied and some of their commercial life in existence. There was much smuggling. Exchanges of prisoners under flags of truce were used by both sides to cover trading with the enemy. Both French and British ships sometimes traded under neutral colours; and Dutch vessels (because until April 1747 the United Netherlands were not formally at war with France) reaped a rich harvest by supplying the French islands. In 1745, when only a single ship from France reached Guadeloupe, 168 from the Dutch island of St Eustatius touched there.[10] Not surprisingly, these subterfuges generated throughout the war, particularly on the British side, much friction between naval commanders intent on cutting off trade with the enemy and colonial leaders, law officers and even governors as well as merchants, who were ready to wink at and even support activities of this kind.

In North America the situation was different. There, a generation or more earlier had already been seen the first real effort by either of the great west European colonial rivals to translate their

8 J. A. Houlding, *Fit for Service: The Training of the British Army, 1715–1795* (Oxford, 1982), p. 13fn.

9 C. Baudi di Vesme, *La Pace di Aquisgrana (1748)* (Turin, 1969), p. 259; Pares, *War and Trade*, p. 390.

10 Pares, *War and Trade*, chap. ix.

antagonism into significant military action in another continent, when in 1711 Britain made an unsuccessful effort to take the French stronghold of Quebec. The war of 1744–8 in this area, however, centred on the capture in June 1745 by a force of New England (mainly Massachusetts) militia, supported by a British naval squadron, of the great French fortress of Louisbourg on Cape Breton island in the Gulf of St Lawrence.[11] There were good reasons why the New Englanders should wish to take it. Founded in 1720, Louisbourg was a base for French privateering against the British cod fisheries off Newfoundland and the trade of the New England colonies in general. This made them willing to contribute to the substantial effort involved in its capture; and William Shirley, the able governor of Massachusetts who was the main driving force behind the enterprise, saw its fall as a step towards the conquest of all French Canada. More important politically was the impression the victory made in Britain. There a public opinion distrustful of commitments in Europe, hostile to Hanover and its alleged influence on British policies, and disillusioned with an expensive and intractable Austrian ally, reacted enthusiastically to the first real British success since the beginning of the struggle with France. 'The surrender of Cape Breton has put our merchants in high spirits', wrote one observer, '. . . being the best managed expedition of any that has been undertaken during the whole course of the war.' After the victory Shirley was given the rank of colonel; William Pepperell, the New England merchant who had led the American militiamen, was knighted; and Commodore Warren, who had commanded the naval force involved, was promoted to rear-admiral. Almost eighteen months later Newcastle was sure that 'The nation is now universally for the war. All parties in Parliament seem to agree in it, and that which has united everybody, I am convinced, is their hopes and expectations of keeping Cape Breton, and distressing and making impression upon the French in North America.'[12] There were even calls in 1745 and 1747 for the annexation of the island by Act of Parliament.

11 There is a detailed account of the siege in M. Mimler, *Der Einfluss kolonialer Interessen auf die Strategie und Diplomatie Grossbritanniens während des Österreichischen Erbfolgekrieges, 1744–1748* (Hildesheim-Zurich-New York, 1983), pp. 48ff. See also Richmond, *The Navy*, ii, 212–16.

12 J. Black, 'Anglo-French Relations in the Mid-Eighteenth Century, 1740–1756', *Francia*, Band 17/2 (1990), 59; Richmond, *The Navy*, iii, 49; R. Harris, *A Patriot Press: National Politics and the London Press in the 1740s* (Oxford, 1993), pp. 223ff.

A French effort to retake the fortress was a disastrous failure. A strong squadron under the duc d'Anville sent for this purpose with a substantial military force in 1746 took three months to cross the Atlantic, was devastated by scurvy and smallpox, lost some 8,000 men in all and achieved nothing. This catastrophe was a striking illustration of the great difficulties in the sailing-ship era of carrying through a successful enterprise of this kind thousands of miles away from Europe. At the same time, however, British hopes of a conquest of Canada proved equally visionary. An expedition set on foot for this purpose never sailed, in part because of prolonged unfavourable winds (always a serious potential difficulty in such undertakings) but also because of the escape of d'Anville's stronger force and pressures to devote more resources to the Netherlands and stiffen Dutch resistance there.[13] The men and ships were finally used in an attack on the French port of L'Orient, the main base of the French East India Company; but this was conspicuously badly planned and ineffective. General St Clair, its commander, had no plan of the town or map of the surrounding country, and no information about the likely opposition or places where the ships might anchor in safety; in any case, the attack was not pressed home when it had the town at its mercy.

To the end of the war, nevertheless, hopes of retaining Louisbourg, the one tangible gain from years of costly national effort, remained high in Britain. Quite apart from the importance of denying the French its use as a base it was possible to argue that it might have some positive commercial value. Warren (who was alleged to have made a huge personal profit of £70,000 when it was taken) hoped that it could be developed as a free port and made a lucrative trading centre.[14] Possession of it might give Britain a monopoly of the Newfoundland fisheries, the greatest 'nursery of seamen' of all, as well as helping to protect the New England colonies. Its return to France, agreed when peace was made at Aix-la-Chapelle, therefore drew a heavy fire of criticism in newspapers and pamphlets and from the opposition in Parliament.[15] Henry Pelham, pacific and pessimistic, had seen almost from the moment of its capture that the strong popular desire to hold it was

13 A. H. Buffington, 'The Canada Expedition of 1746 in Relation to British Politics', *American Historical Review*, 45 (1939–40), 552–80; *The Royal Navy and North America: The Warren Papers, 1736–1752*, ed. J. Gwyn (Navy Records Society, vol. 118: 1973), pp. 276, 377.

14 *The Royal Navy and North America*, p. 169.

15 Mimler, *Der Einfluss*, pp. 191–8.

likely to prove an obstacle to any peace-making. In December 1745 he had already concluded that 'Cape Breton will be a stumbling-block to all negotiation'.[16] Whether in fact the fortress was worth keeping was at least questionable. Charles Knowles, the very able officer who succeeded Warren in command of the North American squadron, thought it 'the most miserable ruinous place I ever beheld', and had no doubt that Britain should not retain 'this expensive, weak fortress of Louisbourg'.[17] Such arguments, however, were irrelevant. The recovery of the fortress by France was unavoidable. The virtual collapse of the Dutch by the end of 1747 had made the French position in Europe in relation to Britain overwhelmingly strong. For the British government, a French evacuation of the Netherlands was essential. The return of Louisbourg, however unpalatable, was the price which had to be paid for this. As tentative peace negotiations got under way d'Argenson laid down in the autumn of 1746 that the recovery of the fortress was for France an essential part of any settlement.[18] Even as late as the spring of the following year it was hoped in London that an abandonment of Saxe's conquests might be bought merely by concessions in Italy; and the original instructions given to the earl of Sandwich, the main British peace negotiator, in August of that year ordered him, if Louisbourg must be handed back to France, at least to hold out for the destruction of its fortifications. But by 1748 there was no hope of achieving even this very limited success.[19] The war in North America, therefore, like that in the Caribbean, ended in stalemate and a reassertion of the prewar situation.

THE STRUGGLE IN INDIA

India, now beginning to emerge as the third great area of Anglo-French imperial rivalry, was until the 1740s completely outside the European conflicts of these two powers; and it seemed at

16 W. Coxe, *Memoirs of the Administration of the Right Honourable Henry Pelham* (London, 1829), i, 284.

17 *The Royal Navy and North America*, pp. 254 fn., 382.

18 *Recueil des Instructions donées aux Ambassadeurs et Ministres de France des Traités de Westphalie jusqu'à la Révolution Française* xxiii (*Hollande* iii) (Paris, 1924), 94.

19 J. M. Sosin, 'Louisbourg and the Peace of Aix-la-Chapelle', *William and Mary Quarterly*, 14 (1957), 516–35.

first possible that it might be equally unaffected by this new struggle. The French East India Company proposed in 1742 that its Indian possessions and those of its English counterpart should be recognised as neutral in any future Anglo-French war; and between November 1742 and May 1743 there were unsuccessful Anglo-French negotiations for the neutralisation of the whole area of the Indian Ocean. Joseph Dupleix, who had become Governor of Pondichéry, the most important of the French trading-stations, in January 1742, heard only at the beginning of December 1744 of the war which had broken out in the previous March. As soon as he received the news, however, he wrote to the councils of the British stations at Madras and Bombay to suggest an agreement banning all hostilities east of the Cape of Good Hope: a few weeks later representatives were sent from the smaller French station at Chandernagore in Bengal to Calcutta with similar proposals.[20] Nothing came of these initiatives; but they show the continuing vitality of the belief that it was possible for two states to be at war in Europe without the hostilities between them necessarily spilling over into other continents. The assumption that conflict between competing empires must inevitably be indivisible and world-wide was emerging but not yet fully established.

In India almost as much as in North America the fighting of 1744–8 was focused on a single episode, in this case the capture of Madras by the French in September 1746. Both sides were still very weak in military and naval terms. In theory in the early 1740s there were about 1,000 French soldiers in India. But desertion and sickness meant that this number was never reached in practice; and the training and morale of this tiny force was poor. The British position was almost equally weak. When Madras surrendered, after offering a very inadequate defence, there were only about 200 European soldiers in the town and the chief gunner died of a heart attack when he saw the French approaching.[21] There were almost ridiculously few casualties on either side during the siege. The last stages of the war saw some effort to devote greater resources to the

20 Ph. Haudrere, 'La Flotte de la Compagnie Française des Indes durant les conflits maritimes du milieu du XVIIIe siècle', in Martine Acerra and others, eds, *Les Marines de guerre européennes, XVIIe – XVIIIe siècles* (Paris, n.d.), p. 271; A. Martin, *Dupleix et l'Inde française, 1742–1749* (Paris, 1923), pp. 223–5.
21 Martin, *Dupleix*, pp. 75–6, 28; R. Beatson, *Naval and Military Memoirs of Great Britain from 1727 to 1783* (London, 1804), i, 311; G. Parker, *The Military Revolution: Military Innovation and the Rise of the West, 1500–1800* (Cambridge, 1988), p. 133.

struggle in the east. The British expedition under Admiral Boscawen which sailed for India early in November 1747 was much the largest yet sent there by any power; yet even this involved only six ships of the line (two of these of merely fifty guns) and a little army of 1,200 soldiers and 800 marines. At sea the British had the better of it, for the French East India Company in these years lost two-thirds of its fleet (which in 1740 had been slightly larger than that of its English rival) and in 1745 was forced to suspend its trade.[22] But this was not a decisive or lasting victory; and on land the struggle was equally indecisive.

In India, therefore, as in America and the Caribbean, neither side could inflict a clear-cut defeat on the other. The undoubted French success at Madras was followed by a violent quarrel over the disposal of the town between Dupleix and the buccaneering Mahé de la Bourdonnais, a former governor of Mauritius with extensive trading experience in India who had led the attack. In 1747–8 three French efforts to capture Fort St David, the main defence of the small British factory at Cuddalore, were failures. Boscawen's attack on Pondichéry in August 1748 was the biggest military operation hitherto in Asia by any European state: with East India Company troops, seamen and a small Dutch contingent as well as the soldiers he had brought from England, he had more than 5,000 men available for the siege.[23] Yet it was equally unsuccessful. When Madras was finally handed back to the East India Company at the beginning of September 1749 the situation reverted, at least on the surface, to what it had been in 1744.

None the less, during these years both British and French had begun to learn a lesson which they were to apply in the future with immensely important effects – that small European forces, disciplined and well-led, could decisively defeat much larger Indian ones. The victory won by the French in October 1746 on the Aydar river near Madras over an army commanded by the son of a local potentate, the nawab of Arcot, was the first example of such a success. Never before had Europeans defeated so numerous an Indian force; and the victorious little French army numbered only 300 Europeans and 700 native levies trained on European lines. The psychological effects of the battle were considerable. It pointed the way towards future developments which in the 1740s were still not fully foreseen. But by 1751 Dupleix's successor in Pondichéry could

---

22 Haudrere, 'La Flotte', pp. 269–70, 272.
23 Beatson, *Naval and Military Memoirs*, i, 391.

tell the French East India Company that 'All my efforts are directed towards attaining for you vast revenues from this part of India, and consequently placing the [French] nation in a position to maintain itself here even when it may lack support from Europe.'[24] The fighting of the 1740s, ineffective as much of it was, had planted the seed of European territorial empire in the east.

BRITISH SUCCESSES AND THE WAR AGAINST FRENCH TRADE

Britain was slow to translate its naval superiority, and the French preoccupation with military success in Europe rather than strength at sea, into decisive naval victory. Gradually, however, Britain's greater seapower asserted itself. From the beginning of 1745 there was a strong squadron, based at Plymouth, cruising in the western approaches to the Channel both to protect British trade and to watch the movements of the French Brest squadron. This was a development which had been foreshadowed in several earlier naval wars, perhaps even as early as the 1650s, and which owed much in this instance to the urgings of Vernon, now commanding the Channel squadron.[25] It meant that these ships were now being used, even if belatedly, in a truly strategic way: the contrast with the deployment of French and Spanish naval strength in 1744–8 almost entirely to protect convoys, which meant that it was used in relatively small and weak detachments, became increasingly marked as the struggle went on. The slow tilting of the balance in favour of Britain can be seen in the fact that many more French than British sailors were taken prisoner during the war. In all, about 31,000 men from the French navy were held in the British Isles at some time in 1744–8; and in May 1747 it was calculated that during the previous three years it had lost as prisoners over 14,000 more men than the British one. Another contemporary estimated that in spite of numerous exchanges of prisoners during the war, there were still in 1748 18,000 men of the French navy in British hands. In March of that year, in an effort to force the British government to agree to a general exchange of all naval prisoners of war, from which France might benefit, the French government suspended the existing agreement under which military prisoners were freely exchanged;

---

24 Parker, *The Military Revolution*, p. 134.
25 *The Vernon Papers*, ed. B. McL. Ranft (Navy Records Society, vol. 99: 1958), pp. 445–6, 451.

but the end of the war was now too close for this to have any effect.[26] Not until 1747, however, were the only decisive naval battles of the entire war fought. Early in May of that year, off Cape Ortegal in northern Spain, British ships under Admiral Anson almost annihilated a much inferior squadron under La Jonquière which was escorting a convoy, capturing all the French men-of-war and a considerable number of the merchantmen. In October, again with a considerable superiority in numbers, a British fleet under Admiral Hawke took most of a French squadron under l'Etanduère which was again escorting a large convoy. Britain's command of the sea was now more effective than ever before during the war; and this meant that its ability to protect its own trade and destroy that of France was correspondingly increased. Between February and early December of 1747 at least twenty-five French privateers were captured in British home waters; and in 1748 sixty-four French and Spanish ones were taken.[27]

Meanwhile, French seaborne trade was increasingly devastated. From 1745 onwards Maurepas had tried to introduce a system of convoys to protect ships involved in the very important trade with the Caribbean; but this soon ran into serious difficulties. From the beginning there were long delays in their sailing, with inevitable losses to the merchants concerned: sometimes cargoes deteriorated or perished as a result. Instead of the planned four convoys each year (two each to Martinique and Saint Domingue) there were never more than two: this meant that they became larger and thus increasingly difficult for their naval escorts to control or protect.[28] Even France's trade with other European states was suffering severely by the later stages of the war from the attentions of the British navy and privateers. This meant, among other things, that French ability to import from the Baltic, the main producing area (usually through Dutch intermediaries), naval stores and, above all, the hard-to-obtain large pine trees which made the best masts and

26 T. J. A. Le Goff, 'L'Impact des prises effectuées par les Anglais sur la capacité en hommes de la marine française au XVIIIe siècle', in *Les Marines de guerre européennes, XVII–XVIII siècles*, p. 108; Olive Anderson, 'The Establishment of British Supremacy at Sea and the Exchange of Naval Prisoners of War, 1689–1783', *English Historical Review*, lxxv (1960), 86; Baudi di Vesme, *La Pace*, p. 257.

27 See the list in Richmond, *The Navy*, iii, 116; C. E. Fayle, 'Economic Pressure in the War of 1739–48', *Journal of the Royal United Services Institution*, lxviii (1923), 436.

28 Pares, *War and Trade*, pp. 311–16.

large spars for warships, was completely destroyed. There was a very sharp rise in the cost of insuring French cargoes (though until near the end of the war, when it was made illegal, a great many of these were insured in Britain; it can be argued that this increased the confidence of French shipowners and their willingness to risk their vessels at sea). Perhaps more significant was the fact that the coming of peace was followed at once by the reappearance in French ports of very large numbers of ships from neutral states – Denmark, Sweden, Prussia and Danzig. Clearly, a large unsatisfied demand for shipping had built up in France during the last years of the war.[29] Spain, with less seaborne trade, had less to lose than France in this way; and the failure of the British in 1741 to take either Cartagena or Havana, focal points of its American trade, was a very important negative success for her. In both Paris and Madrid, and indeed throughout Europe generally, the successful resistance of Cartagena was seen as a great defeat for Britain. None the less, Spain's trade suffered severely. Of the treasure-fleets which still brought it silver from America only one, in 1744, returned from the Caribbean during the whole of the war (another was being prepared in 1748 but reached Spain only after peace had been made). Register-ships, those trading to the Spanish colonies, often the smaller markets there, under government licence, were often captured by the British. One French calculation was that of 118 which sailed from Cadiz between May 1740 and June 1745, sixty-nine were taken.[30]

Not too much should be made of all this. By 1748 there was much distress in France. The duke of Newcastle claimed in March 1748, as the work of peace-making drew to a close, that 'though we have our mortifications, the enemy have theirs also. Their trade is absolutely ruined for the present, and bankrupts swarm in all the great French towns.'[31] He somewhat exaggerated; but in any case, in the undoubted difficulties which France was facing, losses at sea were only a minor element. In what was still a predominantly agricultural economy the poor harvest of 1747 and resulting shortage and high price of food were far more important; and this was a kind of economic pressure with which Britain had nothing at all to do. France's strength lay in its European territories and

29 Baudi di Vesme, *La Pace*, p. 259.
30 Pares, *War and Trade*, pp. 111–14.
31 J. Black, 'British Naval Power and International Commitment: Political and Strategic Problems, 1688–1770', in *Parameters of British Naval Power, 1650–1850*, ed. M. Duffy (Exeter, 1992), p. 48.

its large population. These meant that it could lose much or even all of its overseas trade and still remain the greatest of the great powers, as it was to show very clearly under Napoleon I. British pamphleteers and parliamentary orators during the war liked to exaggerate, sometimes grossly, the extent to which France could be weakened by purely naval pressure. This was an expression of the dislike and distrust of European commitments which was now a deeply rooted tradition in Great Britain, and also of the widespread tendency to overstate the relative importance of colonial and intercontinental trade in general. But their assertions should not be mistaken for facts. The chief French negotiator of the peace of 1748, justifying to Louis XV the ending of a war in the last stages of which France's military position was so strong, said, 'What has led me, sire, to complete the great work of peace is the shortage of food, the depopulation of the state and the disorder of the finances.'[32] Only the last of these factors, and then to a minor extent, could be said to owe anything to the actions of the British navy.

The effects of the struggle at sea on British trade and the British economy are more debatable. As the noisy enthusiasm for war with Spain in the later 1730s had shown very clearly, many contemporaries believed that a successful maritime war was the best of all commercial stimuli, since it would destroy the trade of competitors and forcibly open new markets for British goods. Certainly in retrospect hardly anyone in Britain doubted that the war of 1739–48 had brought some economic advantages. One writer in 1758, for example, claimed that the value of French and Spanish cargoes captured during it had exceeded by £2 million that of the British ones taken.[33] Inevitably the war brought with it costs and losses. A contemporary calculation which has been frequently quoted by historians was that during it 3,238 British merchant ships were captured; but the same reckoning yielded a figure of 3,434 French and Spanish vessels lost, and it may be true, as has been argued,[34] that these were in general more valuable than the British ones. The system of convoys which the British as well as the French

32 Baudi di Vesme, *La Pace*, p. 261.

33 *The Naval History of Great Britain* (London, 1758), iv, 319–20. The aggressive and warlike aspects of British mercantilist thought in this period are well illustrated in G. Neidhardt, *Handel und Krieg in der Britischen Weltpolitik, 1738–1763* (Munich, 1971), pp. 84–97.

34 Fayle, 'Economic Pressure', pp. 440–1.

navy operated often meant, just as it did in France, long delays and interruptions to trade while convoys were assembled and got under way. In 1742, a good case in point, ships destined for Portugal, one of the most important foreign markets for British goods, had to wait almost a year for convoy. In 1744 others going to Jamaica, which were ready to sail in April, did not in fact do so until November.[35] The convoy system also meant that there could be violent price fluctuations as large quantities of such things as West Indian sugar or Virginian tobacco suddenly appeared on the market with the simultaneous arrival in port of a large number of ships, as well as long delays in loading and unloading. The effect of this and other wartime interruptions of peacetime commercial contacts – for example, Britain's inability to use entrepôts such as Antwerp and Cadiz – is impossible to quantify. But these difficulties and complications hampered French at least as much as British trade. The official figures for British exports fell sharply in 1744 under the first impact of war with France. But by 1748 the tonnage of British ships cleared outwards was slightly above the average for 1736–8; and exports soon recovered to a higher level than ever before, though some of this growth was certainly fictitious, the result merely of the supplying of British forces overseas and the payment of subsidies to continental allies.[36]

In British financial life the French declaration of war meant a tightening of the position on the London money market in a way in which war with Spain by itself had not. Government 3 per cent stock, the best single indicator of the financial position, whose price had been around par, fell at once to 92–93; but this was a defensive reaction to unwelcome news rather than the result of any immediate damage to British trade or credit. The one great financial crisis of the war, around the turn of the year 1745–6, when the 3 per cents at one point touched 74, was the product of the Jacobite rebellion and had nothing to do with French activity at sea. The last months of the conflict certainly produced clear signs that years of un-successful struggle were at last having an effect on confidence. By the beginning of April 1748 the 3 per cents had dropped to 77; and it was claimed that as much as 12 per cent was being offered for money in the City: such pressures powerfully strengthened the desire for an early peace. By the end of 1747 Pelham already seriously

35 Fayle, 'Economic Pressure', p. 435.

36 See the figures in G. Chalmers, *Estimate of the Comparative Strength of Great Britain* (London, 1804), p. 117.

doubted whether the country could go on fighting for another year.[37] But in general Britain's financial structure coped well with the war, which added £29 million to the National Debt. It showed during these years that it might even face with some confidence the much greater demands it would have to meet in a few years' time.

The final verdict on the impact of the Austrian Succession struggle on Britain's economic life must therefore be tentative and uncertain. Probably the safest conclusion is that it had some role, though an unspectacular one, in the process by which British trade and imperial profits outstripped those of its competitors. It thus played a minor and indirect part in laying the foundations of Britain's later economic successes.

37 P. G. M. Dickson, *The Financial Revolution in England: A Study in the Development of Public Credit, 1688–1756* (London, 1967), pp. 216–7, 227–8; cf. D. Joslin, 'London Bankers in Wartime, 1739–1784', in *Studies in the Industrial Revolution presented to T. S. Ashton*, ed. L. S. Pressnell (London, 1960), pp. 162–4.

9 THE PEACE OF AIX-LA-CHAPELLE

PEACE FEELERS AND TENTATIVE NEGOTIATIONS,
1745-7

Every great international conflict of old-regime Europe saw while
fighting still went on contacts between the combatants aimed at
achieving an acceptable peace. Feelers were put out, proposals
drawn up, serious and prolonged negotiations embarked on, while
battles were still being fought. The peace settlements of 1678–9, of
1697 and of 1713–14 were all preceded over a period of years by
much diplomatic activity of this kind. The treaty which ended the
war of the Austrian Succession, signed by British, French and Dutch
representatives at Aix-la-Chapelle on 16 October 1748 and by
Spanish, Austrian and Sardinian ones over the following month, was
no exception.

By the end of 1745 it was clear that the central decision of the
war had been taken; and this helped to focus and concentrate efforts
at peace. Prussia was, at least for the foreseeable future, in
possession of Silesia. France, quite apart from the personal idealism
of d'Argenson, had now little to gain from continuing the war. It
could do nothing further in Germany to shake the Habsburg
position there; and in Italy it was fighting, as it always had been, for
the interests of its intractable and unreliable Spanish ally. Many
British politicians and much British public opinion were now
disillusioned by an expensive and generally unsuccessful struggle and
increasingly resentful of the demands and complaints of Austria.
The Dutch, always lukewarm at best in their conduct of the war,
would welcome any settlement which seemed to offer safety and
escape from a conflict they had never wished for. From 1745–6,
therefore, the peace-feelers from various sides which had been in
evidence from early in the war became more frequent and the
negotiations to which they gave rise more serious and prolonged.

In the spring of 1745 a French secret agent, Fournier, was sent to London, ostensibly to buy tobacco there as the farmers-general, the pivots of the French tax system, normally did. He had some indirect contacts with the British government; but the possibility of exploratory talks between London and Paris was shattered by the outbreak of the Jacobite revolt. At the end of the same year a Colonel Larrey was sent, with the agreement of the British government, as the secret and personal emissary of the Dutch Pensionary Van der Heim to sound d'Argenson on possible peace terms. He had three interviews with the French minister but nothing came of these; and on the very last day of the year the French government increased the pressure on the unhappy States-General by revoking the concessions granted to Dutch trade by a Franco-Dutch treaty signed six years earlier. This made a considerable impression in Holland, much the most important of the Dutch provinces from the commercial point of view, so that in February 1746 a second and now official Dutch representative, count Wassenaer-Twickel, was sent to Paris to test the ground once more. In April he was supplemented by a colleague, Jacob Gilles, who was thought more fitted to discuss trading issues, while in May d'Argenson put forward an elaborate set of proposed peace terms.[1] In a typical display of high-mindedness, however, he incorporated in one of its clauses an appeal for an amnesty for the defeated Jacobites. This aroused great indignation in London and thus weakened the position of the ministers, notably Henry Pelham and Lord Harrington, who were prepared to accept d'Argenson's proposals at least as a basis for discussion. These peace-feelers underlined once more the deep disunity which had marked both sides throughout the war. Britain and the Dutch were quite prepared to negotiate without any reference to their Austrian or Sardinian allies, France to do so without any consultation with Spain. This fragmentation of the peace negotiations was to be their most obvious characteristic. More and more the strongest power on each side, Britain on the one and France on the other, took the leading roles, while the others, the

1 Sir R. Lodge, *Studies in Eighteenth-century Diplomacy, 1740–8* (London, 1930), pp. 153–5. Chap. iv of Lodge's book gives much detail on these Franco-Dutch contacts. See also *Receuil des Instructions données aux Ambassadeurs et Ministres de France des Traités de Westphalie jusqu'à la Révolution Française*, xxiii (*Hollande*, iii) (Paris, 1924), 70–4. There is a detailed account of the whole process of peacemaking in R. Browning, *The War of the Austrian Succession* (New York, 1993), chaps 19–20.

Austrians, Dutch, Spaniards and Sardinians, found themselves faced by *faits accomplis* which they had willy-nilly to accept.

The decisive role of the two great west European powers was emphasised when, on 4 October 1746, Lord Sandwich, acting for Great Britain, and the marquis de Puysieulx as the representative of France, met in the Dutch city of Breda. (Gilles was also present as representative of the States-General, but played an inevitably secondary role.) This began a series of peace negotiations which went on intermittently for several months. The Breda meetings were not a peace congress or any real approach to one: though there was much discussion as to whether the representatives of Austria and Sardinia should be admitted, Sandwich himself finally suggested that they should not take part directly but merely be informed by the British, French and Dutch ones of what was going on. Moreover, from the British point of view, these meetings were largely a holding operation. Ministers in London expected little from them. Henry Pelham, the most important and in many ways the ablest member of the government, told the duke of Bedford just before they opened that 'Between you and I [*sic*], I don't imagine this congress will last long. I hope in God we shall have something to propose for carrying on the war, since we are not likely to hit upon any terms of peace.'[2] In London it was hoped that the accession of Ferdinand VI in Madrid, particularly since his wife, a Portuguese princess, came from a political background traditionally favourable to Britain and Austria, might pave the way to a separate peace with Spain. This would break up the already very fragile alliance of the Bourbon powers and seriously weaken the position of France when a final settlement was negotiated. Benjamin Keene, a former envoy to Spain, therefore arrived in Lisbon in the autumn of 1746, accredited to the Portuguese court but with the task of detaching Spain from its French ally. There were also hopes that a successful Austro-Sardinian invasion of Provence, for which the British had pressed,[3] might soon force France into significant concessions.

With a second and even a third string to its bow in this way the British government was in no hurry to bring the Breda negotiations to a successful conclusion. Indeed Sandwich, who completely lacked diplomatic experience, was chosen as its representative in them precisely for that reason: it was felt to be easier for him than for a more hardened negotiator to temporarise and procrastinate until it

---

2 *Correspondence of John, Fourth Duke of Bedford* (London, 1842–6), i, 140.
3 See above, pp. 168–9.

became clear how far either Keene's efforts at Lisbon or those of the allied commanders in southern France had altered the situation. Neither had the hoped-for effect. The revolt in Genoa ended any prospect of success in Provence.[4] Keene in his negotiations with the Spanish ambassador in Lisbon, the duke of Sotomayor, achieved nothing. Ferdinand VI continued to insist on adequate provision for his half-brother; and Keene had been forbidden to make any promise of this kind. (There was some discussion at Breda of the possible establishment of Don Philip in Tuscany; but this had no practical significance.) Moreover, it was clear that Austria would agree to nothing which gave or implied any guarantee to Charles III in Naples of the sort the Spanish government wanted: Maria Theresa's still-cherished hopes of conquering the kingdom made this impossible for Vienna to accept.

The French government was as ready as the British one to divide its opponents by negotiating with each of them separately. At the end of 1746 the duc de Richelieu, when he was sent to Dresden to act as proxy for the dauphin at the marriage-ceremony of the latter with a Saxon princess, had talks with count Brühl to test the ground for a possible separate peace between France and Austria in the making of which Saxony would act as a go-between. This led to an interview on 6 January 1747 between Maria Theresa and count Christian von Loss, the Saxon representative in Vienna, in which the empress made it clear that she was ready to consider a settlement with France; and a few days later Loss was able to send Austrian peace proposals to Dresden. On the evening of 23 January a trusted associate of Brühl, Von Saul, had an interview in the Hofburg with Maria Theresa, who was accompanied by Ulfeld and Bartenstein. This exposed at once what was to remain a major source of friction and difficulty throughout the whole process of peace-making, the continuing deep reluctance of the Habsburg government to give Don Philip the Italian territory which Louis XV and his ministers were demanding for him. Nevertheless, for a time these Saxon efforts seemed to have some chance of bearing fruit.[5]

The year 1747 therefore opened with each side in the war as disunited as it had ever been. When a new Spanish representative, Melchor de Macanaz, arrived at The Hague early in February it became clear that his appointment would do nothing to reduce the mutual dislike and distrust which divided the two Bourbon powers.

---

4 See above, p. 169.

5 (C. F. Vitzthum von Eckstaedt), *Die Geheimnisse des Sachsischen Cabinets, Ende 1745 bis Ende 1756* (Stuttgart, 1866), i, 137–43.

An old man of seventy-seven who had earlier been an advocate of far-reaching reform in Spain, Macanaz had spent the last thirty years in exile in France and the Austrian Netherlands. He deeply resented the decline of Spain's international position during the last two generations or more.[6] He dreamed of restoring to his country the status it had held until the second half of the seventeenth century; and this meant the recovery of the territory Spain had lost since then, including that taken by France. Sandwich reported in February that Macanaz had promised that 'if he finds that France is concerting anything underhand he will go to any length with us except to a declaration of war'. When at the beginning of March the Spaniard demanded admission to the Breda negotiations, or at least a statement of the reasons for his being excluded, this was vetoed by the French: if Macanaz were admitted that would involve the admission also of the Austrian and Sardinian representatives, Harrach and Chavannes, to which France could not agree. His attitude produced a formal French protest in Madrid and brought the tortoise-like progress of the negotiations to a standstill. Sandwich for his part saw the intractability and eccentricities of Macanaz (he spoke, very rapidly, a largely incomprehensible mixture of French and Spanish) as useful in spinning out the proceedings until the new campaigning season, which it was hoped in London would produce better results for the allies than in the past. 'I shall always consider', he told Henry Pelham in April, 'the having delayed the conferences by means of Maccanaz till the opening of the campaign without putting ourselves in the wrong in point of argument as a very essential circumstance in our favour.'[7]

Yet, however bad the relations between the Bourbon powers, this did not mean that a separate peace between Spain and Britain was imminent. A suitable establishment in Italy for Don Philip no longer carried in Madrid quite the emotional charge it had had when Philip V was alive and Elizabeth Farnese therefore able to have a decisive influence on Spanish policy. But the change of regime meant that the recovery of Minorca and Gibraltar, a much more clearly national objective for Spain, now bulked larger than

6 His bitter *Testamento de España* (1740) makes this attitude clear. On his ideas in general, see H. Kamen, 'Melchor de Macanaz and the foundations of Bourbon power in Spain', *English Historical Review*, lxxx (October, 1965), 699–716. His peace-making activities are described in Maria D. G. Molleda, 'El caso Macanaz en el Congreso de Breda', *Hispania*, 18 (1958), 62–128.

7 Lodge, *Studies*, p. 232; N. A. M. Rodger, *The Insatiable Earl: A Life of John Montague, Fourth Earl of Sandwich, 1718–1792* (London, 1992), p. 47.

before; and this impinged directly on British interests and sensitivities as no aspect of the Italian settlement could. The terms of a proposed Anglo-Spanish peace which Macanaz gave to Sandwich and which the latter sent to London early in February 1747 were headed by a demand for the recovery of these two British bases. Several of those involved on the British side were willing to contemplate the abandonment of Gibraltar: Sandwich himself took this line, and there were some efforts to influence public opinion in the same direction. It could be argued that it was sensible to give up a possession which was not worth what it cost to maintain, if such a concession destroyed the Bourbon alliance and helped to revive Britain's valuable trade with Spain.[8] But national pride meant that the abandonment of Gibraltar was never a serious possibility. By the beginning of April Sandwich and Macanaz had reached deadlock on the question; and by late May contacts between them had been broken off.[9]

By the second half of 1747 war-weariness and the cumulating costs of the struggle were turning the minds of all the combatants more and more towards peace. A ministerial conference in Vienna on 20 December decided (with Bartenstein, unyielding to the end, alone dissenting) that 'the worst peace is preferable to beginning another campaign'.[10] Already in July Marshal Batthyany, the new Austrian commander in the Netherlands, had been commissioned to put directly to Saxe preliminary peace terms. In return for recognition of Francis Stephen as emperor and the complete evacuation of the Netherlands by France, Maria Theresa would restore the duchy of Modena, in Austrian hands since 1742, to its ruler, agree to a suitable territorial provision for Don Philip and reaffirm the renunciation of Naples made by her father. A willingness to contemplate such concessions in Italy showed how strong the desire for peace in Vienna was now becoming. In London there was growing pessimism about the likely future course of the war, as the French advance in the Netherlands became more threatening and the financial burden of continuing the conflict more formidable.

8 See, e.g., *National Prejudice Opposed to the National Interest* (London, 1748), which argues along these lines for getting rid of 'that useless place'; and, for a similar argument from an official standpoint, *Correspondence of John, Fourth Duke of Bedford*, i, 315–16.

9 S. Conn, *Gibraltar in British Diplomacy in the Eighteenth Century* (New Haven, Conn., 1942), pp. 148–50.

10 E. Guglia, *Maria Theresia: Ihre Leben und ihre Regierung* (2 vols, Munich–Berlin, 1917), i, 302.

Even in Paris, in spite of the achievements of Saxe, peace now seemed increasingly attractive. The victories of Hawke and Anson and the tightening at last of the British blockade of French ports were now having some effect, though still only a limited one, on France's economic life.[11] The cost of the war was a heavy burden on the country, perhaps a heavier one than on Britain. From 1744 onwards government expenditure was about a third higher than in Britain, whose system of taxation and still more of public finance was much more developed and efficient. By the end of 1746 the French clergy had been asked for a large *don gratuit* of 12 million livres, the *dixième*, the most important direct tax, had been raised by a tenth and the government had borrowed heavily by creating a large quantity of new *rentes*. A year later the cost of bread and all other foodstuffs had risen markedly in Paris.[12] The subsidies paid during the war by France to its allies, Frederick II and some smaller German princes, notably the Elector Palatine, were about the same in money terms as those dispensed by Britain; and, like Britain, France might well feel that it had had rather poor value for them.[13] Count William Bentinck, the principal Dutch negotiator in the final peace-making in 1748, had no doubt, on the basis of his contacts with his French counterparts, that the economic strains of the war were a major reason for France's willingness to make peace.[14] Most important of all, the will to go on fighting was increasingly lacking among the French ministers and in Louis XV himself: France's very strong position *vis-à-vis* the Dutch and British was therefore never exploited to the full.

After the victory at Laufeldt a new French feeler for peace negotiations was put out. The British General Sir John Ligonier, a Huguenot exile who had had a very distinguished military career in his adopted country, had been taken prisoner during the battle. This allowed him to be used as an intermediary between Cumberland and Louis XV, who was himself then with the French army. He was given no peace terms in writing; but it was made clear that any Anglo-French settlement was to be based on the mutual restoration

11 See above, pp. 188–90.

12 *Chronique de la Régence et du Règne de Louis XV (1718–1763), ou Journal de Barbier* (4 vols, Paris, 1885), iv, 203–4, 270.

13 P. G. M. Dickson, *Finance and Government under Maria Theresia, 1740–1780* (Oxford, 1987), ii, 167–9.

14 A. Beer, 'Zur Geschichte der Frieden von Aachen im Jahre 1748', *Archiv für Österreichische Geschichte*, 47 (1871), 98.

of all conquered territory. This initiative could well have led to the signature of preliminary peace terms by Britain and France six months earlier than in fact happened. But William IV of Orange argued that his newly established regime would be fatally weakened if the Dutch were excluded from any Anglo-French negotiations; and in this he was supported by the duke of Newcastle and George II. Newcastle insisted on the need to preserve the unity of the Anglo-Dutch alliance even if this should mean the eventual acceptance of worse peace terms than those the French were now proposing.

The attempt to open negotiations through Ligonier therefore had no immediate result; and Frederick II rather typically thought that France had shown weakness by making such advances and had given its enemies a false impression of its inability to carry on the war.[15] But it was another indication of the way in which, slowly and with much confusion and delay, the belligerents were feeling their way towards peace. The Breda negotiations, after nine months of very intermittent life (there were only five meetings, in all, of the diplomats concerned, all of which broke up over some question of procedure) finally petered out in the early summer of 1747. However, the French and Spanish governments, in a joint message to the Dutch one, proposed that the negotiations be transferred to some suitable neutral city; Aix-la-Chapelle (Aachen) was suggested. Clearly the tortuous process of peace-making would go on. When Puysieulx met Sandwich once more on 11 September, in a convent in Liège, to discuss the terms of a settlement, he showed that France was willing to continue with talks of this kind or even to agree to a general peace congress.

BRITAIN AND FRANCE FORCE THE PACE

By the end of 1747 it was clear that an Anglo-French peace could not be long delayed. On both sides of the Channel the pressures for an end to the war were becoming stronger. Osorio, the Sardinian minister in London, told Gorzegno, the Foreign Minister in Turin, in the first days of January 1748 that the British ministers 'want to hurry on a peace at any price. That is the only thing sure and certain here. All the rest is only confusion and a perpetual flux of

---

15 Duc de Broglie, *Maurice de Saxe et le Marquis d'Argenson* (2 vols, Paris 1891), ii, 338–9, 389–90.

ideas.'[16] In Vienna such a prospect was very unwelcome. Britain and France were now so much the most powerful of the belligerents that Austria could not hope to challenge effectively any settlement made by them. Yet such a settlement was almost certain to include terms which Maria Theresa and her ministers were deeply unwilling to accept. It was very likely to concede to Charles Emmanuel far more than it was felt in Vienna that he was entitled to. It would also probably include some form of guarantee of Prussia's possession of Silesia, something which Frederick II was understandably very anxious to obtain. During the war Maria Theresa had been forced into what she saw as profoundly unjust territorial sacrifices on three occasions, at Breslau, Worms and Dresden. On every one of the three Britain had approved, even urged, the making of these sacrifices: at Worms, in the person of Carteret, Britain had almost dictated the terms. It is not surprising that the empress was unwilling to entrust her interests to an ally whose whole outlook differed so profoundly from her own. The early weeks of 1748, therefore, saw an active Austrian effort to achieve a separate settlement with France, in negotiations carried on mainly through count Johann Adolf von Loss, the Saxon minister in Paris. In mid-February he was sent full powers to sign a peace-treaty. The terms which the empress proposed showed clearly that she still hoped to regain what she had been forced to give up in Italy in 1743, and in a more distant future recover what she had lost in Germany in 1745. Don Philip might have the duchies of Parma and Piacenza (though as imperial fiefs which would return to Habsburg control if he died without male heirs or inherited the throne of either Naples or Spain). But, in return, the territorial concessions made to Sardinia at Worms were to be nullified. Moreover, there was to be no guarantee of Frederick's possession of Silesia, either in the preliminary peace terms or in any final treaty. Acceptance of these terms would have meant the end of the traditional French policy of weakening Habsburg power everywhere and a complete severance of French interests from those of Prussia. It would, in other words, have produced almost a decade earlier something like the situation which had come about by 1756. The French government drew up a counter-proposal which Loss sent to Vienna on 9 March; but before this could be considered by the Austrian ministers France and Britain were well on the way to agreement.

16 D. Carutti, *Storia della Diplomazia della Corte di Savoia* (4 vols, Turin, 1875–80), iv, 305fn.

In the negotiations which began at Aix-la-Chapelle on 17 March 1748 the central thread was that of the Anglo-French settlement. The Spanish government was surprisingly slow in sending its representative, the duke of Sotomayor, who did not arrive until 17 May: this tended to free still further the hands of the marquis de Saint-Séverin, the skilful diplomat of Italian origin who represented France. On the British side, Newcastle, who had for long stubbornly urged the overriding need to safeguard the unity of the anti-French coalition, had now been forced by the near-collapse of the Dutch to change his attitude and accept that peace should be made as soon as possible. Maria Theresa remained very anxious, and with good reason, about the possibility of a separate Anglo-French agreement: on 28 March and again on 4 April, count Wenzel Anton von Kaunitz, now making his first major appearance on the international stage as her representative at Aix, was warned that for this reason the Austrian negotiations with France must on no account be broken off.[17] She was now more and more disillusioned with Britain and ready for a reconciliation with her traditional Bourbon rival. British foreign policy, she told Kaunitz later in April, 'consists of assuring at our expense the greatness of Prussia and Sardinia. These two kings are to be set against the House of Bourbon, one in Germany with his supporters and the other in Italy.'[18] Both the Bourbon powers and their opponents, therefore, were even more disunited than in earlier years. Once more the forces which produced the transformation of 1755–6, with its rather misleading impression of sudden change, can be clearly seen.

France was now in an extremely strong position, diplomatic as well as military. Not only was Saxe victorious. France could now choose to make peace separately with either Britain or Austria and thus weaken still more the already very tenuous alliance of its two great opponents. A settlement with Britain was chosen. Britain, after all, had still some ability to inflict significant losses on France through its dominance at sea and its damaging blockade of French ports. Maria Theresa was a much less threatening enemy. At the end of April Saint-Séverin told Sandwich, quite untruthfully, that Spain and Austria were on the point of signing a separate peace which would allow Maria Theresa, in return for concessions to Don Philip, to recover what she had been forced to give up to Charles Emmanuel. Such an agreement would throw much of European

17 Duc de Broglie, *La Paix d'Aix-la-Chapelle* (Paris, 1892), p. 102.
18 Broglie, *La Paix d'Aix-la-Chapelle*, p. 119.

international relations into the melting-pot: the only way to avoid this was immediate acceptance of preliminary peace terms, most of the details of which had already been settled in the discussions of the previous months.

The result was that Sandwich, with a trepidation understandable in one so young and relatively inexperienced, signed on 30 April a set of peace terms which were the essential step towards ending the war. These provided for an armistice in the Netherlands. But this was not to take effect until six weeks after the peace preliminaries had been signed: this provision allowed the French to take Maastricht on 10 May and thus increase still more the military pressure on the British and Dutch. Between Britain and France there was to be a mutual restoration of conquests: this amounted in effect to an exchange of Louisbourg for Madras. Don Philip, whose claims had throughout the war given rise to such a mountain of diplomatic paper, was to have Parma and Piacenza, and in addition the little duchy of Guastalla. Charles Emmanuel was to gain Vigevano, Anghiera and part of the duchy of Parma. Modena was to be restored to its duke and Genoa was to recover all it had lost during the war: Finale, so coveted by the king of Sardinia, was therefore confirmed as a Genoese possession. The landward defences of Dunkirk were to remain as they were; but those on the seaward side were to be destroyed. The French government, however, rejected absolutely and successfully any repetition of the humiliating condition, incorporated in the Anglo-French peace-treaty of 1713, that a British commissary should observe and verify the work of destruction.[19] The commercial rights claimed by Britain in Spanish America, with all the potentialities for friction they had already shown, were to be re-established. Frederick II's possession of Silesia and Glatz was guaranteed, an important success for him, since the inclusion in the general peace of such a clause and therefore the full international recognition of his annexation of the province had been his major objective in 1747–8. Finally and very significantly, Britain and France agreed that if any other state concerned delayed or refused acceptance of these terms they would none the less put them

---

19 *Receuil des Instructions*, xxiii, 93, 120–1. French efforts, or alleged efforts, to rebuild the fortifications of the town, a great centre of privateering during the wars of Louis XIV, had aroused much uneasiness and strong public feeling in Britain during the 1720s and 1730s; while demands that it be left completely unprotected were seen in France as insulting. The issue, though not now one of great practical importance, had considerable symbolic significance on both sides of the Channel.

into effect. Such a recalcitrant state would forfeit any advantages the treaty might give it. The two great western powers, in other words, were prepared to force the peace they had made on their reluctant and protesting allies.

DISAPPOINTMENTS AND RECRIMINATIONS

Of these the most important, of course, were Austria and Spain. Charles Emmanuel of Sardinia was deeply disappointed by not receiving Piacenza, for which he had hoped, and even more by the denial to him of Finale. The Dutch government, whose representative, William Bentinck, had been allowed to sign the peace preliminaries though he took virtually no part in drafting them, would ideally have liked some guarantee of its barrier fortresses in the Austrian Netherlands comparable to that of Silesia given to Frederick II. But grumbles of this kind Britain and France did not need to take too seriously. Already on 19 April Saint-Séverin had been sure of 'the perfect and entire submission to the will of England' of the Dutch and Piedmontese and had assured his government that 'it is London which rules despotically at The Hague and Turin'.[20] More significant was the anger felt in Madrid. Parma and Piacenza, even with the addition of Guastalla, were much less than Don Philip had been promised in 1743 by the Treaty of Fontainebleau; nor were they an adequate equivalent for Savoy and Nice which the Spanish government, in separate negotiations with Austria, had hoped to obtain for him. The peace terms also destroyed completely any remaining hopes of recovering Minorca and Gibraltar for Spain; and the reassertion of Britain's commercial rights in its American empire seemed an affront to its independence. What power had France to give away its ally's rights and claims in this high-handed way, without even the semblance of consultation? In Paris, relations between Puysieulx and Huescar became so bad that the minister felt physical discomfort when he had to meet the ambassador, while in Aix Sotomayor refused to speak to Saint-Séverin and turned his back when they encountered each other.[21]

Equally bitter and perhaps more justified was the sense of grievance felt by Maria Theresa. For Britain to guarantee to

20 *Receuil des Instructions*, xxiii, 113.
21 Broglie, *La Paix d'Aix-la-Chapelle*, pp. 182–3; C. Baudi di Vesme, *La Pace di Aquisgrana* (1748) (Turin, 1969), pp. 300–1.

Frederick II his ill-gotten gains in Silesia and to Charles Emmanuel his even more resented ones in Italy seemed to her almost deliberate treachery; and the way in which the peace preliminaries had been drawn up without the slightest effort at consultation with Kaunitz also rankled deeply. The fact that the British government was now obviously making efforts to improve relations with Prussia strengthened her sense of betrayal. Though there had been no British diplomatic representation in Berlin since September 1746, a new envoy, Henry Legge, arrived there at the end of April 1748, while Frederick II also clearly wished to bring the two states closer together. In spite of the dislike and contempt he felt for George II he was now offering, as an inducement to conclude an Anglo-Prussian alliance, to support the acquisition by Hanover of the bishopric of Osnabrück and parts of Hildesheim, gains which George much coveted.[22] The empress's resentment broke out in the bitter reproaches she directed at Robinson in a highly-charged interview on 30 April;[23] and early in May the Austrian government protested publicly against the terms agreed in Aix a few days earlier. This deepening of the rifts between its opponents was naturally seen with pleasure in France. 'What seems to me the best aspect of this business', wrote Saint-Séverin to Puysieulx immediately after the preliminaries had been signed, 'is that the courts of Vienna and Sardinia will not forget for a long time the trick which the maritime powers have just played them, and I am putting the final touches to the foundation of distrust and bad feeling which has been laid between our enemies.'[24] British statesmen were well aware that the Austrian alliance, which almost all of them still saw as necessary and as a kind of natural law of international relations, had been strained more severely than ever before. But they could argue that the situation in the Low Countries by the beginning of 1748 was so desperate that they were justified in making a separate peace and disregarding the protests of an ally so expensive and intractable as Maria Theresa. The great military superiority of the French, wrote the duke of Bedford, 'made us catch at any terms at the first offer,

---

22 *Politische Correspondenz Friedrichs des Grossen*, ed. J-G. Droyson *et al.* (46 vols, Berlin 1879–1939), vi, 101.

23 Robinson's account is printed in W. Coxe, *History of the House of Austria from the Foundation of the Monarchy by Rodolphe of Hapsburgh to the Death of Leopold II*, 3rd edn (London, 1847), iii, 353.

24 Broglie, *La Paix d'Aix-la-Chapelle*, pp. 173–4.

without taking our allies with us'.[25] This was an essentially accurate description of what had happened.

Between agreement on preliminary terms by France, Britain and the Dutch and the signature of the final peace-treaty there was an interval of over five months. The French, British and Dutch plenipotentiaries signed the treaty of Aix-la-Chapelle on 18 October; but the reluctance and disappointment of the other belligerents showed itself in the fact that, while the Spanish one did so two days later, that of Austria signed only on 8 November, and that of Sardinia only on the 20th of that month. The conflicts of aim and outlook, and the resulting tensions and resentments, which had so marked both sides throughout the war remained very much alive to its last moments. These summer and autumn months saw no lessening of such feelings; if anything, they became stronger. On 2 August Britain and France agreed that the Russian auxiliaries on whom so many British hopes had been pinned should begin their retreat. In return, an equivalent number of French soldiers were to be withdrawn from the Netherlands. This was directly contrary to the wishes of Maria Theresa, who wanted the Russians to continue their advance or at least to remain in Germany. She argued with obvious force that, once in retreat, they could never be used in western Europe, whereas French regiments, even if they left the Netherlands, would remain close at hand and available for use. Nevertheless, the growing insistence in Britain on reducing public expenditure, typified by Henry Pelham, carried the day. Most significant of all, the convention which provided for the homeward march of the Russians to begin was signed without Kaunitz even being informed of it.

At the end of August Newcastle even proposed a secret British agreement with France and Sardinia to ensure, if necessary by the use of force, the carrying-out of the Italian provisions of the peace preliminaries, the part which Maria Theresa found most humiliating and difficult to swallow. A British squadron, he suggested, might if necessary be sent to the Mediterranean for this purpose.[26] Such a proposal illustrates strikingly the bankruptcy of the Anglo-Austrian alliance: certainly the irritation of many British politicians with what they saw as the dangerous obstinacy of the empress and her advisers was intense. 'The Austrians', declared the deeply unsympathetic Henry Pelham, 'are, and ever were, false, self-interested and proud

25 *Correspondence of John, Fourth Duke of Bedford*, i, 386.
26 Lodge, *Studies*, pp. 368–70, 400.

beggars.'[27] In Vienna resentment of British disloyalty and high-handedness was correspondingly strong. Maria Theresa herself now felt keenly the cumulative disappointments of the war and the failure of so many of her efforts. An Austrian diplomat who returned to the capital after a long absence abroad 'found Her Majesty greatly changed; it seemed to me as though everything disgusted her and that the crown lay heavy on her head'.[28] The influence of Bartenstein and the uncompromising outlook he typified was still great; and his resentment of British attitudes at Breda and Aix-la-Chapelle was bitter.[29] Just as Britain had agreed to send its Russian auxiliaries home without consulting or even informing the Austrians, so the Austro-French convention of 16 September, which provided for the withdrawal by both powers of their forces from the Netherlands, was signed without the knowledge of the British or the Dutch. During the summer there were still some hopes in Vienna that the peace might be given the form of a series of bilateral treaties between different pairs of combatants, as had been done at Utrecht.[30] This, it was felt, might allow Austria to avoid any general guarantee by the powers of the Treaties of Worms and Dresden. But neither the British nor the French government ever contemplated such an expedient; and their control of the peace-making process was now more and more complete. The papal representative in Paris told the Curia just after the conclusion of the preliminaries that the other states involved were now little more than dependants of the two great western ones;[31] though this was something of an exaggeration, it was not a very gross one.

If in Britain there was relief at escaping from a generally unsuccessful war on the best terms which could be reasonably expected, there was a corresponding feeling among many Frenchmen that their government had not exploited to the full France's very strong military position. Saxe himself was understandably piqued that his victories had not been translated into more favourable peace terms. France was surrendering its conquests in the Netherlands, he

27 P. C. Yorke, *Life and Correspondence of Philip Yorke, Earl of Hardwicke, Lord Chancellor of Great Britain* (Cambridge, 1913), i, 675.

28 Guglia, *Maria Theresia*, i, 313.

29 Baudi di Vesme, *La Pace*, pp. 306–7; A. von Arneth, 'Johann Christof Bartenstein und seine Zeit', *Archiv für Österreichische Geschichtsforschung*, 46 (1871), 42.

30 A. Beer, 'Zur Geschichte des Friedens von Aachen in Jahre 1748, *Archiv für Österreichische Geschichte*, 47 (1871), 138.

31 Baudi di Vesme, *La Pace*, p. 283.

told Maurepas a few days after the signature of the preliminaries, while Frederick II was retaining Silesia; and yet Prussia was a far weaker and more vulnerable state than France. Such generosity on the part of Louis XV was a mistake. The duc de Richelieu, now commanding the French garrison in Genoa, also condemned 'the excessive and scandalous haste' with which peace was being made,[32] while what public opinion there was in France was equally critical. 'It seems', wrote the Paris lawyer Barbier, 'that of all the belligerent powers we shall have gained least by this war which has cost us immense sums and the loss of three or four hundred thousand men.'[33] Popular feeling in France, or at least in Paris, was particularly stung by the clause in the treaty by which the French government agreed to expel from its territory Prince Charles Edward Stuart, the leader of the 1745 rebellion. This was felt as a national humiliation; and when in December the prince, who had refused to leave France, was arrested at the Opéra in Paris and forced into exile in Switzerland, this aroused much indignation.

Throughout Europe, indeed, and not least in Britain, there was a similar feeling that the French had failed strikingly to press home their advantages. Frederick II, with his usual acerbity, said that 'France is governed by idiots and ignorant men, since they know so badly how to take advantage of their strong position', while Horace Walpole wrote, 'wonderful it is what can make the French give us such terms, or why they have lost so much blood and treasure to so little purpose'.[34] Two years later Pitt felt that 'if there be any secret in the late affairs of Europe, it is in the question how it was possible for our Ministers to obtain so good a peace as they did'; and there was a considerable feeling that Sandwich had done well, given Britain's weak negotiating position.[35]

Many of the belligerents, therefore, signed the final peace-treaty in anger and disappointment, merely because they had no alternative. Maria Theresa had to agree to a guarantee of the cessions made to Prussia and Sardinia, though she was able to stipulate that the Pragmatic Sanction be mentioned in the treaty as one of the bases of the peace. Spain continued to make difficulties until the last moment over the number of years for which Britain

---

32 Broglie, *La Paix d'Aix-la-Chapelle*, pp. 171–2, 263.

33 Barbier, *Chronique*, iv, 309.

34 Broglie, *La Paix d'Aix-la-Chapelle*, p. 245; *The Yale Edition of Horace Walpole's Correspondence*, xix, (Oxford–New Haven, Conn., 1955), 482–3.

35 *The Parliamentary History of England from the Earliest Period to the Year 1803*, xiv (London, 1813), 695; Rodger, *The Insatiable Earl*, pp. 51–2.

was to recover its rights under the Asiento agreement in compensation for those during which it had been prevented from enjoying them: this relatively minor issue took up much time and effort in the Anglo-French negotiations during the summer months.[36] Spain also raised problems over the terms on which the territories to be given to Don Philip in Italy might revert, at least in form, to the Holy Roman Empire at some future date. Charles Emmanuel was still deeply disappointed by his failure to secure better access to the sea for his territories. But France was now willing, even anxious, to make peace; and Britain was more than ready to accept the terms offered. The French army left Bergen-op-Zoom and Maastricht at the beginning of December. By February 1749 it had evacuated its conquests in Brabant, Flanders and Hainault. One of the most complex and incoherent wars (or rather series of wars) in the history of Europe was ended by a treaty whose making reflected to the full the conflicts and rivalries which had played so great a role during the years of fighting.

36 They were eventually restored for four years; but in 1750 the South Sea Company finally surrendered them in return for a cash payment of £100,000. In this low-key way ended an agreement on which so many hopes had been built and which had absorbed so disproportionate an amount of ministerial and diplomatic time.

10 THE RESULTS OF THE WAR

PRUSSIAN SUCCESS AND HABSBURG REFORM

This long series of struggles had in many ways disappointingly little decisive result. Even before it ended it had come to seem to many observers a depressing example of sterile conflict, the product merely of the ambition and obstinacy of rulers and ministers. 'When one sees the outcome of a war so bloody and costly', wrote a Swiss from the security of neutral Geneva in 1747, 'one must say that princes are cruel and false.'[1] It was all too clear by 1748 that few of the rivalries which had begun and prolonged the war had been ended. Most threatening of all, the struggle between Prussia and Habsburg power in Germany, which Frederick II had set in motion at the end of 1740, was as active and bitter as ever. It had now become one of the fixed points around which international relations in Europe were to turn for generations to come. In it the peace of 1748 was no more than a truce. Neither side pretended that it was more. 'We are entering a house made of cardboard,' said Kaunitz just after he had reluctantly put his signature to the treaty of Aix-la-Chapelle. 'We shall have to see whether we think of making from it something more solid.' On his side Frederick was both more specific and more pessimistic. 'This general pacification', he wrote, 'resembles rather a truce in which all parties profit from a short period of repose and look for alliances to be better placed to take up arms again.' Nor was this pessimism confined to ministers and monarchs. 'Never have the European powers kept such large forces in being as since the last peace at Aix-la-Chapelle,' wrote a Prussian officer a few years later. 'Little or nothing is heard of troop reductions. The states vie with one another in training their troops, and putting officers and men through constant military exercises.

---

1 Baudi di Vesme, *La Pace di Aquisgrana* (1748) (Turin, 1969), p. 423, fn. 243.

We keep our weapons sharp, and follow the principle that a large and well-schooled army is the best rampart of the state.'[2]

The creation of this deep-seated antagonism in the German world was the one profound political change of these years, the one new element which they introduced into the European balance. Brandenburg-Prussia was still in 1748 not a true great power. Its population and economic resources were too small for that. But it was now beginning to have some of the characteristics of one. Its new importance was essentially a military achievement; and on the military level at least it was now crushingly superior to any other German state, the equal of Austria and little inferior even to France or Russia. It was, moreover, a lasting achievement. Never again would Prussia relapse to the second-class status which had been its lot under Frederick William I. No statesman could now shut his eyes to this transformation, however unwelcome he might find it. At the beginning of the Silesian wars the Hanoverian ministers of George II had believed that the electorate was capable of effective armed mediation between Frederick II and Maria Theresa. By the time of the Breslau settlement of 1742, however, they had realised that it could not hope to face Prussia as an equal; and the total defeat of Saxony in December 1745 and the treaty of Dresden made it even clearer that Hanover was now totally overshadowed by its much more powerful neighbour. The intense dislike which both the Empress Elizabeth and Bestuzhev felt for Frederick II was also an indirect tribute to Prussia's success and new potentialities. Bestuzhev at least seems genuinely to have feared that Frederick, once in possession of Silesia, might extend and round off his territories by attacking West Prussia and Danzig and might even try to establish one of his brothers as ruler of the Russian-dominated duchy of Courland.[3] In Paris also, though there was still a comfortable assumption of French military superiority to Prussia, one destined to be shattered in less than a decade, there was a clear realisation that the events of 1741–5 had changed drastically the whole political and military balance in central Europe.

Prussia's quantum leap to a new level of international importance was all the more impressive to contemporaries because it had been so rapid and because it owed nothing to population or

---

2 Duc de Broglie, *La Paix d'Aix-la-Chapelle* (Paris, 1892), pp. 269, 282; C. Duffy, *The Military Experience in the Age of Reason* (London–New York, 1987), p. 15.

3 W. Mediger, *Moskaus Weg nach Europa: Der Aufstieg Russlands zum europäische machtstaat im Zeitalter Friedrichs des Grossen* (Braunschweig, 1952), pp. 224–5.

wealth and everything to organisation and leadership. Its young ruler seemed to have raised it, through his own daring and vision, to a status for which nothing in its history or natural resources had prepared the world. Admiration, sometimes envious and reluctant, for Prussia's army, the engine of its new-found importance, as well as for its ruler, was now becoming widespread. It can be seen in such things as the adoption in its Habsburg rival from the middle of the century onwards, and later in other armies, of Prussian styles of uniform, or in the publication in 1754 of the first English translation of the Prussian army regulations.

Frederick had thus laid the foundations of a Prusso-Austrian, Hohenzollern–Habsburg rivalry, with potent overtones of Protestant–Catholic antagonism, which was to last for well over a century. As one of his most bitter nineteenth-century academic critics claimed, 'King Frederick II not merely destroyed the thousand-year-old empire: he made peace between the Germans impossible.'[4] For generations this 'dualism' in central Europe was to be one of the guidelines of international relations. By his defeat of Maria Theresa in 1741–5, confirmed in the life-and-death struggle of 1756–62, Frederick can be seen, as many of his later admirers among historians saw him, as paving the way for the creation, under the aegis of Bismarck, of a united and Prussian-dominated Germany which was merely a *Kleindeutschland* and from which the Austrian provinces and Bohemia were deliberately excluded. To claim this as a direct result of the Austrian Succession struggle would be a great exaggeration and oversimplification; but it is quite legitimate to see the Silesian wars of the 1740s as the starting-point of a development which was to reach fruition only in the 1870s.[5]

The only significant loser by the war was the Habsburg Empire. It is not surprising, therefore, that the struggle with Prussia stimulated serious efforts to reform its chaotic and irrational administrative structure (or rather structures, since they varied so much in different parts of the empire), the product of generations of local interests and pressures of all kinds. Even before the war had ended Count Friedrich Wilhelm Haugwitz, now Maria Theresa's chief adviser on internal matters, had begun serious efforts to

4 O. Klopp, *Der König Friedrich II von Preussen und seine Politik*, 2nd edn. (Schaffhausen, 1867), p. 128.

5 An attempt is made to survey some of the enormous historical literature on Frederick and to discuss the varying judgements passed on him by historians in M. S. Anderson, *Historians and Eighteenth-Century Europe, 1715–1789* (Oxford, 1979), pp. 131–57.

overhaul the Habsburg finances. Reform and innovation of this kind had one overriding objective – to enable the Habsburg lands to pay for the larger armies needed to protect them against further attack and equip them to fight a war of revenge against Frederick II.[6] Efforts at military reform had also begun before the fighting ended. A committee of leading commanders (it included three field-marshals), headed by Prince Charles of Lorraine, assembled for the first time in February 1748, and over a series of twenty meetings gave the Habsburg army what it had never had before, a standardised system of drill, as well as reforming its very defective accounting methods. Other innovations followed. A military academy for the training of officers, the first of its kind in the Habsburg Empire, was set up in Wiener-Neustadt in 1752. A training-school for military engineers was established in Vienna two years later (the first regulations for the engineer corps had already been issued in 1748). Field-Marshal Prince Liechtenstein, who had distinguished himself in the fighting in Italy, reformed the Austrian artillery in a way which aroused the admiration of Frederick II himself (who had in general a low view of the effectiveness of artillery in warfare): the Austrian 12-pounder field-gun, the best of its kind in Europe, was widely imitated. Moreover, the Habsburg army was to be bigger as well as better. The hereditary provinces in central Europe were now to maintain a standing force of 108,000 men, while Count G. L. Pallavicini produced a plan for the Italian territories which envisaged their providing in wartime 32,000 more, and it was hoped to raise 22,000 in the Austrian Netherlands.[7]

Underlying all this, moreover, was a new and slowly developing feeling that the lands of the monarchy formed some kind of whole, that it was now becoming more than a mere random agglomeration of territories. Even a little before 1740 maps had begun to appear which gave a comprehensive overview of the lands of the Austrian Habsburgs and showed them as 'a clearly defined empire with fixed boundaries and a distinct geographic shape'. The official decision in 1764 to embark on a comprehensive mapping of the entire

6 The formidable complexities of Habsburg financial reform in this period are elucidated, so far as they are ever likely to be, by P. G. M. Dickson, *Finance and Government under Maria Theresia, 1740–1780* (Oxford, 1987), ii, chap. 1.

7 A. von Arneth, *Geschichte Maria Theresias* (10 vols, Vienna, 1863–79), iv, 88, 92–4; Dickson, *Finance and Government under Maria Theresia*, ii, 25. A short account of the Austrian military reforms of this period can be found in *Handbuch zur deutschen Militärgeschichte, 1648–1939*, ed. G. Papke and W. Petter (Munich, 1964–81), iii, 72ff

monarchy, the most ambitious single cartographic project of the eighteenth century, can be seen as an indication of this new governmental attitude.[8] (In Prussia, by contrast, Frederick II, who feared that good maps might help an enemy, discouraged the survey begun by Field-Marshal von Schmettau in 1750.)

A BRITISH OR FRENCH ALLIANCE FOR AUSTRIA?

Improvement of the Habsburg administration and strengthening of the Habsburg army were directed entirely against Prussia. In Italy the territorial position achieved in 1748 remained remarkably stable until the French Revolution. The losses which Maria Theresa accepted there had been a bitter pill to swallow; but swallowed it was. Don Philip was dissatisfied with what he had been given at Aix-la-Chapelle; but neither his half-brother Ferdinand VI nor his father-in-law Louis XV had any intention of provoking a new conflict for his sake. Spain was now freed from any need to pursue in Italy the essentially trivial dynastic ambitions on which it had been forced for so long to waste its resources. It could at last concentrate on strengthening its position at sea and in America, where real national interests were at stake. Austrian hopes of recovering Naples were now more clearly than ever visionary; and in 1752, by the Treaty of Aranjuez, Maria Theresa and Charles Emmanuel guaranteed each other's Italian possessions. For almost half a century, therefore, the Italian peninsula was to be a backwater so far as international relations were concerned. This simplified and even strengthened the position of Austria; but it made Prussia stand out more clearly than ever in Vienna as the supreme, indeed the only, enemy. The energies of the Habsburg monarchy were now concentrated on the strengthening of its core possessions in central Europe and above all on the recovery of Silesia.

This demanded, however, not merely the internal strengthening of the Habsburg monarchy but also the gaining of effective outside support in any future war of revenge. Of its traditional allies, Great Britain and the Dutch, the latter was now clearly useless. Quite apart from the factional struggles which divided the United Netherlands, the Dutch army had lost completely the high reputation won in the war of the Spanish Succession. Could Britain

---

8 J. Vann, 'Mapping under the Habsburgs', in *Monarchs, Ministers and Maps: The Emergence of Cartography as a Tool of Government in Early Modern Europe*, ed. D. Buisseret (Chicago-London, 1992), p. 163.

ever again be a reliable supporter of the Habsburg cause? Given the deep divisions between the two powers which the events of 1741–8 had revealed, the omens were far from good. On several occasions during the war, most noticeably perhaps in the advances made by Harrach to Vaulgrenant in Dresden in December 1745,[9] the idea of isolating Frederick II by some agreement with France had seemed attractive in Vienna. (This was yet another argument against a forward policy in Italy, which would inevitably mean serious friction with the Bourbon powers.) Yet from the British point of view the Austrian alliance was valuable only as a weapon against France. On the other hand, the tentative British efforts to improve relations with Prussia in 1748, which Frederick had warmly welcomed[10] could only strengthen the feeling in Vienna that the government in London was indifferent to Habsburg interests. Each partner in the alliance was therefore now dangerously willing to improve its relations with the enemy of the other.

By the summer of 1748 most of the ministers in Vienna were in favour of some change of system; and Maria Theresa, though as yet unwilling to break with the maritime powers, had decided to improve her relations with France.[11] In March of the following year she ordered each member of the Geheime Conferenz to give in writing his opinion on the direction which the foreign policy of the monarchy should now take. In response Kaunitz towards the end of the month submitted a memorandum in which, supported by Bartenstein, he urged an approach to France to secure not merely its neutrality in a new war with Prussia but also its positive support for the recovery of Silesia. At least equally important for this purpose, in his eyes, was support from Russia, whose international import-ance, he impressed on Maria Theresa in 1751, had in recent years grown spectacularly.[12] This could be achieved without threatening the more and more threadbare relationship with Britain; but any genuine Austro-French *rapprochement* would almost certainly deal it a death-blow. There were still forces in Vienna which wanted to restore and maintain good relations with Britain; and feeling there improved when in the spring of 1749 Newcastle persuaded the

---

9 See above, pp. 151–2.

10 See above, p. 205.

11 Guglia, *Maria Theresia: Ihre Leben und ihre Regierung* (2 vols, Munich–Berlin, 1917), i, 308–9.

12 *Europa im Zeitalter Friedrichs des Grossen*, ed. B. R. Kroener (Munich, 1989), p. 83.

cabinet, against the advice of his thrifty younger brother, to pay the final instalment of the wartime subsidy to Maria Theresa.[13] Nevertheless, Kaunitz's whole attitude was underlain by a determination to free the Habsburg monarchy from what could be easily, and indeed justifiably, seen as a humiliating dependence on Britain. When in May 1753 he became chancellor, replacing count Ulfeld, who had held the post for a decade, it was clear that a major reorientation was under way. Bartenstein, though many of his objectives were essentially similar to those of Kaunitz (who said 'I believe Herr von Bartenstein and I want the same thing, but by different means') now lost his influence over foreign policy.[14] New attitudes and new men were in the ascendant in Vienna. This new situation was to culminate, rather fortuitously, in the Austro-French agreement of 1 May 1756, the decisive step in the 'Diplomatic Revolution' which began in that year. This agreement astonished many observers: but they were perhaps surprised largely because so many earlier suggestions for something of this kind had come to nothing.

On the British side there was much less readiness to discard the Austrian alliance. Over the last few years it had come under increasing strain. It had also proved expensive: by 1748 subsidies to foreign allies, of whom Austria was by far the most important, accounted for a sixth of all British war expenditure. Yet in London it was very difficult to envisage dispensing with the alliance entirely. Newcastle had played a significant role in the fall of Carteret in 1744; but his ideas on foreign policy did not differ very much from those of the man he had helped to overthrow. Indeed, he had throughout his political career been a steady and rather uncritical supporter of the traditional friendship with Austria. In the 1730s, for example, he had opposed Walpole's failure to support Charles VI in the Polish Succession struggle. He was well aware of Britain's need, if it were to win its maritime and colonial struggle with France, of continental allies which could divert to land warfare some of the resources of the great enemy, for 'France will outdo us at sea, when they have nothing to fear by land'. More important still, the vulnerability to French attack of Hanover in 1741 and the Netherlands in 1745–8 had driven home the need for such allies. Even after the Aix-la-Chapelle settlement and the resentment it and

13 R. Browning, 'The British Orientation of Austrian Foreign Policy, 1749–1754', *Central European History*, i (1968), 299–323.
14 Grete Klingenstein, *Der Aufstieg des Hauses Kaunitz* (Göttingen, 1975), pp. 284–8, 298.

the manner of its making had aroused in Vienna, Newcastle was still unrealistic enough to refer to Britain's 'old alliance' as 'the only solid system in Europe'. The misunderstandings with Austria, he believed, could be smoothed over, particularly if Bartenstein could be got rid of; and he looked forward to an alliance of Britain, Austria, Russia and the Dutch which he hoped other German states, in particular Saxony, might join.[15] If relations with Prussia could be improved it might even be possible to persuade Frederick II to join a traditional anti-French combination of this kind.

Considerable efforts were made to breathe new life into the relationship with Vienna, which was strongly supported by George II, still deeply hostile to the king of Prussia, and his Hanoverian ministers. In 1749 Britain acceded to the public articles of the Austro-Russian treaty of 1746, though not to the secret ones which looked forward to a new war with Prussia. In the same year an effort was begun to regain the good graces of Maria Theresa by securing the election of her eldest son, the Archduke Joseph, as King of the Romans and thus ensuring his succession to the imperial title on the death of his father, Francis Stephen. In 1749–51 there were negotiations with the electors of Cologne, Bavaria and Saxony to secure their support for the archduke in return for British, Dutch or Hanoverian subsidies; but the scheme was a failure. It was opposed by France (one significant secondary motive behind it was probably that of giving the German states somewhat greater unity and thus making them less vulnerable to French influence). It was equally unwelcome to Frederick II, always alert to oppose anything which seemed to threaten a strengthening of the Habsburg position in Germany. Even in Vienna there was little enthusiasm for it; to support it strongly would endanger the better relations with France which were now increasingly desired there.[16] Not until 1764, in a very different political environment and without help from Britain, did Joseph become King of the Romans.

---

15 P. C. Yorke, *Life and Correspondence of Philip Yorke, Earl of Harwicke, Lord Chancellor of Great Britain* (Cambridge, 1913), ii, 23; *The Private Correspondence of Sir Benjamin Keene*, ed. Sir R. Lodge (Cambridge, 1933), p. 21; *Archives ou Correspondance inédite de la Maison d'Orange-Nassau*, 4th ser., i, ed. Th. Bussemaker (Leyden, 1908), 192–5.

16 There is a useful discussion in R. Browning, 'The Duke of Newcastle and the Imperial Election Plan, 1749–1754', *Journal of British Studies*, 7 (1967–8), 28–47, and in the same author's *The Duke of Newcastle* (New Haven, Conn.–London, 1975), chap. v.

The war of the Austrian Succession therefore made international relations more fluid by eroding old assumptions and certainties. In Vienna the opposition to France which had well over two centuries of tradition behind it now seemed increasingly irrelevant and a hindrance in coping with the new situation facing the Habsburgs in central Europe. For Britain the sudden rise of Prussia meant that there was now a second German power for possible use as a weapon against France, even if few people in London were as yet prepared to think seriously in these terms. It is possible, then, without an excessive use of hindsight, to see clear foreshadowings of the sudden change in international alignments which was to take place only a few years later.

COLONIAL STALEMATE; LIMITED MILITARY INNOVATION

In Europe, therefore, the war had some significant results. This is not true of the parallel colonial and maritime struggle which Britain carried on during these years with Spain and, from 1744, with France. The hopes with which the Spanish war had begun in 1739 of easy and lucrative conquests, and a resulting great expansion of British trade, proved completely illusory. The Spanish possessions in America proved far less vulnerable than had been believed in London; and they were defended not only by their own considerable strength but by the natural obstacles which impeded every expeditionary force sent to the Caribbean – the yellow fever which so quickly killed off soldiers and sailors, sometimes in thousands; the rum which often assisted its ravages; the hurricanes which could almost in a moment cripple or even destroy a naval squadron. The Anglo-French struggle for empire was equally indecisive. From it, as a later historian said, the rivals 'gained nothing but the experience of each other's strength and power'.[17] The capture of Louisbourg and the naval victories of 1747 belatedly succeeded in reducing France's transatlantic trade to a mere trickle. But they were for Britain only a modest return for what they cost; and they were counterbalanced by the loss of Madras and the failure to make any real impression on the French West Indian islands.

After 1748 there were clearly still important and unresolved colonial rivalries between the two powers which contained the seeds

17 W. Coxe, *Memoirs of Horatio, Lord Walpole* (London, 1802), p. 359.

of future conflict. In particular, the failure in the peace negotiations to fix more clearly colonial boundaries in North America (though this would in practice have been very difficult) opened the way to a new struggle: in 1755–6, as this erupted, the ministers then in power in Paris were very critical of Puysieulx for his failure in this respect.[18] On both sides renewed imperial and naval conflict was taken for granted from the moment peace was made. France had lost twenty-three ships of the line during the war against only nine lost by Britain; but new building meant that when it ended it had still about forty, the number with which it had entered the naval struggle in 1744. In 1749–54 thirty-eight more were built, so that France began the Seven Years War with sixty-three (though by then Britain had 142). In Spain there was an even more determined effort to rebuild the country's naval strength. The new chief minister, Ensenada, who came to power in 1746 with the accession of Ferdinand VI, at once pressed the new king to strengthen the navy and calculated that, given eight years of peace, fifty ships of the line could be built in Spain and across the Atlantic in Havana. In 1752–3 20 million pesos were spent on new building of this kind, so that by 1754 Spain had a very respectable fleet of forty-five ships of the line and sixteen frigates. So many skilled workmen were recruited abroad (mainly in Britain and the Dutch Republic) to help restore its naval strength that one historian has spoken of 'an avalanche of foreigners' in these years.[19]

In military terms the war of the Austrian Succession was much less dramatic than the truly desperate struggle which Prussia had to face for several years after 1757. It produced no really over-whelming victories on the battlefield, apart perhaps from that of Leopold of Anhalt-Dessau over the Saxons at Kesselsdorf in December 1745 and the strategically unimportant one of the Sardinians over the French on the Assietta ridge in July 1747. Frederick II was well aware of the desirability of fighting if possible short and decisive campaigns. He knew that Prussia, however effective its military organisation, would still find it very difficult to bear the cost of a long and expensive war. His search for a peace with Maria Theresa almost from the moment his army crossed the Silesian frontier shows this clearly; and in later years (for example in his *Generalprinzipien vom Kriege* of 1748) he stressed the need for

---

18 Baudi di Vesme, *La Pace*, p. 265.

19 J. Lynch, *Bourbon Spain, 1700–1808* (Oxford, 1989), pp. 166, 176–8; J. P. Merino Navarro, *La Armada española en el siglo XVIII* (Madrid, 1981), p. 69.

Prussia's wars to be short and sharp. Yet it is at least arguable that his campaigns in 1741–2 and 1744–5, though his tactics on the battlefield were usually aggressive, aimed at attrition, at exhausting his enemies rather than annihilating them.[20]

It is doubtful, indeed, whether he ever had the resources needed to destroy a Habsburg army on the battlefield. In most of the battles he fought during these years he did not command more than 40,000 men; and of these up to two-fifths might become casualties even in victory. Both at Mollwitz and Chotusitz the Prussians lost almost as many men killed and wounded as their opponents: Hohenfriedberg was Frederick's one victory of the war in which the balance of casualties was heavily in his favour. On several occasions – in the first days of 1741, in February 1742, in September 1744 – he was able to make rapid and superficially impressive advances into Habsburg territory; but this was the result merely of the lack of effective opposition. As soon as he found himself facing a substantial enemy force this freedom of action vanished. Frederick's real achievement was one of organisation, in ensuring that his army was more efficiently supplied, clothed and paid than those it fought. In the Netherlands, again, though Saxe won an impressive series of battles, he commanded in each of them larger forces than those available to Cumberland, Prince Charles of Lorraine and the other allied generals, and forces which had the enormous advantage of unity of command and purpose.

Some of the impression of indecisiveness, of failure to win clear-cut victory and often to follow up adequately success when it was achieved, may stem from the fact that so many of the commanders concerned were elderly, sometimes very old, men. In the naval struggles of these years Sir Charles Wager, the First Lord of the Admiralty, was seventy-three in 1739, while Sir John Norris became commander of the British Channel squadron in February 1744 when he was in his mid-eighties and De La Court, the French commander in the indecisive battle off Toulon in the same year, was also an octogenarian. On land Traun, to whom the Habsburg cause owed so much, was close to seventy in 1744, the year of his greatest success, while on the British side Lord Stair, who commanded in the

---

20 The question of whether Frederick, whatever his own claims, was ever able to think in Napoleonic terms of a single crushing blow against Austria is discussed in K. Lehmann, 'Ermattungsstrategie – oder nicht?' *Historische Zeitschrift*, cli (1935), 48–86. For a shorter treatment, see M. Kitchen, *A Military History of Germany from the Eighteenth Century to the Present Day* (Bloomington, Ind.–London, 1975), pp. 24–5.

Netherlands in 1743, had been born in 1673, as had his successor, Marshal Wade. Even Ligonier, the best British general of these years, had first seen service as early as the 1690s, and Leopold of Anhalt-Dessau was almost seventy when he won at Kesselsdorf in 1745. Of course age did not by any means necessarily imply incompetence. But this gallery of elderly generals and admirals strengthens the impression of a war which, in the way it was fought, looked back to the days of Marlborough and Prince Eugene rather than forward. The same, indeed, is true of many of the policies and ambitions of the belligerents. The French onslaught on Maria Theresa from 1741 onwards, as so many historians have pointed out, was rooted in a centuries-old tradition which was now becoming more and more difficult to justify, while the anti-French combination of Britain, Austria, Piedmont and some of the German Protestant states at which Carteret aimed in 1743 was strongly reminiscent of that formed against Louis XIV in 1701 and the following years.

The Austrian Succession struggles none the less saw at least two military innovations of importance. One was the first significant use of divisions, relatively large, self-contained units of all arms. The splitting of an army into these often made for easier movement in difficult country and might also confuse the enemy as to the main point at which an attack was to be launched. The French and Spanish armies in Italy sometimes made effective use of this form of organisation, notably in the campaigning of 1744: the French plan for the invasion of Piedmont in that year, drawn up by Pierre-Joseph de Bourcet, an outstanding staff officer and military theorist, is the clearest example.

Much more eye-catching and interesting to contemporaries, however, was the considerable use now being made by several armies of light troops of a kind hitherto little seen in western Europe. From early in their invasion of Silesia the Prussians found themselves harassed, their communications threatened and their supplies interrupted, by *grenzers* and *pandours*, irregular units originally raised largely in the Habsburg military frontier areas in Croatia, which soon became known and feared for their mobility and their propensity to plunder and destroy.[21] 'The men look scarcely human', wrote an English lady after seeing a body of Croat irregulars in the Netherlands in 1748, 'the swarthiness of their

---

21 For British comments on their effectiveness, see *Gentleman's Magazine*, xi (1741), 222; xii (1742), 277, 332, 501, 548–9, 605.

complexions, their size, their whiskers, the roughness of their dress, without linen, and with bare arms and legs, two or three brace of pistols stuck into their belts, beside other arms, and their method of turning their heads and eyeballs all the same way to look at their general as they march, all this combined together gives them a fierceness not to be described.' At least one well-informed later commentator believed that without these exotic supporters the Habsburg monarchy would have collapsed in the crisis of the early 1740s.[22] Similar light forces soon made their appearance in the other theatres of conflict: the hussars, the cavalry form which they took, made a particular appeal to the imagination of contemporaries and soon gave rise to a distinctive style of uniform as well as of fighting. From 1743 onwards light and irregular troops appeared in the Habsburg forces in the Netherlands, while Saxe (who had himself gained considerable experience of this form of warfare during the earlier Habsburg struggles with the Turks) introduced light infantry units into the French army. In 1742–3 Charles Emmanuel used in the Alps irregulars, often armed peasants, whom one French observer thought 'at least as awkward in these mountainous countries as the pandours of the Queen of Hungary'.[23]

Even in pitched battles light troops of this kind were sometimes employed to considerable effect – by Charles Emmanuel at Camposanto in 1743 and at Fontenoy two years later by Saxe. In 1747 the *grenzer* units were for the first time fully incorporated into the Austrian army, while two years later the military frontier began to be administered directly by the Hofkriegsrat in Vienna. These areas had now become 'a vast military reservation from which the new Austrian state and its centralised bureaucracy was able to draw a reliable and devoted soldiery', while by 1763, it has been claimed, a quarter of the Habsburg army 'qualified for the description of light troops'.[24] By the 1750s and 1760s light forces were an established part of many European armies. The one notable (and significant) exception was that of Prussia, where Frederick II believed that their use, because of the relative freedom and powers of independent initiative they often enjoyed, would lead to a great

22 Duffy, *The Military Experience*, p. 272; H. G. Mirabeau, *Système militaire de la Prusse* (London, 1788), p. 17.

23 *Chronique de la Régence et du Règne de Louis XV (1718–1763) ou Journal de Barbier* (4 vols, Paris, 1885), iii, 550.

24 G. E. Rothenberg, *The Austrian Military Border in Croatia, 1522–1747* (Urbana, Ill., 1960), p. 123; J. Childs, *Armies and Warfare in Europe, 1648–1789* (Manchester, 1982), p. 117.

increase in desertion from his regular regiments in which discipline was so brutally strict. The use which could be made of them in reconnaissance, in raiding and harassing an enemy's flanks and communications, soon became a recognised and much-discussed aspect of military theory: in the second half of the eighteenth century about fifty books on *'la petite guerre'* of this kind made their appearance.[25] In purely military terms, therefore, as well as in political ones, the Austrian Succession struggles, untidy and in many ways inconclusive as they were, had real significance and saw important change and the emergence of new potentialities.

25 Among the better-known examples are Captain M. de Grandmaison, *La Petite Guerre, ou traité du service des troupes légères en campagne* (Paris, 1756); Captain Jeney, *Le Partisan, ou l'art de faire la Petite Guerre* (The Hague, 1759); de Platen, *Le Husard, ou courtes maximes de la Petite Guerre* (Berlin, 1761); (Sir William Young), *An Essay on the Command of Small Detachments* (?London, 1766). For works on irregular warfare and light troops published in English after 1763, see J. A. Houlding, *Fit for Service: The Training of the British Army, 1715–1795* (Oxford, 1981), pp. 221–3. There is a useful study of Austrian light infantry during the eighteenth century in J. Kunisch, *Der kleine Krieg: Studien zum Heerwesen des Absolutismus* (Wiesbaden, 1973); and a good deal of information about the use of such units in the later part of the century can be found in Duffy, *The Military Experience*, chap. 7.

CHRONOLOGY

1703	Pactum Mutuae Successionis attempts to regulate Habsburg succession.
1713	
April	Pragmatic Sanction issued by Emperor Charles VI.
1739	
January	Abortive Anglo-Spanish agreement.
October	War declared between Great Britain and Spain.
November	British capture Portobello.
1740	
May	Death of Frederick William I, accession of Frederick II.
October	Death of Charles VI: death of Empress Anna, fall of Bühren.
December	Frederick II invades Silesia.
1741	
January	Almost all Silesia in Prussian hands.
March	Mission of Belleisle to Germany begins.
March–April	Unsuccessful British attack on Cartagena.
April	Battle of Mollwitz.
May	Spanish-Bavarian treaty of Nymphenburg.
June	Franco-Prussian treaty of alliance: Maria Theresa crowned queen of Hungary.
July	Sweden declares war on Russia: Franco-Bavarian invasion of Austrian provinces.
September	George II signs convention with France for neutrality of Hanover.
October	Convention of Klein-Schnellendorf.

November	Accession of Empress Elizabeth, fall of Ostermann: first landing of Spanish forces in Italy: Prague captured by French and Bavarians.
December	Frederick II invades Moravia.

1742

January	Resignation of Walpole: Elector Charles Albert becomes Emperor Charles VII.
February	Austrians capture Munich: Austro-Sardinian agreement.
May	Battle of Chotusitz.
June	Austria and Prussia agree preliminary peace terms at Breslau.
August	Great Britain forces Neapolitan withdrawal from the war in Italy.
November	Anglo-Prussian defensive alliance signed.
December	French retreat from Prague.

1743

January	Death of Cardinal Fleury.
February	Battle of Camposanto.
June	Austrians recapture Munich: battle of Dettingen.
June–July	Abortive Anglo-Austrian negotiations at Hanau.
September	Treaty of Worms signed by Great Britain, Austria and Sardinia.
October	Treaty of Fontainebleau (Second Family Compact).

1744

February	Indecisive naval battle off Toulon.
March	French plan for invasion of Great Britain abandoned: France declares war on Great Britain and Hanover.
May	Union of Frankfurt formed: France declares war on Austria.
August	Frederick II invades Bohemia: Austrians retreat from Alsace.
November	Fall of Carteret.
November–December	Prussian retreat from Bohemia.

1745

January	Death of Emperor Charles VII: Great Britain, Austria, Saxony and the Dutch Republic sign the Treaty of Warsaw.
April	Austria and Bavaria make peace by the Treaty of Füssen.
May	Battle of Fontenoy.
June	Battle of Hohenfriedberg: British capture Louisbourg.
July	Jacobite rebellion begins in Scotland.
September	Grand Duke Francis Stephen becomes Emperor Francis I: battle of Soor.
October	Secret Franco-Sardinian negotiations begin.
December	Spaniards capture Milan: battle of Kesselsdorf: Treaty of Dresden.

1746

February	French plan for invasion of Great Britain abandoned.
March	Sardinians capture Asti.
June	Austro-Russian defensive alliance signed: battle of Piacenza.
July	Death of Philip V, accession of Ferdinand VI.
September	Austrians capture Genoa: French capture Madras.
October	Battle of Rocoux: Breda peace negotiations begin.
December	Revolt in Genoa.

1747

January	Fall of d'Argenson.
May	Orangist revolution in the Dutch Republic: Anson defeats La Jonquière.
June	Anglo-Russian convention for the supply of Russian auxiliary troops.
July	French defeated on the Assietta ridge (Exilles): battle of Laufeldt.
September	French take Bergen-op-Zoom.
October	Hawke defeats l'Etanduère.
November	Second Anglo-Russian convention for the supply of Russian auxiliary troops.

1748	
January–April	Austrian efforts to achieve a separate peace with France.
March	Aix-la-Chapelle negotiations begin.
April	Anglo-French peace preliminaries signed.
May	French capture Maastricht.
October	Britain, France, Spain and the Dutch Republic sign the Treaty of Aix-la-Chapelle.
November	Austria and Sardinia sign the Treaty of Aix-la-Chapelle.

BIBLIOGRAPHY

Much has been written on the war of the Austrian Succession; but its complexity and the way in which its ramifications extended to different parts of Europe and the outside world help to explain a notable lack of general studies. In English, however, there is now Reed Browning, *The War of the Austrian Succession* (New York, 1993), which appeared after this book had been completed and was in the process of publication. It is a comprehensive and balanced account which provides a detailed narrative, particularly of military events.

The struggle for power in Germany in 1740–45, the central theme during these years, is covered in detail in F. Wagner, *Kaiser Karl VII und die grossen Mächte* (Stuttgart, 1938), which is thorough and based on wide-ranging archival research. Sir R. Lodge, *Studies in Eighteenth-century Diplomacy, 1740–8* (London, 1930), takes up the story only in 1743 and is concerned essentially with British policy and based on British archives only. Nevertheless, it throws much light on the period it covers.

R. Butler, *Choiseul*, i, *Father and Son, 1719–1754* (Oxford, 1980), which was intended to form the first volume of a very large-scale study of the French statesman, is much wider in scope than its title suggests: though centred on French policy it ranges widely, and sometimes approximates to a general study of many aspects of the war.

There is a vast literature on Frederick II, one of the two central figures in the European struggle; but no secondary work is an adequate substitute for the relevant volumes of *Politische Correspondenz Friedrichs des Grossen*, ed. J. G. Droysen and others (Berlin, 1879–1939), which is excellently edited and an indispensable source of information about international relations during his reign. Of the biographies of the king the largest is R. Koser, *Geschichte Friedrichs des Grossen* (6th and 7th edns, 4 vols, Stuttgart-Berlin, 1921), of which the first two volumes are relevant here. Shorter and easier to use is A. Berney, *Friedrich der Grosse;*

Entwicklungsgeschichte eines Staatsmannes (Tübingen, 1934): while the king's own *Histoire de mon temps*, which appeared as the first volumes of the *Oeuvres historiques de Frédéric II, Roi de Prusse* (Berlin, 1846), though written long after the events it describes, still throws interesting and important light on them.

On Maria Theresa, the heroine of the war, the relevant volumes of A. von Arneth, *Geschichte Maria Theresias* (10 vols, Vienna, 1863–79), are still indispensable in spite of their age, particularly because of the copious extracts from documents printed in them. E. Guglia, *Maria Theresia: Ihre Leben und ihre Regierung* (2 vols, Munich–Berlin, 1917), of which the first volume covers this period, makes considerable use of Arneth and remains very useful in spite of its age.

The military aspects of the war in Europe are made accessible to the English reader in three books by C. Duffy – *Frederick the Great: A Military Life* (London, 1985); *The Army of Frederick the Great* (Newton Abbot, 1974) and *The Army of Maria Theresa* (London, 1977) – while the same author's *The Wild Goose and the Eagle: A Life of Marshal von Browne, 1705–1757* (London, 1964) is an interesting study of one of the more successful commanders on the Austrian side. The military achievements and failures of France are covered in detail in a narrative way in the second volume of comte P. V. C. de Pajol, *Les Guerres sous Louis XV* (Paris, 1882); and there is much that is relevant to the same subject in *Histoire militaire de la France*, ii, *De 1715 à 1871*, ed. J. Delmas (Paris, 1992): this is part of a great four-volume collective work under the general editorship of A. Corvisier. An important recent work is J-P. Bois, *Maurice de Saxe* (Paris, 1992). *Handbuch zur deutschen Militärgeschichte, 1648–1939* ed. G. Papke and W. Petter (6 vols, Munich, 1964–81) provides in its first and third volumes much information on the social and administrative aspects of German armies during this period: it says nothing, however, about military operations.

Perhaps the best brief discussion in English of Frederick II's ideas on warfare is R. R. Palmer, 'Frederick the Great, Guibert, Bülow: From Dynastic to National War', in *Makers of Modern Strategy*, ed. P. Paret (Oxford, 1986).

French policy during the war has attracted a good deal of attention from historians, though much of the writing on it was published many years ago. Its origins and first stages are very competently treated in two works by a French army officer, M. Sautai: *Les Préliminaires de la Guerre de la Succession d'Autriche* (Paris, 1907) and the first volume, the only one to appear, of *Les Débuts de la Guerre de la Succession d'Autriche* (Paris, 1909). The same ground is covered much more briefly in English in A. M. Wilson, *French Foreign Policy during the Administration of Cardinal Fleury* (Cambridge, Mass., 1936). In the 1880s and 1890s the Duc de Broglie produced a series of narrative histories of French foreign policy during the 1740s: *Frédéric II et Marie Thérèse, 1740–1742* (Paris, 1883); *Frédéric II et Louis XV, 1742–1744* (2 vols, Paris, 1885); *Marie-Thérèse impératrice, 1744–1746* (2 vols, Paris, 1888); *Maurice de Saxe et le Marquis d'Argenson* (2 vols, Paris, 1891); and *La Paix d'Aix-la-Chapelle* (Paris, 1892). They were written when the impression made by the defeat of France by Prussia in 1870–1 was still fresh; and throughout them there runs the argument that France made a fatal mistake during these years by contributing so much to the rise of a power which was in the long run to be so damaging to its international position. They have therefore in many ways a distinctly old-fashioned feel. None the less, they still contain much useful information. The old and excessively schematic E. Zevort, *Le Marquis d'Argenson et le Ministère des Affaires Etrangères du 18 Novembre 1744 au 10 Janvier 1747* (Paris, 1880) remains the only large-scale secondary work on the most original and idealistic foreign minister of the eighteenth century: d'Argenson's ideas can be followed in the four volumes of his *Journal et mémoires*, ed. E. J. B. Rathery (Paris, 1859–67). On a more general level, the relevant parts of M. Antoine, *Louis XV* (Paris, 1989) are useful.

On French relations with the Jacobites the most recent study is F. J. McLynn, *France and the Jacobite Rising of 1745* (Edinburgh, 1981), while the very strained relationship with the other major Bourbon power is still best followed in the last volume of A. Baudrillart, *Philippe V et la Cour de France* (5 vols, Paris, 1890–1902).

On British policy during much of the war the most detailed guide remains the book by Lodge mentioned above. The relevant parts of R. Browning, *The Duke of Newcastle* (New Haven, Conn.–London, 1975) provide an account of the domestic background to British diplomacy, as does the older J. B. Owen, *The Rise of the Pelhams* (London, 1975). U. Dann, *Hanover and Great Britain, 1740–1760* (Leicester–London, 1991) is short and useful, while the relatively secondary issue of Gibraltar is the subject of a short chapter in S. Conn, *Gibraltar in British Diplomacy in the Eighteenth Century* (New Haven, Conn., 1942).

On the fruitless British military exertions in Europe there are: F. H. Skrine, *Fontenoy and Great Britain's Share in the War of the Austrian Succession* (Edinburgh–London, 1906); Hon. E. Charteris, *William Augustus, Duke of Cumberland, His Early Life and Times (1721–1748)* (London, 1913); and the more recent and wider-ranging R. Whitworth, *Field-Marshal Lord Ligonier: A Story of the British Army, 1702–1770* (Oxford, 1958).

Russia, though never itself a combatant, loomed large in the minds of the combatant governments; its importance is elucidated in W. Mediger, *Moskaus Weg nach Europa: Der Aufstieg Russlands zum europäischen Machtstaat im Zeitalter Friedrichs des Grossen* (Braunschweig, 1952), a massive and thorough study.

On the rather pathetic figure of the Emperor Charles VII there is, apart from the work of Wagner, the shorter and more biographical P. C. Hartmann, *Karl Albrecht – Karl VII: glücklicher Kurfürst, unglücklicher Kaiser* (Regensburg, 1985); while D. B. Horn, 'Saxony in the War of the Austrian Succession', *English Hitorical Review*, xliv (1929), though it is confined to the later years of the war, is almost the only work in English on the significant role played by this state.

The Dutch Republic's inglorious role in the war is discussed in the old but still useful A. Beer, 'Holland und der Österreichische Erbfolge-Krieg', *Archiv für Österreichische Geschichte*, 46 (1871) and the very short P. Geyl, 'Holland and England in the War of the Austrian Succession', *History*, New Series, x (1925–6). For those who can read Dutch there is the same author's *Willem IV en Engeland tot 1748* (The Hague, 1925).

On the Habsburg–Bourbon struggle in Italy, S. Wilkinson, *The Defence of Piedmont, 1742–1748: A Prelude to the Study of Napoleon* (Oxford, 1927) is useful though it is the work of a military historian and concerned primarily with the fighting in the peninsula. On the complex diplomacy involved the fourth volume of D. Carutti, *Storia della Diplomazia della Corte di Savoia* (4 vols, Rome–Turin–Florence, 1875–80) is still essential.

There is a large literature on several aspects of the maritime and colonial struggle outside Europe; only a few titles will be mentioned here. The most recent discussion of the outbreak of war between Britain and Spain is P. Woodfine, 'The Anglo-Spanish War of 1739', in *The Origins of War in Early Modern Europe*, ed. J. Black (Edinburgh, 1987), while for much of the background Jean O. MacLachlan, *Trade and Peace with Old Spain, 1667–1750* (Cambridge, 1940) is useful. The outstanding work on international conflict in the Caribbean, however, is R. Pares, *War and Trade in the West Indies, 1739–1763* (Oxford, 1936): a recent specialised study is R. Harding, *Amphibious Warfare in the Eighteenth Century: The British Expedition to the West Indies, 1740–1742* (London, 1991).

The war on the American continent is covered in G. S. Graham, *Empire of the North Atlantic: The Maritime Struggle for North America* (Toronto, 1950).

On the struggle at sea there is the old and rather unsatisfactory G. Lacour-Gayet, *La Marine militaire de la France sous le règne de Louis XV* (Paris, 1902) and the much better and more detailed H. W. Richmond, *The Navy in the War of 1739–48* (3 vols, Cambridge, 1920).

The beginnings of Anglo-French competition for empire in India can be followed in A. Martin, *Dupleix et l'Inde française, 1742–1749* (Paris, 1923) and the first volume of Sir G. Forest, *The Life of Lord Clive* (2 vols, London, 1918), while on the general background there is the excellent H. Furber, *Rival Empires of Trade in the Orient, 1600–1800* (Minneapolis–Oxford, 1976).

On the peace negotiations at Aix-la-Chapelle and the preliminaries to them there is much information in the book by Lodge mentioned above. C. Baudi di Vesme, *La Pace di Aquisgrana (1748)* (Turin, 1969) is a collection of articles published in the *Bolletino Storico-Bibliografico Subalpino* in 1967–9 and therefore lacking a clear structure; but it is based on a very wide range of materials, notably from Italian archives. The relevant pages of N. A. M. Rodger, *The Insatiable Earl: A Life of John Montague, Fourth Earl of Sandwich, 1718–1792* (London, 1993) cover Sandwich's part in the peace negotiations of 1746–8. The old A. Beer, 'Zur Geschichte des Friedens von Aachen im Jahre 1748', *Archiv für Österreichische Geschichte*, 47 (1871) is still useful: it is a substantial article of almost 200 pages, of which just over half consists of illustrative documents.

The best general study of the development of the new international alignments stimulated by the war is still D. B. Horn, *Sir Charles Hanbury Williams and European Diplomacy (1747–58)* (London, 1930), while on aspects of this process the same author's 'The Duke of Newcastle and the Origins of the Diplomatic Revolution', in *The Diversity of History: Essays in Honour of Sir Herbert Butterfield*, ed. J. H. Elliott and H. G. Koenigsberger (London, 1970); W. J. McGill, 'The Roots of Policy: Kaunitz in Vienna and Versailles, 1749–53', *Journal of Modern History*, 43

(1971); and R. Browning, 'The Duke of Newcastle and the Imperial Election Plan, 1749–1754', *Journal of British Studies*, 7 (1967–8), may be mentioned.

The development of light and irregular forces which was the main military legacy of the war can be followed in a British context in E. Robson, 'British Light Infantry in the Mid-eighteenth Century', *Army Quarterly*, 63, no. 2 (1952), and P. E. Russell, 'Redcoats in the Wilderness: British Officers and Irregular Warfare in Europe and America', *William and Mary Quarterly*, 3rd series, xxxv (1978).

The very large subject of war in general during this period, the problems of waging it and its impact on society, are discussed in J. Childs, *Armies and Warfare in Europe, 1648–1789* (Manchester, 1982); G. Parker, *The Military Revolution: Military Innovation and the Rise of the West, 1500–1800* (Cambridge, 1988); A. Corvisier, *Armies and Societies in Europe, 1494–1789* (Bloomington, Ind.–London, 1989); and M. S. Anderson, *War and Society in Europe of the Old Regime, 1618–1789* (London, 1987). C. Duffy, *The Military Experience in the Age of Reason* (London–New York, 1987) brings together much material which illustrates the realities of battle and the soldier's life; while the administrative and economic repercussions of international conflict for an individual state are penetratingly discussed in J. Brewer, *The Sinews of Power: War, Money and the English State, 1688–1783* (London, 1989).

MAPS

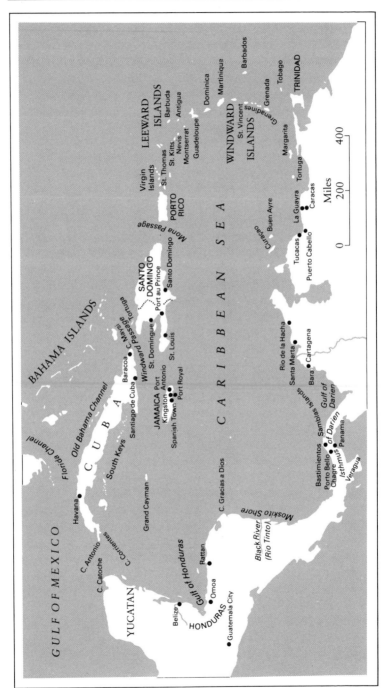

1. The West Indies

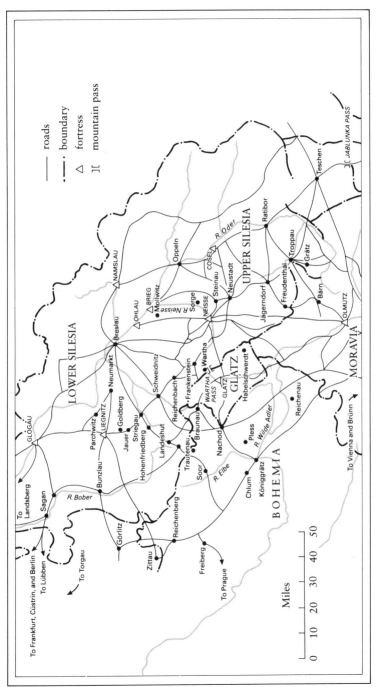

2. Silesia

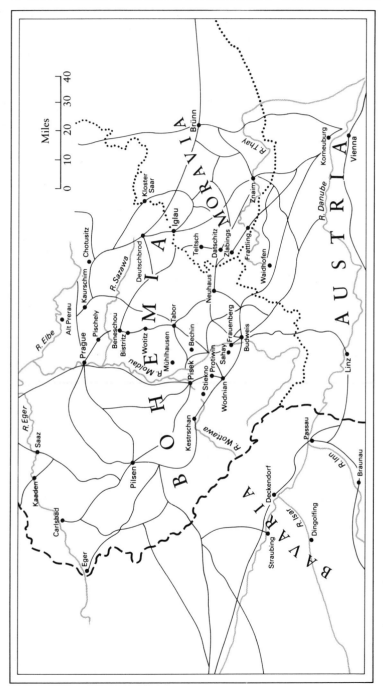

3. Bohemia, 1742

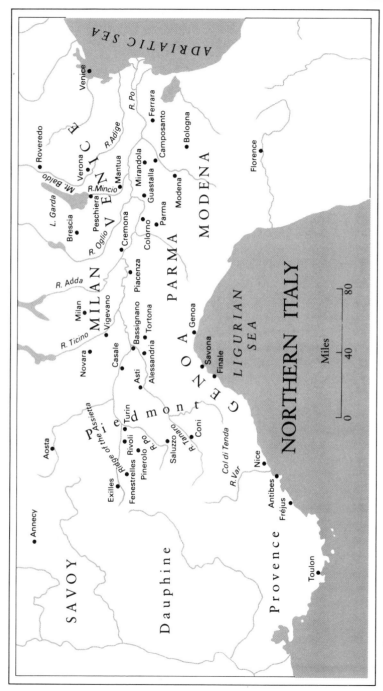

ADRIATIC SEA

Venice

R. Po

Ferrara

Camposanto

Bologna

Roveredo

R. Adige

Verona

Mantua

Mirandola

Mt. Baldo

R.Mincio

Peschiera

Guastalla

MODENA

Modena

Florence

L. Garda

Brescia

R. Oglio

Cremona

Colorno

Parma

R. Adda

Piacenza

Milan

Vigevano

Bassignano

Tortona

Genoa

LIGURIAN

SEA

R. Ticino

Novara

Casale

Asti

Alessandria

Savona

Finale

NORTHERN ITALY

Ridge of the Assietta

Turin

Coni

Miles

80

Aosta

Exilles

Rivoli

Pinerolo

Saluzzo

Col di Tenda

40

Fenestrelles

R. Var

Nice

Annecy

Antibes

Fréjus

0

SAVOY

Dauphine

Provence

Toulon

4. Northern Italy

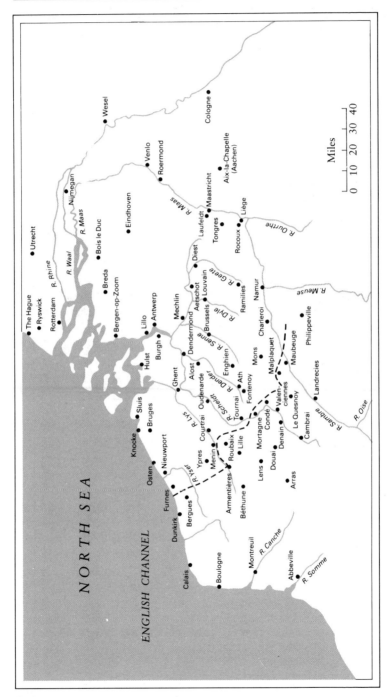

5. Flanders and the Netherlands

INDEX